DIVINATION

MOSELEY ROAD INC.
International Rights and Packaging
22 Knollwood Avenue
Elmsford, NY 10523
www.moseleyroad.com

President Sean Moore
Art and editorial director Lisa Purcell
Cover designer Lisa Purcell
Contributing writer Nancy J. Hajeski

Printed in China

ISBN 978-1-62669-212-1

25 24 23 22 21 1 2 3 4 5

DIVINATION

EVERYTHING YOU WANT TO KNOW ABOUT PREDICTING YOUR FUTURE

ALIDA SOMERS

mri

Moseley Road, Inc.
Elmsford, New York

Contents

FORTUNE-TELLING for a MODERN AGE

The desire to foretell the future stems from many causes. In times of calm and boredom, we may look to the stars or the cards to see if something is coming along to shake things up a bit and get us motivated. In times of crisis, a check of the tea leaves or a gaze into the crystal ball might just afford us hope for a better tomorrow and a way to carve a path to that better day. In this book, we will look at some of the major systems of fortune-telling, from astrology to casting with various objects and reading cards, palms, or tea leaves. It is meant as a sampler of the many ways you can use divination, offering guides to their methods and meanings. Not every form will resonate with you. You may find that a deck of tarot cards are just pretty pictures, but a handful of gemstones sets your intuition into overdrive. With a bit of practice, you can find the method that feels right for you and do further, in-depth research.

Is divination real? That question may never have a definitive answer, but the many divination methods out there speak to our deep desire to see the paths ahead of us. Whether empirically "real" or not, what divination offers us is a way to clarify the issues in our lives, to make us think about the questions we need answered. It is a way to let ourselves not just drift along, accepting whatever comes. No fortune is inevitable, and no method of fortune-telling can give us exact answers. It instead suggests options and alternatives we can evaluate so that we can carve out our paths forward. Divination offers us a map, but we can focus on the routes that matter.

C·H·A·P·T·E·R 1
READING the FUTURE
in the HEAVENLY BODIES

ASTROLOGY and DIVINATION

The study of the stars and planets has long been believed to offer us insights into the future.

The night sky has held a fascination for human beings for many millennia. Those illuminated astral bodies moving through their stately seasonal arcs enthrall us; the orbiting Moon, appearing so near at times, beckons to us. Planets align, come close, then appear to drift away. While the earth around us feels finite, the sky is vast, limitless. It is no wonder, then, that early seers and prophets looked to the heavens for omens, and that Earth's relationship with the Sun, Moon, planets, and stars furnished ancient societies with both the means to predict the future and calculate the passage of time.

ASTROLOGY AND HOROSCOPES

Horoscopic astrology, which is the ancestor of modern Western astrology, was born in the Mediterranean region and the Near East, gestating in Babylonia, Egypt, Greece, and Rome. As the centuries passed, the passion for astrology rose and fell. By the late 19th and early 20th centuries a renewed interest in astrology occurred in many countries, and today the discipline remains enormously popular. At least 80 branches of astrology are in use today. Within these are different schools of practice and further subsets that employ varied techniques. In this chapter, you will become acquainted Western astrology, as well the Chinese zodiac.

Many people still scoff at astrology and label it a pseudoscience, but the practice can become a reassuring presence in a person's life, offering counsel and providing signposts toward a more productive and even prosperous future. If you earnestly study the stars, ultimately, you, like multitudes before you, will come to understand that the wisdom revealed by the movement of heavenly bodies can uplift your spirits, make you open to new encounters, teach you caution when needed, and inspire you to take your destiny into your own hands.

An astrological clock, with golden zodiac symbols dating to the 1490s, graces the Torre dell'Orologio, or St. Mark's Clock Tower, on the Piazza San Marco in Venice, Italy.

ASTROLOGICAL CHARTS

An astrological, or natal, chart maps out the position of the planets, the Sun, and the Moon at the moment of your birth. They are essentially road maps of your life, plotting your personality, talents, skills, and potentials. They are complicated undertakings, but there are many online resources that allow you to plug in your relevant data and then generate a chart based on that info. You'll just need the date, time, and place of your birth. Let the website do the complicated mathematics.

READING YOUR CHART

Most websites generate a chart in a circular format, which is the easiest to read for non-experts, along with tables that indicate the positions of various elements within the chart. The basic chart is built from 12 wedges that represent the 12 Houses associated with each zodiac sign. There are several main placements that you should focus on.

Sun Sign

This is indicated by the Sun glyph (☉). Look for it on your chart, noting which house and sign it appears in. Most of us are familiar with our Sun signs and their associated characteristics.

Ascendant, or Rising Sign

This is indicated by an "AC." The ascendant is the sign rising over the eastern horizon at the time and place of your birth. Directly opposite is the descendant, which represents the western horizon and what is setting. The wedge in which the ascendant falls is also called the first house, and it is where the chart begins. You then move counterclockwise through to the 12th house.

Moon Sign

This is indicated by the Moon glyph (☽). Locate it on your chart, noting which house and sign it appears in. Its location informs you about your feelings, intuition, and unconscious.

Houses

Houses represent the path of the planets as they moved across in the sky at the time of your birth. Around the outer ring glyphs of the major zodiac signs will be scattered, each corresponding to a single house. Each house represents a different aspect of your life.

- *1st* You at birth; your inherent physical and psychological qualities. Planets and signs found in the first house greatly impact your personality.
- *2nd* Security, money, and comfort
- *3rd* Communication, thought, and self-expression
- *4th* Your roots, home, family, and property
- *5th* Fun, spontaneity, romance, and hobbies
- *6th* Health and physical well-being
- *7th* Long-term relationships and serious commitments
- *8th* Regeneration and rebirth; also loss, intimacy, and transformation
- *9th* Higher powers; also long-distance travel.
- *10th* The future; also career and status
- *11th* Hopes and dreams; also the collective consciousness, including friends and society
- *12th* Secrets and mysteries; the unconscious, subconscious, and spirituality

The 12 HOUSES

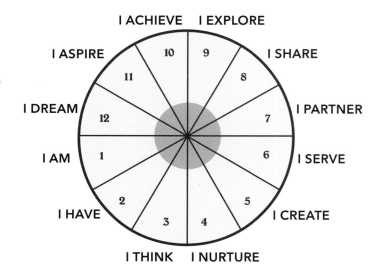

GLYPHS

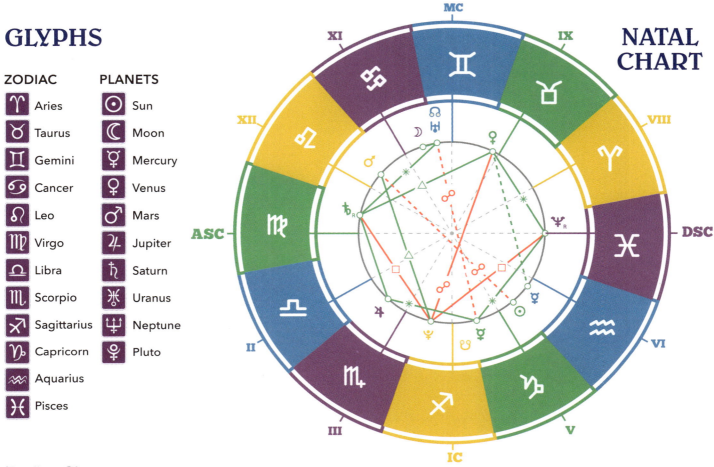

NATAL CHART

ZODIAC

♈	Aries
♉	Taurus
♊	Gemini
♋	Cancer
♌	Leo
♍	Virgo
♎	Libra
♏	Scorpio
♐	Sagittarius
♑	Capricorn
♒	Aquarius
♓	Pisces

PLANETS

☉	Sun
☽	Moon
☿	Mercury
♀	Venus
♂	Mars
♃	Jupiter
♄	Saturn
♅	Uranus
♆	Neptune
♇	Pluto

Zodiac Signs

Within the houses, there will be glyphs representing the signs of the zodiac, indicating whether they were rising or setting. The glyphs' positions afford a snapshot of the sky at the time of your birth.

- *Aries* Excitement and adventure
- *Taurus* Pleasure, beauty, and sensuality
- *Gemini* Wit, intellect, and versatility
- *Cancer* Moodiness, sensitivity, and empathy
- *Leo* Enthusiasm, generosity, and courage
- *Virgo* Carefulness and the analytical
- *Libra* Diplomacy, harmony, and fairness
- *Scorpio* Strength, jealousy, and control
- *Sagittarius* Philosophy and positivity
- *Capricorn* Practicality and discipline
- *Aquarius* Social consciousness and affection
- *Pisces* Emotions, sentiment, and intuition

Planets

Planetary glyphs also appear scattered within the house wedges, with their placement determining their signification. Their movements are said to affect the events of your daily life.

- *The Sun* Your identity and ego
- *The Moon* Feelings, perception, and intuition
- *Mercury* Logic and communication
- *Venus* Love and enjoyment; the feminine
- *Mars* Aggression, passion, the masculine
- *Jupiter* Luck, confidence, and integration
- *Saturn* Responsibility, order, and rules
- *Uranus* Higher thought, personal growth, and individuality
- *Neptune* Idealism, spirituality, and imagination
- *Pluto* Change, sexuality, and inner growth

The SUN SIGNS

These familiar signs are the ones the Sun was in on the day of our birth.

In the Western zodiac, birth signs are often referred to as Sun signs. This is because a person's astrological sign is based on which constellation the Sun was "in" on their day of birth. (Each constellation extends 30 degrees across the ecliptic, and the Sun remains in each sign for approximately 30 days.) The name is also used because the Sun symbolically represents light, hope, vitality, and love. The term *Sun sign* can be used interchangeably with *zodiac sign* or *star sign*.

The 12 signs of the zodiac were originally conceived by the Babylonians in the first half of the first millennium BC. Even though ancient astronomers believed the Sun was merely one of the celestial bodies that orbited around the earth, they understood its crucial role as the provider of light and warmth.

THE BIRTH OF SUN SIGNS

It is likely 17th-century Englishman William Lilly was the first newspaper astrologer, but the publication of daily or monthly horoscopes truly began in England in 1930. This was when the *Sunday Express* asked noted astrologer R. H. Naylor to write a horoscope for newborn Princess Margaret, younger sister to the future Queen Elizabeth II. The thrust of his prediction was that her life would be "eventful"— pretty much a given. When the horoscope generated a positive public response he was assigned a column, "What the Stars Foretell," an idea that was soon being appropriated across the globe, and thus horoscopic astrology found its seemingly permanent niche in the public's reading habits.

The SUN SIGNS and CONSTELLATIONS

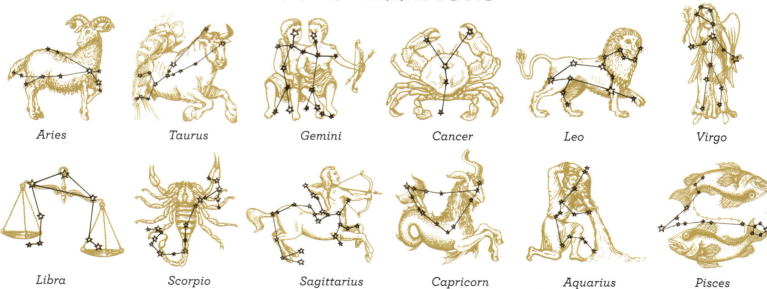

Aries   Taurus   Gemini   Cancer   Leo   Virgo

Libra   Scorpio   Sagittarius   Capricorn   Aquarius   Pisces

Naylor decided he needed a simplified version of Western astrology that would be suitable to a newspaper column. Sun signs was what he came up with, a system that takes into account only the position of the Sun in a given zodiac constellation at the time of a person's birth.

He created a basic guide that named each Sun sign, showed its symbol, and provided its English name, its element, its modality, its polarity—features that most followers of horoscopes are familiar with—but he further listed an approximate span of time showcasing the seasonal phenomena that accompanied each sign. This is significant because it harks back to one of the original uses of astrology: the prediction of agricultural markers.

- *Aries* – Vernal Equinox
  (Mar 21 to day before Corn Rain)
- *Taurus* – Corn Rain
  (April 20 to day before Corn Forms)
- *Gemini* – Corn Forms
  (May 21 to day before Summer Solstice)
- *Cancer* – Summer Solstice
  (June 21 to day before Great Heat)
- *Leo* – Great Heat
  (July 24 to day before End of Heat)
- *Virgo* – End of Heat
  (Aug 23 to day before Autumnal Equinox)
- *Libra* – Autumnal Equinox
  (Sept 23 to day before First Frost)
- *Scorpio* – First Frost
  (Oct 23 to day before Light Snow)
- *Sagittarius* – Light Snow
  (Nov 23 to day before Winter Solstice)
- *Capricorn* – Winter Solstice
  (Dec 22 to day before Great Cold)
- *Aquarius* – Great Cold
  (Jan 20 to day before Vernal Showers)
- *Pisces* – Vernal Showers (
  Feb 19 to day before Vernal Equinox)

SUN SIGN AFFILIATES

Each Sun sign is associated with and affected by one of four elements, one of three modalities, one of two polarities, and one or more planets. The four elements assigned to the Sun signs can briefly be described thus: air signs thrive on ideas and information; fire signs are aflame with passion and power; water sign plunge into emotions and memories; and earth signs are generally grounded, practical, and stable. But there are also affiliated symbols such as birthstones, colors, and plants that each zodiac sign has acquired over time.

Many of us start the day with a peek at a horoscope app.

Insight The term *horoscope* comes from the Greek *hõra* ("time" or "hour") and *scopos* ("observer"). Ideally, horoscopes are based not just on a birth date and time, but also on a location, because these data points are needed to determine the precise alignment of planets and stars.

Sun Sign: ARIES

The first sign of the zodiac, its motivations are to survive and to be independent, and its motto would be "I am."

Aries is the baby of the zodiac, the first sign in the wheel, originally positioned at 0 degrees of the ecliptic band. Like most babies, its energies, attributes, and liabilities are softened somewhat. As a fire sign, it can seem like more of an ember than an outright conflagration. Still, there is impulsivity in good measure, and a brash eagerness to start projects. Finishing, however, is another matter.

The Sun, which represents life force and essence, is exalted in Aries. When a planet or luminary is exalted in a sign, that means it has the greatest power to achieve its potential.

POSITIVE TRAITS

This sign combines the courage of Mars the Warrior with creativity, spontaneity with confrontation. They are the perfect choice to dive into a situation while keeping their eyes on the goal. If a project needs a forceful, can-do achiever who will fight for a cause or a dynamic leader who loves a challenge, look no further. Stylistically they want to start trends, raise eyebrows, or be the first through the door at all the new hot spots.

NEGATIVE TRAITS

Like its namesake, a Ram can be brusque and aggressive, with a manner that often lacks subtlety or finesse. Expect a certain impatience and even the infant's "I want it now!" attitude. They may overlook or ignore the consequences for their hair-trigger or hot-headed reactions, but others probably won't.

ROMANCE OUTLOOK

When an Aries falls in love, acting like a passionate fool is not out of the question. Whirlwind courtships are also quite common as is some measure of promiscuity and bad choices . . . yet once an Aries gives their heart away in a grounded and mature relationship, the connection is often for life.

This zodiac sign is represented by the Ram, which embodies the Aries tendency to meet life head-on. The Aries symbol (♈) is a glyph meant to resemble the Ram's head and horns.

Mars is the ruling heavenly body of Aries.

The Aries constellation is located in the northern celestial hemisphere between Pisces to the west and Taurus to the east.

Best Matches

Those born under the sign of Aries blend well with companion fire signs Sagittarius, Leo, and other Aries. Yet the complimentary air signs of Gemini, Libra, and Aquarius have a history of providing the best long-term love matches. The signs that might lead to romantic woes are Taurus, Cancer, Capricorn, and sometimes other Aries.

CAREER OUTLOOK

As staff members, Aries individuals are capable of working and thinking independently and can be decisive, confident, and results-oriented. During a crisis, they are quick to respond, and when facing a tough deadline, they bring their competitive A-game. Careers that would work well for those born under the sign of Aries include public relations specialist, communications manager, retail store manager, magazine editor, real estate agent, hair stylist, sales representative, holistic healthcare practitioner, registered nurse, and defense attorney.

ARIES at a Glance

REPRESENTED BY
The Ram

DATES
Mar 21 – Apr 19

SYMBOL
♈ = Horns of a ram

RULING HOUSE
First

RULING PLANET
Mars

ELEMENT
Fire

QUALITY
Cardinal

POLARITY
Positive

SPIRIT COLOR
Red

GEMSTONE
Diamond

LUCKY NUMBERS
1, 6, 7, 10, 15, 25

LUCKY DAY
Tuesday

SEASON
Spring

FLOWERS/HERBS
- Thistle
- Poppy

TRAITS
- Adventurous
- Confident
- Self-Centered
- Impulsive

COMPATIBILITY
- Gemini
- Sagittarius
- Leo

TAROT CARDS
- The Emperor
- King of Wands

Sun Sign: TAURUS

The second sign of the zodiac, its motivations are to be secure and consistent, and its motto would be "I establish."

Taurus arrives directly after "baby" Aries, and as a result Taureans can sometimes act like the least mature of the three earth signs. This fixed sign craves comfort and wants to be surrounded by beautiful things . . . and is willing to focus its earthly energies to ensure such pleasures. The Moon is exalted in Taurus, meaning its power to inspire the imagination and creativity is at its peak.

POSITIVE TRAITS

These goal-oriented lovers of possessions are like all earth signs in that they value tangibles. Naturally sensuous and patient, the Taurean may take their sweet time to accomplish a task, yet they can be a skilled artisan or builder. Many Taureans have a resonant voice and enjoy singing or public speaking.

NEGATIVE TRAITS

The Bull is frequently stubborn, and it resists change, traits those born under this sign possess. Although they can be stingy or childishly selfish, Taureans are usually generous with those they hold dear. The notion of giving things away has to be purposely cultivated, however. Weight gain may become a problem if the Taurean diet is not monitored closely.

ROMANCE OUTLOOK

The Venus-ruled Taurean in love is sensual and loyal, willing to share some of the luxuries they crave with their special person. With their sweet natures and generous inclinations toward lovers, Taureans make some of the best romantic catches in the zodiac. They want the best not only for themselves but also for their cherished ones. On the other hand, partners of certain Taureans may need to avoid becoming a carefully guarded "possession" or feeling smothered by their constant physical and emotional attention and need for hugs and kisses.

This zodiac sign is represented by the Bull, which is as stubborn as those born under this sign. The Taurus symbol (♉) is a glyph meant to resemble the Bull's head with large curvy horns.

Venus is the ruling heavenly body of Taurus.

The Taurus constellation, located in the northern celestial hemisphere, is most famous for its red giant star, Aldebaran, as well as the Pleiades star cluster.

Best Matches

The Bull insists on loyalty, stability, intimacy, and commitment in their relationships, and they will only get along with a few other Sun signs. The best bets are the earth signs Virgo and Capricorn, as well as other Taureans, and two water signs, Cancer and Pisces. Scorpio is also a water sign, but opposite Taurus on the zodiac wheel, which if matched with this sign can lead to clashes.

CAREER OUTLOOK

Taureans bring excellent qualities to a job. They are methodical and practical, as well as professional and grounded, and have proven to be skilled planners and organizers. They don't mince words on the status of an assignment and are able to visualize projects still in the early stages. Some careers that goal-oriented Taureans might excel at include retail banker, project manager, landscape photographer, art director, interior designer, chef, restaurant manager, entertainer/performer, makeup artist, and museum curator.

TAURUS at a Glance

REPRESENTED BY
The Bull

DATES
Apr 20 – May 20

SYMBOL
♉ = Horns of a bull

RULING HOUSE
Second

RULING PLANET
Venus

ELEMENT
Earth

QUALITY
Fixed

POLARITY
Negative

SPIRIT COLOR
Deep green

GEMSTONE
Emerald

LUCKY NUMBERS
1, 2, 3, 7, 10, 12, 19

LUCKY DAY
Friday

SEASON
Spring

FLOWERS/HERBS
- Daisy
- Lily

TRAITS
- Persistent
- Security-loving
- Jealous
- Inflexible

COMPATIBILITY
- Cancer
- Capricorn
- Pisces

TAROT CARDS
- The Hierophant
- Queen of Pentacles

Sun Sign: GEMINI

The third sign of the zodiac, its motivations are to learn and interact, and its motto would be "I communicate."

The first of the air signs, Gemini earns its affiliation with its ruling planet Mercury, as those born under the sign can be quite mercurial. With this duality in mind, a person's positive traits may sometimes be perceived as negatives: their versatility can read as shallowness, their ambition as ruthlessness, their youthfulness as immaturity, and their speed at performing tasks as impatience.

POSITIVE TRAITS

Geminis are the quick-witted intellectuals, the curious seekers of novelty, the identifiers of trends—in short, people who are adaptable, friendly, and fun. Because they are outgoing, enthusiastic, and intelligent, they are often a joy to be around, especially at social gatherings.

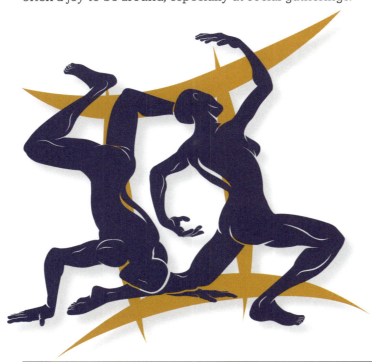

NEGATIVE TRAITS

This Twins sign can include some capricious flip-flopping and even tricksterish behavior. Geminis might be drama queens or party boys lacking the motivation or appropriate focus for really important projects. But they also like to learn and swiftly absorb new information. Yes, there are times they can be two-faced, but many non-Geminis also "code-switch" . . . putting on professional voices on the phone, watching their language around elderly relatives, and offering polite untruths to acquaintances.

ROMANCE OUTLOOK

A Gemini looking for love is playful and fun, flirting and thrilled by meeting new people, yet they can also be slow to give their hearts. Their protective instincts insist they take time to know potential partners before making any kind of emotional commitment. Sometimes love actually takes them by surprise. As creative, dynamic personalities, they themselves can be very easy to love, plus they are known for supporting their partners' goals and aspirations.

Best Matches

The strongest matches are generally considered to be Aries, Leo, Libra, and Aquarius. The least compatible signs with Gemini are probably Virgo and Pisces.

This zodiac sign is represented by the Twins, which stands for the duality of a Gemini. The Gemini symbol (♊) is a glyph of two lines joined together, resembling the Roman numeral II, signifying the Twins.

Mercury is the ruling heavenly body of Gemini.

The Gemini constellation, located in the northern celestial hemisphere, is fairly easy to spot northeast of the Orion constellation and between Taurus and Cancer.

Then again, statistically Gemini women are most likely to marry another Gemini men (there is that duality again) and also least likely to part with them, but they will divorce a Scorpio, Sagittarius, and Aquarius at a higher rate than the other signs. Men are also most likely to marry other Geminis and have a higher-than-average divorce rate with Capricorns, but are least likely to part from Taurus, Gemini, and Scorpio.

CAREER OUTLOOK

On the job, Geminis can bank on their strong communication skills. They are logical thinkers who love ferreting out information via search engines and flexible performers who find multitasking a breeze. Their witty, clever personalities and poise in the spotlight make them ideal as seminar leaders, fundraisers, or blog hosts. Some of the careers that Geminis might excel at include communications consultant, news reporter, event DJ, equity trader, dance instructor, director of photography, web analytics developer, patent agent, interpreter, and content writer.

GEMINI at a Glance

REPRESENTED BY
The Twins

DATES
May 21 – Jun 20

SYMBOL
♊ = Roman numeral II

RULING HOUSE
Third

RULING PLANET
Mercury

ELEMENT
Air

QUALITY
Mutable

POLARITY
Positive

SPIRIT COLOR
Yellow

GEMSTONE
Alexandrite

LUCKY NUMBERS
3, 5, 7, 12, 16, 23, 39

LUCKY DAY
Wednesday

SEASON
Spring

FLOWERS/HERBS
- Tansy
- Yarrow

TRAITS
- Versatile
- Intellectual
- Superficial
- Inconsistent

COMPATIBILITY
- Libra
- Aquarius
- Aries

TAROT CARDS
- The Lovers
- Knight of Swords

Sun Sign: CANCER

The fourth sign of the zodiac, its motivations are to heal and nurture, and its motto would be "I care."

Cancer is a cardinal sign that falls at the beginning of summer. As the first elemental water sign, Cancer may tend toward shallow depths, but it is brimming with life. Cancerians are ruled by the Moon, which heightens maternal or paternal instincts and often makes them into caregivers, nest-builders, and home lovers.

POSITIVE TRAITS

Cancers are all about emotion, frequently—and a little selfishly—their own. They become absorbed in their moods, and this can make them cautious around new people. Yet the very sensitivity that restricts them at times also gifts them with intuition, creativity, and a great capacity to care . . . for people, animals, and causes.

They are wise, empathetic, keepers of family lore, and storehouses of surprising hidden strength. Watch a weepy Cancer take charge in an emergency and be amazed. They can also sense undercurrents and read between the lines, making them excellent BS detectors.

NEGATIVE TRAITS

The moody Crab can be an irritable crybaby and may throw temper tantrums out of frustration or from suspecting that their words were misunderstood. They are also emotionally clingy and may restrict the free movement of others in their family circle.

ROMANCE OUTLOOK

The Cancer in love is self-protective, yet Moon Children are also known to fall very quickly and so may rush into relationships. This is a highly sensitive and nurturing sign, which often means Cancers are tender lovers who express their caring in ways that might never occur to other signs. They are unlikely to bail at the first hint of trouble but prefer to dig in and try to work things out. Some Cancerians can be intrusive "helicopter" parents who smother their offspring with worry; these moms and dads need to work extra hard to open those crab claws and let go.

This zodiac sign is represented by the Crab, which embodies the self-protective nature of those born under this sign. The Cancer symbol (♋) is a glyph meant to represent the Crab's claws.

The Moon is the ruling heavenly body of Cancer.

Although visible in both hemispheres, the Cancer constellation is faint to the naked eye, lying between Leo and Gemini.

Best Matches

The best love matches for Cancer are generally considered to be Taurus, Virgo, Scorpio, and Pisces; the least promising signs are Aries and Libra. Two Cancers coming together can easily overdo it in the sweet romance department, which can lead to anxiety . . . and sugar shock.

CAREER OUTLOOK

Cancerians are among the most loyal workers out there. Add to that trait their creativity, concern for coworkers, and ability to bring a team or family spirit to projects . . . and their worth escalates. They are also skilled financial managers, and they are extremely intuitive when it comes to anticipating problems before they happen or finding solutions for them once a problem arises. Ideal positions for Moon Children include chief executive officer, childcare worker, content editor, attorney, physical therapist, regional planner, interior designer, computer systems analyst, and art gallery manager.

CANCER at a Glance

REPRESENTED BY
The Crab

DATES
Jun 21 – Jul 22

SYMBOL
♋ = Claws of a crab

RULING HOUSE
Fourth

RULING PLANET
The Moon

ELEMENT
Water

QUALITY
Cardinal

POLARITY
Negative

SPIRIT COLOR
White

GEMSTONE
Ruby

LUCKY NUMBERS
2, 4, 6, 8, 20, 26

LUCKY DAY
Sunday

SEASON
Summer

FLOWER/HERB
- Water lily
- Morning glory

TRAITS
- Emotional
- Imaginative
- Overemotional
- Clinging

COMPATIBILITY
- Virgo
- Scorpio
- Pisces

TAROT CARDS
- The Chariot
- King of Cups

Sun Sign: LEO

The fifth sign of the zodiac, its motivations are to perform and lead, and its motto would be "I shine."

As a fire sign, the spirited Leo usually understands its own power enough to control it. That's a good thing, because their larger-than-life personalities and conceit often need to be tamed—or at least toned down. It should also be noted that no one can fault them for dreaming big and that their intentions are almost always good.

POSITIVE TRAITS

It is no wonder the classic Leo—vivacious, theatrical, driven, and intense—seeks the spotlight. Even in a less visible setting they remain proud, glamorous, and regal. At home among family they are big-hearted and expressive, on the job ambitious and unafraid of challenges. They crave adventure and have no problem facing risks.

NEGATIVE TRAITS

Lions always compete to win. They can be egomaniacs who steal the show, pompous asses acting like they are better than everyone, vengeful children, or bossy control freaks. They may challenge the wrong person who will quickly put them in their place—even lions have to give way to other animals on occasion. They can also manifest a false confidence that comes across as prideful. Finally, they resist change and are reluctant to take advice.

ROMANCE OUTLOOK

Leo is the sign that rules the human heart, so it's not surprising that as lovers they are passionate and demonstrative . . . once they let down their guard. It is said they know they are in love when they finally put the needs of their partner before their own. On the downside, Leos can be jealous and possessive, requiring a patient paramour to calmly reassure them. They are also known to stray and can even end up as promiscuous alley cats.

This zodiac sign is represented by the Lion, which is as bold as those born under this sign. The Leo symbol (Ω) is a glyph is meant to represent the Lion's head, mane, and tail.

The Sun is the ruling heavenly body of Leo.

Leo is a highly recognizable constellation, and is fairly easy to find in the northern celestial hemisphere, because the "pointer stars" of the Big Dipper point to Leo.

Best Matches

The Lion matches up well with all three air signs—Libra, Gemini, and Aquarius. When Leos are paired with other Leos, or other fire signs for that matter, the couple might generate too much scorching energy, resulting in struggles for dominance. If there is mutual respect, however, Leos and fire sign Sagittarians have a history of finding enduring love.

CAREER OUTLOOK

These powerful natural leaders may rise to advanced positions in many fields. Their take-charge attitude, dynamism, and fearlessness make them ideal military or law enforcement officers, teachers, stockbrokers, politicians, researchers, and sportsmen and women. Their histrionic side often situates them in the arts. Career paths for a Leo might include advertising executive, broadcaster, actor, stand-up comedian, event planner, special education teacher, fashion designer, graphic or production artist, personal trainer, dog trainer, and business coach.

LEO at a Glance

REPRESENTED BY
The Lion

DATES
Jul 23 – Aug 22

SYMBOL
Ω = A tail from a circle

RULING HOUSE
Fifth

RULING PLANET
The Sun

ELEMENT
Fire

QUALITY
Fixed

POLARITY
Positive

SPIRIT COLOR
Gold

GEMSTONE
Peridot

LUCKY NUMBERS
2, 3, 5, 11, 14

LUCKY DAY
Sunday

SEASON
Summer

FLOWERS/HERBS
- Chamomile
- Sunflower

TRAITS
- Generous
- Enthusiastic
- Bossy
- Dogmatic

COMPATIBILITY
- Sagittarius
- Aries
- Gemini

TAROT CARDS
- Strength
- Queen of Wands

Sun Sign: VIRGO

The sixth sign of the zodiac, its motivations are to maintain and fix, and its motto would be "I serve."

Compared to the fiery lions that precede them, logical, practical Virgos might seem to suffer by comparison. But they bring much to the table in terms of positive qualities and are less wearing to be around than those demanding Lions. Their constellation, a long-haired maiden bearing a sheaf of wheat, symbolizes the bounty that Virgo can provide. As an earth sign, Virgos are sensual; being ruled by Mercury makes them quick-witted and articulate, with a fine sense of humor—in other words, good communicators.

POSITIVE TRAITS

Virgos understand the value of hard work and are conscientious on the job. They seek a level of precision and purity in all things and feel safest following a routine. Like Mercury the Messenger, the Virgo hurries from place to place, busy organizing, planning, implementing. This independent sign is convinced it can accomplish anything . . . and it is often right. Yet in spite of their achievements, Virgos also know how to remain humble and kind. There is also a traditional belief that Virgo produces more attractive people than any other sign of the zodiac.

NEGATIVE TRAITS

The fastidious Virgin can be a relentless critic; this applies to self-criticism as well as judgment of others. While they are quite observant, Virgo vigilance can easily devolve into anxiety. They can also seem square, uptight, too solicitous, and hesitant to try new ideas. Caution is their watchword, and they back it up with a stubborn streak. If their negative traits become too extreme, Virgos can develop obsessive-compulsive behaviors that might require professional intervention.

ROMANCE OUTLOOK

Virgos are sincere but discriminating when it comes to romance, seeking the kind of love where souls, minds, and bodies blend effortlessly. Virgos might be guarded about their inner feelings at first, but that is to protect themselves until trust develops. Once that

This zodiac sign is represented by the Maiden, or Virgin, which embodies the modesty inherent in a Virgo. This Virgo symbol (♍) is a glyph of an M with an inward twist to signify the introspection inherent in the Maiden.

Mercury is the ruling heavenly body of Virgo.

Visible in both hemispheres, Virgo is the largest constellation of the zodiac and the second-largest of all constellations, behind Hydra.

barrier is down, Virgos pay great attention to their partners, even to the point of trying to assist them in self-improvement plans.

Best Matches

Virgo's best matches are Taurus, Cancer, Scorpio, and Capricorn. Taurus, especially, wants to show the Virgo that true love really does exist. The least compatible signs are Gemini and Sagittarius. Two Virgos together can be lackluster: they tend to let their conservative, rational side prevail and so dismiss deep emotions.

CAREER OUTLOOK

Virgos are planners and organizers with strong verbal skills. They also know how to sit and listen, which can be a rarity in the business world. They are marvels at solving problems and handling crises and can be supportive team leaders. Their most promising career options include veterinarian, laboratory technician, environmentalist, biologist, accounting analyst, social worker registered nurse, nutritionist, and life coach.

VIRGO at a Glance

REPRESENTED BY
The Virgin or Maiden

DATES
Aug 23 – Sep 22

SYMBOL
♍ = Letter M with a loop

RULING HOUSE
Sixth

RULING PLANET
Mercury

ELEMENT
Earth

QUALITY
Mutable

POLARITY
Negative

SPIRIT COLOR
Indigo

GEMSTONE
Emerald

LUCKY NUMBERS
2, 6, 8, 15, 20, 35

LUCKY DAY
Wednesday

SEASON
Summer

FLOWERS/HERBS
- Wintergreen
- Hazel

TRAITS
- Modest
- Analytical
- Fussy
- Conservative

COMPATIBILITY
- Taurus
- Cancer
- Capricorn

TAROT CARDS
- The Hermit
- Knight of Pentacles

Sun Sign: LIBRA

The seventh sign of the zodiac, its motivations are to balance and analyze, and its motto would be "I relate."

Those born to this air sign are often the aesthetes of the zodiac—cultured, refined, intellectual, sensitive, and attracted to the glories of art or nature. These connoisseurs of life are ruled by Venus, the planet that oversees love, beauty, and money, but they are not profligate in their pursuits of same. No, their psyche is more rational—they need to create equilibrium in all aspects of their life.

POSITIVE TRAITS

Few are more stylish or sophisticated than Libras, with their love of art and fashion. Talkative Libras enjoy being around other people and are known for being cooperative, open-minded, and willing to compromise. Charm is their middle name. This makes them excellent diplomats. They make interesting, clever friends and at home are always in the mood for group activities. They also know how to act as peacemakers when there is family discord.

NEGATIVE TRAITS

The Scales, symbolizing the ability to keep everything in balance, may also indicate someone evading confrontation. Maintaining the peace doesn't work when strong feelings need a healthy outlet. Libras also analyze everything and can fritter away hours weighing the pros and cons of an issue. This comes from their need to please everyone. When things go awry, Libras might feel like the whole world is against them. With their need to find a point of connection with everyone, they may seem shallow, but they normally don't lack depth. Ultimately, their tendency to be self-centered can make them unreliable and even flighty at times.

ROMANCE OUTLOOK

Libras tend to be "in love with love." This might sound romantic and thrilling, but their strong desire for excitement and beauty also means they are prone to getting "love drunk" and losing good judgment. They are happy to engage in numerous lighthearted flings with a series of partners, but they are quite choosy if and when they desire to settle down. And once they are truly in love, they take commitment very seriously.

This zodiac sign is represented by the Scales, which stands for the just nature of a Libra. The Libra symbol (♎) is a glyph of a horizon line, with the Sun rising above it, meant to suggest the balance of the Scales.

Venus is the ruling heavenly body of Libra.

The Libra constellation is located in the southern celestial hemisphere between Scorpius to the east and Virgo to the west.

Best Matches

Libras get along best with Gemini, Leo, Sagittarius, and Aquarius partners. Cancer and Capricorn are their least compatible options. Because Libra is one of the most engaging signs, it makes sense that a Libra-Libra match would have great potential.

CAREER OUTLOOK

Libras are natural leaders who shine when they are allowed the autonomy to be creative. They do best when left alone to generate ideas but might depend on a willing team to help them with follow-through, not always a Libra strong point. They sometimes make good collaborators or team players and know how to network to further an agenda. With their sense of design and balance, they often gravitate to the arts and also make excellent teachers. Careers ideas for Libras include interior decorator, journalist, municipal court judge, mediator, public relations specialist, customer service representative, graphic artist, web designer, and brand marketing consultant.

LIBRA at a Glance

REPRESENTED BY
The Scales

DATES
Sep 23 – Oct 22

SYMBOL
⚖ = Sun over a straight line

RULING HOUSE
Seventh

RULING PLANET
Venus

ELEMENT
Air

QUALITY
Cardinal

POLARITY
Positive

SPIRIT COLOR
Pink

GEMSTONE
Opal

LUCKY NUMBERS
1, 5, 6, 7, 10, 14, 24

LUCKY DAY
Friday

SEASON
Autumn

FLOWERS/HERBS
- Pansy
- Primrose

TRAITS
- Diplomatic
- Idealistic
- Indecisive
- Gullible

COMPATIBILITY
- Aquarius
- Gemini
- Sagittarius

TAROT CARDS
- Justice
- King of Swords

Sun Sign: SCORPIO

The eighth sign of the zodiac, its motivations are to regenerate and penetrate, and its motto would be "I transform."

This is an intense sign; those born under it tend to be brooding but also very magnetic. Think of Scorpio as the original angsty emo Goth. Like its fellow water signs, Cancer and Pisces, Scorpio is intuitive and insightful, but in this case, it can also be secretive and enigmatic. A Scorpio may easily figure out what is going on in a specific situation, but they will not be the first one to share that knowledge. Ruled by the warlike planet Mars, this sign engineers its attacks with precision.

POSITIVE TRAITS

Those who admire Scorpios find them soulful and profound, truth-seekers who are rarely cowed. They can be skilled healers, but are also drawn to the occult, hidden processes of the world. No surprise, they enjoy mysteries, express dark emotions, and brag that they would be at home in the underworld. Yet they can be brave and honest and are able to muster up the drive to succeed in a number of arenas. Their loyalty to friends knows no bounds.

NEGATIVE TRAITS

Scorpios can be tough-minded, aggressive, and quick to respond to provocation. Remember, these creatures will sting if they feel threatened. They are frequently ambitious and can turn resentful, even vengeful, if they feel slighted. They may have a hard time trusting others or getting others to trust them.

ROMANCE OUTLOOK

Even when in love, Scorpios can be guarded. This makes them extremely beguiling to members of the opposite sex, who invariably want to break down those barriers. Scorpios enjoy being in control and are capable of mesmerizing potential lovers, and then drawing them into their orbit until the two are closely bonded. This may sound manipulative, but don't pity their "victims"— Scorpios are reputed to be the most intimate, passionate, and creative lovers in the zodiac. On the other hand, they are often possessive, prone to jealousy and suspicion.

This zodiac sign is represented by the Scorpion, which embodies the prickly nature of a Scorpio. The Scorpio symbol (♏) is a glyph of an M with a barbed tail turning upward to resemble the Scorpion's stinger.

Pluto is the ruling heavenly body of Scorpio.

One of the brightest constellations, Scorpio lies close to the southern horizon in the Northern Hemisphere; in the Southern, it lies high in the sky near the center of the Milky Way.

Best Matches

Scorpios need independent, ambitious, loyal, and understanding partners. They are most compatible with the water signs Cancer and Pisces and the earth signs Capricorn and Virgo. They should probably avoid Sagittarius, Gemini, and Libra. Needless to say, two Scorpios can light up the bedroom, but they do have marriage potential, providing they can turn down the intensity and learn how to be open with each other.

CAREER OUTLOOK

The Scorpion brings to bear its sharp focus and strong observation skills to keep on top of developing situations. It can also intuit what is going on behind the scenes and intervene if needed. Scorpios will offer enduring loyalty once their trust is won, and as leaders they will quickly flex their power and set boundaries. Career options include psychologist/psychiatrist, surgeon, medical examiner, pharmacist, engineer, attorney, musician, appraiser, massage therapist, realtor, mortgage banker, and financial analyst.

SCORPIO at a Glance

REPRESENTED BY
The Scorpion

DATES
Oct 23 – Nov 21

SYMBOL
♏ = Letter M with a barb

RULING HOUSE
Eighth

RULING PLANET
Pluto

ELEMENT
Water

QUALITY
Fixed

POLARITY
Negative

SPIRIT COLOR
Black

GEMSTONE
Topaz

LUCKY NUMBERS
2, 3, 5, 8, 20, 21, 41

LUCKY DAY
Tuesday

SEASON
Autumn

FLOWERS/HERBS
- Black poppy
- Love-lies-bleeding

TRAITS
- Passionate
- Magnetic
- Jealous
- Secretive

COMPATIBILITY
- Libra
- Leo
- Gemini

TAROT CARDS
- Death
- Queen of Cups

Sun Sign: SAGITTARIUS

The ninth sign of the zodiac, its motivations are to experience and explore, and its motto would be "I master."

Sagittarius is the third and final fire sign. If Aries is the struck match and Leo the glowing campfire, Sagittarius is the roaring bonfire. It is also a mutable sign, dealing with adaptability and flexibility, the perfect complement to the Sagittarian penchant for change and transformation. Ruled by Jupiter, the planet of expansion, this energetic sign is always looking for novel places to travel, new languages to learn, and fresh ideas to try out, typically with a total lack of inhibition. Still, who doesn't adore a shooting star who has no selfishness or greed?

POSITIVE TRAITS

These eternal optimists just gush with enthusiasm . . . and why shouldn't they? Archers are rare among humans in that they are able to transform their thoughts and dreams into real actions. They also love to collect people, hosting parties, organizing road trips, showing up with an entourage at movie premieres or book signings. Any holiday gatherings become an art form then they are in charge. They are noted for their generosity, idealism, and great senses of humor, as well as endless curiosity and open minds.

NEGATIVE TRAITS

Archers are not known for their patience or diplomacy, and their critical arrows often hit the mark. Their judgments can be frank, to the point of hurting people's feelings. They often promise more than they can deliver, leading to disappointment and frustration in their friends and family members. Their desire for never-ending personal growth can make them seem flighty, fickle, or even unstable.

ROMANCE OUTLOOK

Sagittarians value freedom almost more than anything else. But this passionate sign also enjoys having fun with romantic partners and places a premium

This zodiac sign is represented by the Archer, or Centaur, which is a paradoxical character so like those born under this sign. The Sagittarius symbol (♐) is a glyph of an arrow pointing upward, resembling the arrow of the Archer.

Jupiter is the ruling heavenly body of Sagittarius.

With many bright stars that make it visible to the naked eye, Sagittarius is the largest constellation in the southern skies and 15th-largest of all.

on those who tend to be more sexually adventurous. Archers in love are loyal and dedicated, especially with partners who are intelligent, expressive, and sensitive.

Best Matches

Sagittarius matches up well with the other two fire signs—Aries and Leo, as well as with Libra and Aquarius. Their least compatible signs are generally considered to be Virgo and Pisces.

CAREER OUTLOOK

Slotting well into positions of leadership or authority, Sagittarians are big-picture thinkers and fearless risk takers. Their people skills make them popular, and their super-charged personalities draw staff together into effective teams. Yet even working alone, they bring that trademark enthusiasm to any project. Career paths include architect, teacher, hospitality manager, entrepreneur, publishing manager, Uber driver, environmental engineer, freelance writer, travel consultant, global project manager, and sports coach.

SAGITTARIUS at a Glance

REPRESENTED BY
The Archer

DATES
Nov 22 – Dec 21

SYMBOL
♐ = Arrow

RULING HOUSE
Ninth

RULING PLANET
Jupiter

ELEMENT
Fire

QUALITY
Mutable

POLARITY
Positive

SPIRIT COLOR
Bronze

GEMSTONE
Turquoise

LUCKY NUMBERS
4, 5, 9, 22, 23, 45

LUCKY DAY
Thursday

SEASON
Autumn

FLOWERS/HERBS
- Elder
- Yew

TRAITS
- Straightforward
- Intellectual
- Tactless
- Restless

COMPATIBILITY
- Aries
- Aquarius
- Leo

TAROT CARDS
- Temperance
- Knight of Wands

Sun Sign: CAPRICORN

The tenth sign of the zodiac, its motivations are to produce and succeed, and its motto would be "I achieve."

This is the last of the earth signs, and its symbol is the "sea goat," a mythical creature with the head and forelegs of a goat and the hind end of a fish. Like the stubborn goat, that will not be kept from any place it wishes to go, the Capricorn uses all its means to forge ahead toward a goal and rarely lets anything stand in its way. Urgency underlies much of what it does; there is no faith in second chances. These individuals are born managers and tend to be traditionalists with serious natures. The influence of ruling planet Saturn, which represents structure and discipline, makes Capricorns practical and responsible, but also emotionally aloof and even cold.

POSITIVE TRAITS

Resourceful, hard-working Capricorns are often considered pillars of society. They crave acceptance in the established order. They value tangible results and are willing to strategize in order to achieve them. They are typically independent, but at home they relish time spent with family, enjoy listening to or performing music, and look for quality craftsmanship in their possessions. Their emotional connections to childhood memories are ever-present. They make loyal, reliable, and lasting friends, providing those in their circle understand boundaries and don't probe too deeply.

NEGATIVE TRAITS

Capricorns often come across as know-it-alls or condescending. They can be pessimistic, always fearing the worst. If crossed, they can also carry a grudge and withhold forgiveness. Many maintain a long mental list of things and people they don't like.

ROMANCE OUTLOOK

The Capricorn in love can be earthy but remains status-minded. Their walls are high and hard to breech, but once they are won over, they stay committed. Even then, though, their demeanor can be confusingly remote or lacking in compassion. But their track record as devoted partners and providers for the home is

This zodiac sign is represented by the Sea-Goat, which embodies the Capricorn ability to rise to the occasion. The Capricorn symbol (♑) is a glyph of the hoof and curving body and tail of the Sea-Goat.

Saturn is the ruling heavenly body of Capricorn.

One of the faintest constellations, Capricorn sits in the southern celestial hemisphere among other water-themed constellations, including Pisces and Aquarius.

stellar. They are especially good at being hands-on boosters for their mates' endeavors.

Best Matches

Capricorns tend to be ambitious and persistent, even while dating. Men want partners who seamlessly fit into their lives; women want one who makes them smile. The best potential matches are Taurus, Virgo, Scorpio, and Pisces. Signs to be wary of are Aries and Libra.

CAREER OUTLOOK

Capricorns set high standards for themselves and others. This makes them excellent, if demanding, managers. Loyalty and a strong work ethic are often more valuable to them in a staff member than skill or intellect. Order and neatness also impress them. They set long-term goals and have the stamina to meet them. Career paths that best suit include chief executive officer, human resources manager, business analyst, financial planner, architect, copywriter, foreign affairs specialist, and intelligence analyst.

CAPRICORN at a Glance

REPRESENTED BY
The Sea-Goat

DATES
Dec 22 – Jan 19

SYMBOL
♑ = A hoof and tail

RULING HOUSE
Tenth

RULING PLANET
Saturn

ELEMENT
Earth

QUALITY
Cardinal

POLARITY
Negative

SPIRIT COLOR
Brown

GEMSTONE
Sapphire

LUCKY NUMBERS
1, 7, 9, 10, 16, 36, 52

LUCKY DAY
Saturday

SEASON
Winter

FLOWERS/HERBS
- Hemlock
- Burdock

TRAITS
- Reserved
- Humorous
- Pessimistic
- Miserly

COMPATIBILITY
- Taurus
- Pisces
- Virgo

TAROT CARDS
- The Devil
- King of Pentacles

Sun Sign: AQUARIUS

The eleventh sign of the zodiac, its motivations are to network and envision, and its motto would be "I socialize."

The water bearer is the third air sign and can be much more fanciful or cerebral than its two predecessors. As a fixed sign, it is resistant to outside influences. Often preferring their internal world, Aquarians can be quiet and shy, even coming across as eccentric. They have a need to help others and stand up for causes they believe in. With Uranus as their ruling planet, they may be timid, abrupt, or even pugnacious, but the planet also endows them with a clear sense of the future. They typically see the world as teeming with possibilities and are usually focused on the big picture, the large-scale projects.

POSITIVE TRAITS

Aquarians may the ones you watch ambling down the street styled with unconventional glamour: scarves, boots, ethnic jackets, slouchy hats—the Boho, tuned-in visionary. They are open-minded, quirky, and friendly in a vaguely distant way. Yet they are also keen thinkers who relish a mental challenge and use their minds at every opportunity. Because they enjoy company, they work to establish a community. As friends, they are good listeners and can also view conflicting issues from both sides, which makes them skilled problem solvers.

NEGATIVE TRAITS

When they are lost in their dream world, Aquarians may run from emotional demands. Their love of theorizing can blind them to the realities of daily life and impact their ability to connect with people. They can also be uncompromising and temperamental.

ROMANCE OUTLOOK

An Aquarian in love can be unconventional. Their natural tendency is to cherish their freedom and avoid constraint. This means it can take time for them to trust another person in order to achieve intimacy. For this to occur, they must consciously work at expressing their emotions in an honest manner. Flirtation, to them, may consist of intellectually stimulating discourse. On the other hand, they make loyal and committed lovers, with little or no jealousy, who consider their partners their equals.

This zodiac sign is represented by the Water-Bearer, which stands for the Aquarian desire to share knowledge with the world. The Aquarius symbol (≈) is a glyph of two zig-zag lines representing lightning bolts or waves.

Venus is the ruling heavenly body of Aquarius.

Although it appears in both hemispheres and is the 10th-lagest constellation, Aquarius has no particularly bright stars and can be difficult to view with the naked eye.

Best Matches

This sign does well romantically with Gemini, Libra, and Sagittarius. A match of two Aquarians can be exciting and liberating, but one or both partners may not understand traditional sexual taboos or roles. Intimacy, or lack thereof, may also be a problem for them. The less-promising signs for love are Taurus, Cancer, Scorpio, and Capricorn.

CAREER OUTLOOK

Aquarians won't thrive in job situations that squelch their rather spacey natures. They need to be placed among people who value and encourage their assets: out-of-the-box thinking, originality, the ability to build teams and see both sides of a conflict, fair-mindedness, and a spirit of fun and community. Career options might include teacher, research scientist, social worker, industrial engineer, mechanical designer, computer programmer, software developer, astronomy or physics professor, fiction writer, and personal stylist.

AQUARIUS at a Glance

REPRESENTED BY
The Water-Bearer

DATES
Jan 20 – Feb 18

SYMBOL
≈ = Waves

RULING HOUSE
Eleventh

RULING PLANET
Venus

ELEMENT
Earth

QUALITY
Fixed

POLARITY
Positive

SPIRIT COLOR
Aquamarine

GEMSTONE
Amethyst

LUCKY NUMBERS
2, 8, 9, 11, 17, 18, 35

LUCKY DAY
Saturday

SEASON
Winter

FLOWER/HERB
- Dandelion
- Rowan

TRAITS
- Original
- Inventive
- Unpredictable
- Detached

COMPATIBILITY
- Sagittarius
- Libra
- Gemini

TAROT CARDS
- The Star
- Queen of Swords

Sun Sign: PISCES

The twelfth sign of the zodiac, its motivations are to dream and spiritualize, and its motto would be "I imagine."

Pisces is the last water sign and the final sign of the zodiac. It could be said that in this position it has absorbed every practical guideline and emotional lesson from the previous 11 signs. This might account for Pisces being the most perceptive, empathetic, and intuitive sign, those born to it navigating like their fish namesake through the labyrinths of the human psyche. The distant planet Neptune gives them mystical qualities, while their former ruling planet, majestic Jupiter, may still offer remnants of luck and spiritual growth. As a mutable sign, it is ready to adapt to new ideas or trends, which it welcomes and accepts.

POSITIVE TRAITS

These generous, caring souls are loyal, devoted family members who also provide selfless friendship. Pisceans can be artistic, as well as musical, and they enjoy any type of visual media. Sublime thoughts and spiritual musings attract them. Not surprisingly, Pisceans like swimming and other water sports. Most people find them enchanting, even if they are frequently caught woolgathering.

NEGATIVE TRAITS

Pisceans often feel at risk—like a lost child—and have a tendency to play the martyr or victim. As mystics and dreamers they can seem out of touch with reality, sometimes even unreachable. They like to be alone, an odd preference for such a giving sign. They do not like criticism, cruelty, or past mistakes being dredged up.

ROMANCE OUTLOOK

When Pisces fall in love, they tend to become hopelessly smitten. Those born under this sign are not flirts or players when it comes to romance, but instead gentle, passionate lovers who require a real connection with a partner. They know how to express their feelings if an issue needs discussing, but they can also be blindly loyal.

This zodiac sign is represented by the Fish, which embodies the drifting, hard-to-pin-down nature of a Pisces. The Pisces symbol ()-() is a glyph of arcs bisected by a straight line, resembling two fish tied together.

Neptune is the ruling heavenly body of Pisces.

Located in the northern celestial hemisphere, Pisces is the 14th-largest constellation overall. With its very faint stars, it is hard to see with the naked eye.

Best Matches

Pisces may find lasting love with Taurus, fellow water signs Cancer and Scorpio, and Capricorn. There is less likelihood of success with Gemini and Sagittarius. A Pisces-Pisces match may seem like a fairytale coupling between two dreamers, but their "soft" personalities might cause difficulty as they try to shift from friends to lovers. Yet, their mutual understanding of each other's needs can make them extremely compatible in bed.

CAREER OUTLOOK

Pisces tend to be imaginative and creative. On the job they are typically hard-working problem-solvers, dedicated and compassionate. They are not aggressive go-getters but will use their empathetic people skills to motivate staff. They will also go beyond the 9-to-5 bounds to complete assignments. Pisces career paths include attorney, architect, filmmaker, veterinarian, psychologist, physical therapist, musician, librarian, wedding/events photographer, social worker, human resources coordinator, and game designer.

PISCES at a Glance

REPRESENTED BY
The Fish

DATES
Feb 19 – Mar 20

SYMBOL
♓ = Swimming fish

RULING HOUSE
Twelfth

RULING PLANET
Neptune

ELEMENT
Water

QUALITY
Mutable

POLARITY
Negative

SPIRIT COLOR
Mauve

GEMSTONE
Aquamarine

LUCKY NUMBERS
3, 5, 8, 12, 14, 26

LUCKY DAY
Thursday

SEASON
Winter

FLOWER/HERB
- Dogwood
- Narcissus

TRAITS
- Sensitive
- Intuitive
- Escapist
- Vague

COMPATIBILITY
- Libra
- Gemini
- Sagittarius

TAROT CARDS
- The Moon
- Knight of Cups

The CHINESE ZODIAC

This ancient form of Eastern divination has influenced many other forms of astrology.

Chinese astrology, which is based on birth year, rather than birth day, extends for a 60-year cycle, also known as the sexagenary cycle or the Stems-and-Branches. This cycle is made up of 12 yearly animal symbols, each associated with five different elements.

THE FIVE ELEMENTS THEORY

The Five Elements Theory stems from the belief that the elements play a crucial role in the balance of the universe and that all things that arise from and return to the universe are composed of them, forming a cycle of creation and destruction. The elements are as follows.

- *Wood* (木 mù) Born with a desire to explore
- *Fire* (火 huǒ) Inspired by excitement
- *Earth* (土 tǔ) Motivated to secure foundations
- *Metal* (金 jīn) Driven to create order
- *Water* (水 shuǐ) Compelled to form emotional bonds

This cycle repeats every 60 years and has done so since it was first used to record years in the middle of the third century BC. Although this method of numbering days and years no longer has a role in modern Chinese timekeeping, it is still used in the names of historic events and plays a key role in Chinese astrology and fortune-telling.

ANIMALS OF THE ZODIAC

The 12 animals of the zodiac all carry equal weight. Some animals might seem less impressive than others—how does one compare a rabbit to a dragon or a rat to a tiger?—but they are accorded the same importance. Each has its own innate strengths and inevitable weaknesses. Each animal is also designated as either yin (female nature) or yang (male nature).

METHOD

When preparing a natal chart, you need to know the querent's age and birth year according to the Chinese lunar calendar—for example, for a child born in 2021 its Chinese birth year is 4719—as well as their "true animal" and the element for their birth date. The problem here is that the ancient Chinese week contained 10 days, which makes calculating these indicators quite difficult. Fortunately, there are now online calculators that translate the Chinese calendar.

RAT **OX** **TIGER** **RABBIT** **DRAGON** **SNAKE**

"TRUE ANIMALS"

In addition to the yearly zodiac symbols that indicate certain qualities, more detailed information is given by further breaking the year into months, days, and hours—together called the Four Pillars. This reveals the inner animal, the true animal, and the secret animal. After viewing the these "hidden" animals in their natal charts, people are often less confused about why certain of their traits are manifested outwardly while others remain more contained or repressed.

Birth Month

The lunar month determines the inner animal, which indicates the less-obvious characteristics a person possesses but rarely shares with others. The year is divided into 24 two-week solar terms, and each animal is linked to two of these solar terms.

- *Rat* Dec 7 to Dec 21 and Dec 22 to Jan 5
- *Ox* Jan 6 to Jan 19 and Jan 2 to Feb 3
- *Tiger* Feb 4 to Feb 18 and Feb 19 to Mar 5
- *Rabbit* Mar 6 to Mar 20 and Mar 21 to Apr 4
- *Dragon* Apr 5 to Apr 19 and Apr 20 to May 4
- *Snake* May 5 to May 20 and May 21 to Jun 5
- *Horse* Jun 6 to Jun 20 and Jun 21 to Jul 6
- *Goat* Jul 7 to 22 and Jul 23 to Aug 6
- *Monkey* Aug 7 to Aug 22 and Aug 23 to Sep 7
- *Rooster* Sep 8 to Sep 22 and Sep 23 to Oct 7
- *Dog* Oct 8 to Oct 22 and Oct 23 to Nov 6
- *Pig* Nov 7 to Nov 21 and Nov 22 to Dec 6

> **Insight** Because the Chinese New Year is determined by the lunar calendar and does not occur on a specific date—it falls between January 21 and February 20—it is necessary to check when each new year begins.

Birth Day

This indicates the querent's true animal, which represents the sort of person an individual will grow into as an adult.

- *Monday* Sheep
- *Tuesday* Dragon
- *Wednesday* Horse
- *Thursday* Rat, Pig
- *Friday* Rabbit, Snake, Dog
- *Saturday* Ox, Tiger, Rooster
- *Sunday* Monkey

Birth Hour

The time of birth indicates the secret animal, which signifies who a person is at their very core—their truest nature. A 24-hour period is divided into 2-hour segments each represented by a zodiac animal.

- *Rat* 23:00 to 00:59
- *Ox* 01:00 to 02:59
- *Tiger* 03:00 to 04:59
- *Rabbit* 05:00 to 06:59
- *Dragon* 07:00 to 08:59
- *Snake* 09:00 to 10:59
- *Horse* 11:00 to 12:59
- *Goat* 13:00 to 14:59
- *Monkey* 15:00 to 16:59
- *Rooster* 17:00 to 18:59
- *Dog* 19:00 to 20:59
- *Pig* 21:00 to 22:59

HORSE **GOAT** **MONKEY** **ROOSTER** **DOG** **PIG**

THE 60-YEAR CYCLE

The following table shows the 60-year cycle matched up to the Western calendar for the years 1924–2043. This is only applied to the Chinese Lunar calendar. Each of the Chinese lunar years are associated with a combination of the 10 Heavenly Stems and the 12 Earthly Branches, which make up the 60 Stem-Branches in a sexagenary cycle. The chart also indicates which element aligns with each year.

	YEAR 1924–1983	ELEMENT	CELESTIAL STEM	EARTHLY BRANCH	ANIMAL	YEAR 1984–2043
1	02-05 1924–01-23 1925	Yang Wood	甲	子	Rat	02-02 1984–01-21 1985
2	01-24 1925–02-12 1926	Yin Wood	乙	丑	Ox	01-22 1985–02-08 1986
3	02-13 1926–02-01 1927	Yang Fire	丙	寅	Tiger	02-09 1986–01-28 1987
4	02-02 1927–01-22 1928	Yin Fire	丁	卯	Rabbit	01-29 1987–02-16 1988
5	01-23 1928–02-09 1929	Yang Earth	戊	辰	Dragon	02-17 1988–02-05 1989
6	02-10 1929–01-29 1930	Yin Earth	己	巳	Snake	02-06 1989–01-26 1990
7	01-30 1930–02-16 1931	Yang Metal	庚	午	Horse	01-27 1990–02-14 1991
8	02-17 1931–02-05 1932	Yin Metal	辛	未	Goat	02-15 1991–02-03 1992
9	02-06 1932–01-25 1933	Yang Water	壬	申	Monkey	02-04 1992–01-22 1993
10	01-26 1933–02-13 1934	Yin Water	癸	酉	Rooster	01-23 1993– 02-09 1994
11	02-14 1934–02-03 1935	Yang Wood	甲	戌	Dog	02-10 1994–01-30 1995
12	02-04 1935–01-23 1936	Yin Wood	乙	亥	Pig	01-31 1995–02-18 1996
13	01-24 1936–02-10 1937	Yang Fire	丙	子	Rat	02-19 1996–02-06 1997
14	02-11 1937–01-30 1938	Yin Fire	丁	丑	Ox	02-07 1997–01-27 1998
15	01-31 1938–02-18 1939	Yang Earth	戊	寅	Tiger	01-28 1998–02-15 1999
16	02-19 1939–02-07 1940	Yin Earth	己	卯	Rabbit	02-16 1999–02-04 2000
17	02-08 1940–01-26 1941	Yang Metal	庚	辰	Dragon	02-05 2000–01-23 2001
18	01-27 1941–02-14 1942	Yin Metal	辛	巳	Snake	01-24 2001–02-11 2002
19	02-15 1942–02-04 1943	Yang Water	壬	午	Horse	02-12 2002–01-31 2003
20	02-05 1943–01-24 1944	Yin Water	癸	未	Goat	02-01 2003–01-21 2004
21	01-25 1944–02-12 1945	Yang Wood	甲	申	Monkey	01-22 2004–02-08 2005
22	02-13 1945–02-01 1946	Yin Wood	乙	酉	Rooster	02-09 2005–01-28 2006
23	02-02 1946–01-21 1947	Yang Fire	丙	戌	Dog	01-29 2006–02-17 2007
24	01-22 1947–02-09 1948	Yin Fire	丁	亥	Pig	02-18 2007–02-06 2008
25	02-10 1948–01-28 1949	Yang Earth	戊	子	Rat	02-07 2008–01-25 2009
26	01-29 1949–02-16 1950	Yin Earth	己	丑	Ox	01-26 2009–02-13 2010

27	02-17 1950-02-05 1951	Yang Metal	庚	寅	Tiger	02-14 2010-02-02 2011
28	02-06 1951-01-26 1952	Yin Metal	辛	卯	Rabbit	02-03 2011-01-22 2012
29	01-27 1952-02-13 1953	Yang Water	壬	辰	Dragon	01-23 2012-02-09 2013
30	02-14 1953-02-02 1954	Yin Water	癸	巳	Snake	02-10 2013-01-30 2014
31	02-03 1954-01-23 1955	Yang Wood	甲	午	Horse	01-31 2014-02-18 2015
32	01-24 1955-02-11 1956	Yin Wood	乙	未	Goat	02-19 2015-02-07 2016
33	02-12 1956-01-30 1957	Yang Fire	丙	申	Monkey	02-08 2016-01-27 2017
34	01-31 1957-02-17 1958	Yin Fire	丁	酉	Rooster	01-28 2017-02-15 2018
35	02-18 1958-02-07 1959	Yang Earth	戊	戌	Dog	02-16 2018-02-04 2019
36	02-08 1959-01-27 1960	Yin Earth	己	亥	Pig	02-05 2019-01-24 2020
37	01-28 1960-02-14 1961	Yang Metal	庚	子	Rat	01-25 2020-Feb. 11 2021
38	02-15 1961-02-04 1962	Yin Metal	辛	丑	Ox	02-12 2021-01-31 2022
39	02-05 1962-01-24 1963	Yang Water	壬	寅	Tiger	02-01 2022-01-21 2023
40	01-25 1963-02-12 1964	Yin Water	癸	卯	Rabbit	01-22 2023-02-09 2024
41	02-13 1964-02-01 1965	Yang Wood	甲	辰	Dragon	02-10 2024-01-28 2025
42	02-02 1965-01-20 1966	Yin Wood	乙	巳	Snake	01-29 2025-02-16 2026
43	01-21 1966-02-08 1967	Yang Fire	丙	午	Horse	02-17 2026-02-05 2027
44	02-09 1967-01-29 1968	Yin Fire	丁	未	Goat	02-06 2027-01-25 2028
45	01-30 1968-02-16 1969	Yang Earth	戊	申	Monkey	01-26 2028-02-12 2029
46	02-17 1969-02-05 1970	Yin Earth	己	酉	Rooster	02-13 2029-02-02 2030
47	02-06 1970-01-26 1971	Yang Metal	庚	戌	Dog	02-03 2030-01-22 2031
48	01-27 1971-02-14 1972	Yin Metal	辛	亥	Pig	01-23 2031-02-10 2032
49	02-15 1972-02-02 1973	Yang Water	壬	子	Rat	02-11 2032-01-30 2033
50	02-03 1973-01-22 1974	Yin Water	癸	丑	Ox	01-31 2033-02-18 2034
51	01-23 1974-02-10 1975	Yang Wood	甲	寅	Tiger	02-19 2034-02-07 2035
52	02-11 1975-01-30 1976	Yin Wood	乙	卯	Rabbit	02-08 2035-01-27 2036
53	01-31 1976-02-17 1977	Yang Fire	丙	辰	Dragon	01-28 2036-02-14 2037
54	02-18 1977-02-06 1978	Yin Fire	丁	巳	Snake	02-15 2037-02-03 2038
55	02-07 1978-01-27 1979	Yang Earth	戊	午	Horse	02-04 2038-01-23 2039
56	01-28 1979-02-15 1980	Yin Earth	己	未	Goat	01-24 2039-02-11 2040
57	02-16 1980-02-04 1981	Yang Metal	庚	申	Monkey	02-12 2040-01-31 2041
58	02-05 1981-01-24 1982	Yin Metal	辛	酉	Rooster	02-01 2041-01-21 2042
59	01-25 1982-02-12 1983	Yang Water	壬	戌	Dog	01-22 2042-02-09 2043
60	02-13 1983-02-01 1984	Yin Water	癸	亥	Pig	02-10 2043-01-29 2044

YEAR of the RAT

Those born in the Year of the Rat are survivors who are adaptable and energetic.

The Rat is the first sign in the 12-year zodiac cycle and so also beings a new 60-year sequence. Unlike many countries, where rats are reviled, in China they are respected for their many survival skills and quick wits, and so the Rat sign indicates a courageous, enterprising person. Status and financial gratification are often their greatest motivators.

POSITIVE TRAITS

Rats are shrewd, clever, resourceful, and instinctive when faced with adversity. At other times they are calm and perceptive, with keen observational skills. Their honesty and loyalty make them easy to get

ELEMENTS	YEARS	TRAITS
WOOD RAT	• 1924 • 1984	• Independent • Traditional • Popular
FIRE RAT	• 1936 • 1996	• Energetic • Brave • Self-disciplined
EARTH RAT	• 1948 • 2008	• Honest • Self-assured • Resolute
METAL RAT	• 1960 • 2020	• Self-aware • Active • Persuasive
WATER RAT	• 1912 • 1972	• Intelligent • Tenacious • Observant

along with. They are lively, intelligent, curious, and imaginative. Not surprisingly, they require a lot of mental stimulation or they can get restless. As the first sign in the cycle, the Rat manifests leadership qualities and are adept at handling responsibility. They also have a well-developed sense of self-preservation and are nothing if not survivors. They like stability,

NEGATIVE TRAITS

Rats can be opportunistic, and they might even take advantage of an event or person if a goal requires it. Their egos sometimes prod them to take on more than they can handle, meaning they don't always

The Rat is the 1st of the Chinese zodiac animals.

Jupiter is the ruling planet of the Rat.

meet their commitments. Rats dislike making small talk, playing pointless head games, and anything that makes them feel insecure.

ROMANCE OUTLOOK

The Rat is one of the four zodiac signs that is blessed in their love life. They are often more good-looking than average and have little trouble attracting the potential partners. They place a premium on feeling secure and do not enjoy all the uncertainties a new romance may bring. Still, they are tender, caring partners, and when they finally commit to a relationship, it can become quite intense, especially in the beginning. If things cool off, however, their partner needs to reinvigorate the romance before the Rat becomes suspicious or despondent.

Best Matches

Rats can be long-term lovers with Oxes, Monkeys, and Dragons, but should give a wide berth to Horses and Roosters. A Snake is destined to be a good friend, while a Goat is either a perfect match or an enemy.

CAREER OUTLOOK

With their leadership qualities, Rats reign in the workplace. They rarely make mistakes due to their rigorous reviewing processes, yet they manage to maintain harmonious interpersonal relationships. Some ideal jobs for Rat people include artist, author, doctor, teacher, lecturer, marine engineer, architect, fashion designer, and photographer. They can also perform well in service industries and the fundraising and finance fields.

RAT at a Glance

MANDARIN NAME
SHU

YEARS
1912, 1924, 1936, 1948, 1960, 1972, 1984, 1996, 2008, 2020, 2032

RULING PLANET
Jupiter

POLARITY
Yang

LUCKY NUMBERS
2, 3

LUCKY DAYS
4th, 13th and 30th of lunar month

LUCKY DIRECTIONS
Southeast, northeast

SEASON
Winter

COLORS
- Gold
- Blue
- Green

GEMSTONE
Garnet

FLOWER
Lily

WESTERN COUNTERPART
Sagittarius

YEAR of the Ox

Those born in the Year of the Ox are hard workers who are loyal and tenacious.

Occupying second position in the Chinese zodiac, the Ox sign reflects traditional conservative values. Lovers of the home, they are loyal and compassionate. Like their namesakes, Oxes achieve their goals by patient, persistent effort. Never flashy, they rely on their sensible natures to guide them. They are also rarely influenced by those around them, sticking to their tried-and-true methods and performing well within their own capabilities.

POSITIVE TRAITS

Oxes are renowned for their strength, diligence, dependability, and determination. They are also known

ELEMENTS	YEARS	TRAITS
WOOD OX	• 1925 • 1985	• Restless • Decisive • Outspoken
FIRE OX	• 1937 • 1997	• Clever • Versatile • Practical
EARTH OX	• 1949 • 2009	• Honest • Prudent • Resolute
METAL OX	• 1961 • 2021	• Hardworking • Active • Popular
WATER OX	• 1913 • 1973	• Ambitious • Tenacious • Observant

to loyal, honest, responsible, hard-working, and logical. Ox women make traditional, faithful partners who value their children's education. With their strong personalities, they are also capable of career success. Ox men are mature, idealistic, ambitious, and patriotic, with a strong sense of accountability. They attach great importance to their families and to their work.

NEGATIVE TRAITS

Oxes are not great at communicating with others, and often decide it is not worth the effort to exchange ideas with others. They tend to be stubborn and stick to their own ways of doing things.

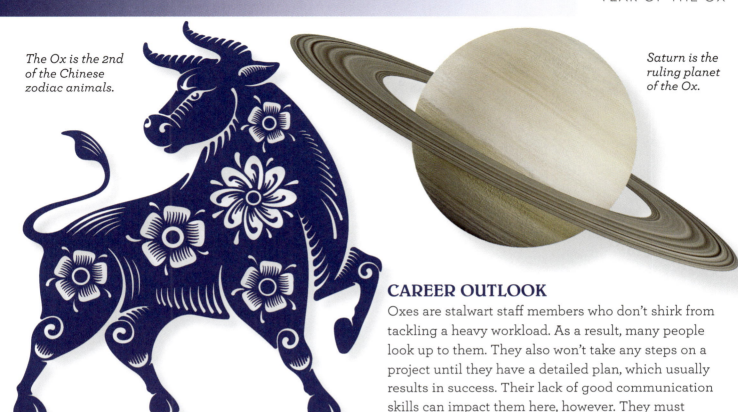

The Ox is the 2nd of the Chinese zodiac animals.

Saturn is the ruling planet of the Ox.

CAREER OUTLOOK

Oxes are stalwart staff members who don't shirk from tackling a heavy workload. As a result, many people look up to them. They also won't take any steps on a project until they have a detailed plan, which usually results in success. Their lack of good communication skills can impact them here, however. They must learn to open up and share ideas. Possible careers for Oxes include lawyer, doctor, teacher, author, social worker, writer, editor, government officer, policeman, technician, politician, office clerk, and consultant.

ROMANCE OUTLOOK

Oxes are not pleasure seekers or party animals. They dislike idle chitchat and avoid parties or crowded gatherings. When they do date, they rarely flirt and are not prone to talk about their feelings, preferring to show how they feel. Anyone interested in marrying an Ox may have a long wait; this sign dislikes change and must feel sure that they are making a most suitable marriage before popping the question. Sadly, Ox marriages have a tendency to fall apart, possibly because Oxes are dominant and inflexible, or because they blame others for their shortcomings. Those who are coupled with Oxes may need to coach them on how to maintain a loving relationship of equal partnership.

Best Matches

The Ox is most compatible with the Rat, Snake, Monkey, and Rooster. The least promising signs are Tiger, Dragon, Horse, and Sheep. Oxes fit together quite well with other Oxes. The Pig, meanwhile, has the potential to be either a great match or a disaster.

OX at a Glance

MANDARIN NAME
NIÚ

YEARS
1925, 1937, 1949, 1961, 1973, 1985, 1997, 2009, 2021

RULING PLANET
Saturn

POLARITY
Yin

LUCKY NUMBERS
8, 9, 3

LUCKY DAYS
13th and 27th of lunar month

LUCKY DIRECTIONS
Southeast, south, north

SEASON
Winter

COLORS
- Red
- Blue
- Purple

GEMSTONE
Aquamarine

FLOWER
Tulip

WESTERN COUNTERPART
Capricorn

YEAR of the TIGER

Those born in the Year of the Tiger are optimists who are brave and passionate.

The Tiger is primarily a sign of power. Those born under this sign are courageous, determined, and persistent, but also cautious. With their sharp senses and keen observation skills they make good leaders, and because they are both forthright and fair, they are able to help others sort out their problems. Frank in speaking out, they quickly gain the trust of others.

POSITIVE TRAITS

People born in a year of the Tiger are brave, competitive, and confident. They are very charming and well-liked by others. But sometimes they are likely to be impetuous, irritable, and overindulged.

ELEMENTS	YEARS	TRAITS
WOOD TIGER	• 1914 • 1974	• Compassionate • Expansive • Open
FIRE TIGER	• 1926 • 1986	• Optimistic • Independent • Impulsive
EARTH TIGER	• 1938 • 1998	• Adventurous • Reasonable • Level headed
METAL TIGER	• 1950 • 2010	• Enthusiastic • Indecisive • Open-minded
WATER TIGER	• 1962 • 2022	• Self-confident • Quick-witted • Creative

NEGATIVE TRAITS

Tigers are authoritative and stubborn and rarely go back on a statement. In social relationships, they always try to take a dominant role. Even in other relationships, they may display a high-handed manner. Once they make up their minds, they are hard to dissuade from a course of action. They are not good communicators and don't do well at networking. They either talk too much or don't talk at all. And even though they typically know a lot of people, they have very few truly close friends. They may also be unpredictable. Most people who are close to Tigers know that understanding, patience, and tact are often needed.

Uranus is the ruling planet of the Tiger.

Far left: The Tiger is the 3rd of the Chinese zodiac animals.

ROMANCE OUTLOOK

Some Tigers have trouble showing deep affection to their partners because they lack a sense of romance. Other Tigers can be tender in love and even sentimental. They enjoy the feeling of being loved, but can become too enthusiastic, which can make their partner uncomfortable or overpowered. Male tigers know how to impress with their air of command. Females are more judgmental, with a strict sense of right and wrong. Tiger partners need to remain active to keep up with this sign's need for adventure.

Best Matches

Tigers pair up well with Dragons, Horses, or Pigs, but should probably steer clear of Oxes, other Tigers, Snakes, or Monkeys. A Tiger-Tiger match is not recommended because it can generate a lot of conflict.

CAREER OUTLOOK

In China the Tiger is known as the "king of animals," and so it makes sense that Tiger signs are considered strong candidates for management positions. As senior staff members, they are respected by others and also enjoy being the center of attention. In their early years, however, Tigers are prone to have rocky careers that smooth out as they gain maturity. This is when they find their true direction and soon acquire wealth. With their boundless enthusiasm, Tigers expend a lot of energy at work, which means they need to take time to refresh themselves outside of work—or risk burning out. Promising careers for Tigers include advertising agent, office manager, travel agent, life coach, sports coach, actor, writer, artist, pilot, flight attendant, musician, comedian, and chauffeur.

TIGER at a Glance

MANDARIN NAME
HŬ

YEARS
1926, 1938, 1950, 1962, 1974, 1986, 1998, 2010, 2022

RULING PLANET
Uranus

POLARITY
Yang

LUCKY NUMBERS
1, 3, 4

LUCKY DAYS
16th and 27th of lunar month

LUCKY DIRECTIONS
South, east, southeast

SEASON
Spring

COLORS
- Blue
- Gray
- Orange

GEMSTONE
Sapphire

FLOWER
Anthurium

WESTERN COUNTERPART
Aquarius

YEAR of the RABBIT

Those born in the Year of the Rabbit are go-getters who are generous and witty.

The Rabbit might seem like an unexciting sign. After all, pet rabbits are sweet and cuddly. But in the wild, rabbits are clever, fast, agile, and vigilant—skilled at surviving the threat of predators, as well as adapting to the encroachments of civilization on their meadow habitats. They persevere; rarely feeling discouraged, they keep working on solutions until they achieve success. These are all enviable characteristics.

POSITIVE TRAITS

Rabbits tend to be gentle, quiet, sensitive, and elegant, yet they are also alert and quick. They can be quite intuitive, have good memories, and enjoy using humor.

ELEMENTS	YEARS	TRAITS
WOOD RABBIT	• 1915 • 1975	• Clever • Lively • Shrewd
FIRE RABBIT	• 1927 • 1987	• Broad-minded • Smart • Intuitive
EARTH RABBIT	• 1939 • 1999	• Frank • Ambitious • Resourceful
METAL RABBIT	• 1951 • 2011	• Kind-hearted • Imaginative • Enthusiastic
WATER RABBIT	• 1963 • 2023	• Gentle • Amiable • Impulsive

Because they can't stand to be bored, they are good at organizing special occasions or creating romantic moments. Male Rabbits are polite and sincere. Female Rabbits, who are often quite pretty, are demure and good-hearted. Rabbits are also considered one of the luckiest signs—each month has three lucky days, when chances for good fortune will increase.

NEGATIVE TRAITS

Rabbits can be superficial, stubborn, and melancholy. Although they are open, they are overly discreet and rarely reveal their thoughts to others. They are prone to anxiety and often seek ways to escape reality.

The Rabbit is the 4th of the Chinese zodiac animals.

Neptune is the ruling planet of the Rabbit.

Meanwhile, they if are too cautious when they need to act, they miss legitimate opportunities.

ROMANCE OUTLOOK

Rabbits are known for their fertility. This might explain why this is one of the four signs that is blessed in love relationships. Rabbits may be quiet, but they are usually quite good-looking, with polished manners. They never have trouble meeting potential partners, even though they can be shy at first. Male rabbits value a stable home with few conflicts. Female rabbits are outgoing and quite social, although they are thoughtful and treat everyone well.

Best Matches

This sign pairs well with Ox, Goat, Snake, and Pig. Rabbit and Rat matches can be iffy, but compelling if they work out. Rabbit-Rabbit matches can feel like magic, like the perfect tasteful romance. The downside is that the couple will spend a lot of time fretting about finances. Matches with the least potential are Rooster, Monkey, and Horse.

CAREER OUTLOOK

At work, Rabbits are intelligent, skillful, patient, responsible, and quick. Still, they are not very competitive, and rely on their merits to rise up the ladder. Some Rabbits can be creative; others are good at handling precision work or overseeing quality control. Possible career choices include: literature or art teacher, psychologist, nurse, writer, minister, judge, dog or cat breeder, electronics engineer, business consultant, translator, quality inspector, and nanny.

RABBIT at a Glance

MANDARIN NAME
TÙ

YEARS
1927, 1939, 1951, 1963, 1975, 1987, 1999, 2011, 2023

RULING PLANET
Neptune

POLARITY
Yin

LUCKY NUMBERS
3, 4, 6

LUCKY DAYS
26th, 27th, and 29th of lunar month

LUCKY DIRECTIONS
East, southeast, south

SEASON
Spring

COLORS
- Red
- Pink
- Purple

GEMSTONE
Pearl

FLOWER
Jasmine

WESTERN COUNTERPART
Pisces

YEAR of the Dragon

Those born in the Year of the Dragon are leaders who are ambitious and popular.

Number 5 of the Chinese zodiac animals is the only supernatural creature in the group. Due to this, the Dragon is considered the most vital and powerful sign in the zodiac. In Chinese culture it traditionally symbolizes power, nobility, honor, luck, and success. These positive qualities are often combined, however, with a hot temper and a sharp tongue. In past times, Dragons were thought to be natural leaders due to their ambition and dominant natures.

POSITIVE TRAITS

Dragons exhibit courage, tenacity and intelligence, along with enthusiasm and confidence. They face up

ELEMENTS	YEARS	TRAITS
WOOD DRAGON	• 1964 • 2024	• Introverted • Talented • Taciturn
FIRE DRAGON	• 1916 • 1976	• Smart • Ambitious • Adaptable
EARTH DRAGON	• 1928 • 1988	• Smart • Enterprising • Hardworking
METAL DRAGON	• 1940 • 2000	• Natural • Straightforward • Unpredictable
WATER DRAGON	• 1952 • 2012	• Persevering • Far-sighted • Vigorous

to challenges and are not afraid to take risks. These are the people you want on your team—at work or play.

NEGATIVE TRAITS

Dragons are sometimes seen as aggressive, and when angry, they are definitely not open to criticism. They rarely consider themselves irritating and arrogant, though those around them may disagree.

ROMANCE OUTLOOK

The Dragon in love can be surprisingly idealistic, generous, and even passive. Unfortunately, they unrealistically seek perfection in every aspect of

Mars is the ruling planet of the Dragon.

The Dragon is the 5th of the Chinese zodiac animals.

life, including romance. Many hopeful lovers pursue Dragons, which can make them smug and arrogant. They will often marry late, seeking partners who are elegant, intelligent, and compassionate. Praise is sure to win over a Dragon.

Best Matches

Dragons will likely make a good match with Rats, Roosters, and Monkeys. Far less successful are matches with Oxes, Goats, or Dogs in which love eventually fades away. Pigs make good friends, and Dragon-Dragon matches are more promising for lasting friendships than for real love connections.

CAREER OUTLOOK

Repetitive jobs are not suitable for Dragons, who need more scope to utilize their many talents. Jobs related to imagination or creativity are right up their alley. With their strong ability to communicate they might consider careers in teaching, journalism, broadcasting, or writing. They also thrive in leadership positions, such as managers or department heads. As team

players, however, they can sometimes lack a spirit of cooperation. Suitable jobs include architect, politician, economist, doctor, quality inspector, financier, athlete, pharmacist, electrician, priest, artist, and actor.

DRAGON at a Glance

MANDARIN NAME
LÓNG

YEARS
1928, 1940, 1952, 1964, 1976, 1988, 2000, 2012, 2024

RULING PLANET
Mars

POLARITY
Yang

LUCKY NUMBERS
1, 6, 7

LUCKY DAYS
1st and 16th of lunar month

LUCKY DIRECTIONS
East, north, northwest

SEASON
Spring

COLORS
- Gold
- Silver
- White

GEMSTONE
Amethyst

FLOWER
Hyacinth

WESTERN COUNTERPART
Aries

YEAR of the SNAKE

Those born in the Year of the Snake are deep thinkers who are perceptive and intelligent.

According to Chinese culture, the Snake is the most mysterious and intuitive of the zodiac animals. They act upon their own judgment, and because they are so private, they rarely talk about their motivations or their reasons for any of their decisions. Very goal-oriented, they dislike failure and really strive to avoid it at all costs. Snakes are quite fond of material pleasures, and they prefer the highest-quality items, but they also happen to hate shopping.

POSITIVE TRAITS

Snakes are thought to be intelligent and wise, usually well-educated, as well as decent, sophisticated, and

ELEMENTS	YEARS	TRAITS
WOOD SNAKE	• 1905 • 1965	• Orderly • Intelligent • Refined
FIRE SNAKE	• 1917 • 1977	• Smart • Insightful • Communicative
EARTH SNAKE	• 1929 • 1989	• Calm • Self-controlled • Forthright
METAL SNAKE	• 1941 • 2001	• Determined • Courageous • Confident
WATER SNAKE	• 1953 • 2013	• Clever • Creative • Lively

humorous and droll. They are effective communicators, even though they usually say only what is necessary to convey an idea. In leadership roles they tend to show creativity and responsibility.

NEGATIVE TRAITS

Like snakes in nature, zodiac Snakes have a reputation for malevolence. What is more likely to be true is that they are catty, harsh, suspicious, and stingy when it comes to money. They are prone to overspending and not being able to maintain a budget. They also go through lazy, low-energy periods just as snakes in the wild do when molting.

The Snake is the 6th of the Chinese zodiac animals.

Venus is the ruling planet of the Snake.

ROMANCE OUTLOOK

At first the Snake in love may be quite romantic, enthusiastic, and loyal. Alas, they also have intimacy issues—Snakes do not have a lot of friends, mainly because they are hard to know and keep many of their feelings bottled up inside. Yet once a Snake is committed to a partner, they will open up and become responsive. If they become too connected, they have to watch out for jealous or obsessive behavior.

Best Matches

Snakes have a high level of compatibility with Dragons and Roosters. They don't share good chemistry with Tigers, Rabbits, Goats, or Pigs. A Snake-Snake match usually works well because they can trust each other and build on that foundation.

CAREER OUTLOOK

Snakes are in demand in jobs that require creativity and diligence. They tend to become job-hoppers, however, if they get bored, which happens frequently. They are clutch performers who enjoy jobs that offer complex problems to solve and tight deadlines. They prefer to work alone, however, and can get stressed by team dynamics or group demands. When starting a business, they do better after taking on a partner to handle the meet and greets. Good career choices for Snakes include research scientist, analyst, investigator, politician, mediator, teacher, painter, potter, jeweler, astrologer, musician, dietitian, psychologist, and sociologist.

SNAKE at a Glance

MANDARIN NAME
SHÉ

YEARS
1929, 1941, 1953, 1965, 1977, 1989, 2001, 2013, 2025

RULING PLANET
Venus

POLARITY
Yin

LUCKY NUMBERS
2, 8, 9

LUCKY DAYS
1st and 23rd of lunar month

LUCKY DIRECTIONS
Northeast, southwest, south

SEASON
Summer

COLOR
- Black
- Red
- Yellow

GEMSTONE
Opal

FLOWER
Orchid

WESTERN COUNTERPART
Taurus

YEAR of the HORSE

Those born in the Year of the Horse are socializers who are cheerful and perceptive.

The horse appears in many Chinese myths and legends as a figure of admiration or strength, and so it is fitting that the zodiac sign of the Horse is one of high charisma with a rare ability to overcome obstacles. Horses can liven up social occasions or bring harmony to a heated discussion with their verbal skills. An excess of energy can make them unruly or rebellious children, but they soon mature into focused achievers.

POSITIVE TRAITS

Horses possess great vitality, zeal, and a passion for life, and they tend to exhibit an interest in a wide range of pursuits. Warm-hearted and generous, they

ELEMENTS	YEARS	TRAITS
WOOD HORSE	• 1954 • 2014	• Freedom-loving • Observant • Imaginative
FIRE HORSE	• 1966 • 2026	• Smart • Energetic • Passionate
EARTH HORSE	• 1918 • 1978	• Pure • Kind-hearted • Unselfish
METAL HORSE	• 1930 • 1990	• Affectionate • Bold • Outgoing
WATER HORSE	• 1942 • 2002	• Kind • Considerate • Empathetic

make friends easily. Courageous Horses often provide positive role models for younger members of their family and social circle.

NEGATIVE TRAITS

Horses love to spend money. Creating a savings account to prepare for a rainy day can be very difficult for them. They are also too frank at times, not considering the other person's feelings when they speak out. Horses are very bad at keeping secrets, which can affect their business dealings. If they don't achieve something quickly, they have a tendency to give up. They are also vain and clothes-proud.

The Horse is the 7th of the Chinese zodiac animals.

Mercury is the ruling planet of the Horse.

ROMANCE OUTLOOK

Horses are noted for falling in love quickly, but once in love they can be torn by indecision: they yearn for their childlike freedom but enjoy intimate connections. Once a Horse has accepted the relationship, they will readily display their confidence to their partner. Male Horses can be especially romantic; women born under this sign are flirtatious but rarely promiscuous. Faithfulness is part of their nature. Horses enjoy touching, but are not overly sexual: they are more interested in romantic wooing.

Best Matches

Horses pair best with Tigers, Rabbits, and Goats. They should avoid Rats and Oxes. Horse-Horse matches have a lot of potential—they are very compatible at first but may find that their mutual dislike of housekeeping leads to a messy house—and maybe a messy breakup. Horse-Dog connections also start out well, but Dogs may soon judge Horses to be fickle and superficial.

CAREER OUTLOOK

The Horse's high level of energy, ability to learn new things, and strong leadership skills may allow it to rise early in its career. Horses can be shrewd, intent on self-improvement and meeting their goals. They know they can rely on the friends they made on the way up to always have their backs. Possible career choices include architect, scientist, sales rep, events planner, publicist, politician, entrepreneur, art gallery manager, public speaker, journalist, translator, securities trader, performer, and tour operator.

HORSE at a Glance

MANDARIN NAME
MǍ

YEARS
1930, 1942, 1954, 1966, 1978, 1990, 2002, 2014, 2026

RULING PLANET
Mercury

POLARITY
Yang

LUCKY NUMBERS
2, 3, 7

LUCKY DAYS
5th and 20th of lunar month

LUCKY DIRECTIONS
Northeast, southwest, northwest

SEASON
Summer

COLOR
- Yellow
- Green
- White

GEMSTONE
Topaz

FLOWER
Calla lily

WESTERN COUNTERPART
Gemini

YEAR of the GOAT

Those born in the Year of the Goat are altruists who are sympathetic and even-tempered.

Sometimes known as the Sheep or Ram, this sign typically indicates a gentle or mild-mannered soul, one who prefers to travel in groups, but avoids the center spotlight. Soft-hearted Goats are not pushovers, however, and they know how to defend themselves against attack.

POSITIVE TRAITS

Goats are calm and dependable, with kind hearts and good minds. Although they may seem passive, never underestimate the interior toughness of a Goat. When they have a goal in mind, they can persevere, and when knocked down, they have the resilience to recover

ELEMENTS	YEARS	TRAITS
WOOD GOAT	• 1955 • 2015	• Amicable • Gentle • Compassionate
FIRE GOAT	• 1907 • 1967	• Sentimental • Frank • Honest
EARTH GOAT	• 1919 • 1979	• Righteous • Honest • Just
METAL GOAT	• 1931 • 1991	• Principled • Kind-hearted • Responsible
WATER GOAT	• 1943 • 2003	• Trustworthy • Altruistic • Self-sacrificing

and get right back up. Their opinions are usually well thought out, and they tend to stick to them. One reason they seem quiet is that they like being alone with their own thoughts. They are surprisingly fashion conscious and enjoy following the latest styles, but they are not snobbish about wealth.

NEGATIVE TRAITS

Those born under this sign can be a bit timid and passive. They can also be moody and vain and resist spending money. Goats often judge things by their surface appearance and don't look deeper. Goats value their privacy and have trouble opening up.

The Goat is the 8th of the Chinese zodiac animals.

The Moon is the ruling planet of the Goat.

ROMANCE OUTLOOK

Even when Goats fall in love, they can still have trouble expressing their feelings. The men make sincere, romantic lovers, but they can also act childish. The women are attractive and considerate of their partners, but they also are too polite to refuse suitors who don't appeal to them. They tend to take any criticism to heart. All Goats need encouragement from caring partners to open up and create true intimacy.

Best Matches

Goats pair best with a Rabbit, Horse, or Pig. The worst matches may be with an Ox, Dragon, Snake, or Dog. A Goat-Goat match has traditionally been considered an almost perfect pairing—both parties will enjoy giving their opinions about art and music, planning for their home, and even sharing work as colleagues.

CAREER OUTLOOK

Goats are creative and intuitive, always a valued combination in the workplace. They are quick to acquire professional skills, but prefer working in a team, especially with Horse signs. Status and power don't really motivate them. They are not quick to volunteer but will lead a group if asked. Career options include pediatrician, actor, daycare or grade school teacher, interior designer, florist, hairstylist, musician, editor, illustrator, and art history professor.

GOAT at a Glance

MANDARIN NAME
YÁNG

YEARS
1931, 1943, 1955, 1967, 1979, 1991, 2003, 2015, 2027

RULING PLANET
The Moon

POLARITY
Yin

LUCKY NUMBERS
2, 7

LUCKY DAYS
7th and 30th of lunar month

LUCKY DIRECTIONS
East, southeast, south

SEASON
Summer

COLOR
- Red
- Brown
- Purple

GEMSTONE
Emerald

FLOWER
Primrose

WESTERN COUNTERPART
Cancer

YEAR of the MONKEY

Those born in the Year of the Monkey are pioneers who are active and humorous.

Those born under the Monkey sign are smart, cheerful, and energetic, but their curiosity and playfulness also incline them to mischief. Like their animal namesakes, they are also known for being adaptable and flexible. Although they can be clever and creative, they don't always choose the proper ways to display their talents.

POSITIVE TRAITS

Monkeys are considered loyal, wise, and caring, Their characteristic insight, intuition, and forethought often appear while they are still quite young. With their upbeat, amiable personalities, they raise the mood of a room just by entering it.

ELEMENTS	YEARS	TRAITS
WOOD MONKEY	• 2004 • 1944	• Helpful • Self-assured • Stubborn
FIRE MONKEY	• 2016 • 1956	• Intelligent • Adventurous • Irritable
EARTH MONKEY	• 1968 • 2028	• Frank • Optimistic • Fearless
METAL MONKEY	• 1980 • 2040	• Clever, • Confident • Talented,
WATER MONKEY	• 1992 • 1932	• Quick-witted • Attention-seeking • Haughty

NEGATIVE TRAITS

Restless monkeys may become impatient and irritable around those who are less active, and they are easily frustrated. These masters of hijinks look for opportunities to have fun with others, but their pranks can go overboard and hurt people's feelings. Monkeys can't always read their audience. They can be eccentric or sly, which does not endear them to everyone.

ROMANCE OUTLOOK

Monkeys find humorous and intelligent partners to be the most appealing. Male Monkeys are willing to help their partners in both life and work. Their joy for life

The Monkey is the 9th of the Chinese zodiac animals.

The Sun is the ruling planet of the Monkey.

helps to dispel any gloom. They do require their loved ones to create an atmosphere of affection and caring at home. Female Monkeys dislike giving up their freedom. It takes a powerful attraction and a promise of stability for them to change and become part of a loving team. All Monkeys need partners who can stimulate them and keep them on their toes.

Best Matches

Statistics show that a Monkey's best chances for happy, harmonious pairing are with Ox, Dragon and Rabbit. Rats are also possibilities—they push the Monkey to succeed in business. Unpromising combinations are with the Tiger, Pig, and Snake signs. Monkey-Monkey matches start out very well, with lots of shared traits, but both partners need to realize that egotism and jealousy could shake them out of their bliss.

CAREER OUTLOOK

Monkeys are competent, goal-oriented performers who show strong leadership potential. These quick learners and innate problem-solvers can be surprisingly scheming when it comes to moving up the ladder at work. Monkeys tend to be short-sighted;

if they become distracted or bored, they can lose sight of project goals. Careers that play to a Monkey's strengths include most types of freelance work, such as editor, artist, or journalist, also entertainer, musician, DJ, event planner, social director, linguist/translator, shop owner, stockbroker, teacher, and athlete.

MONKEY at a Glance

MANDARIN NAME
HÓU

YEARS
1932, 1944, 1956, 1968, 1980, 1992, 2004, 2016, 2028

RULING PLANET
The Sun

POLARITY
Yang

LUCKY NUMBERS
4, 9

LUCKY DAYS
14th and 28th of lunar month

LUCKY DIRECTIONS
North, northwest, west

SEASON
Autumn

COLOR
- Gold
- White
- Blue

GEMSTONE
Peridot

FLOWER
Chrysanthemum

WESTERN COUNTERPART
Leo

YEAR of the ROOSTER

Those born in the Year of the Rooster are extroverts who are active and dynamic.

Roosters are natural mixers, and with their active, amusing, talkative personalities, it is no wonder they are popular. They tend to be very attractive and are quite comfortable being the center of attention. Still, in spite of seeming strong and courageous, Roosters need reassurance and validation from those close to them.

POSITIVE TRAITS

Roosters are hardworking, resourceful, and creative, as well as loyal. These deep thinkers are typically honest, bright, ambitious, capable, and warm-hearted. Few things can sidetrack them when engaged on a mission; if thwarted they can be fierce.

ELEMENTS	YEARS	TRAITS
WOOD ROOSTER	• 1945 • 2005	• Active • Vibrant • Tender
FIRE ROOSTER	• 1957 • 2017	• Trustworthy • Responsible • Dynamic
EARTH ROOSTER	• 1909 • 1969	• Generous • Trustworthy • Popular
METAL ROOSTER	• 1921 • 1981	• Forceful • Brave • Persevering
WATER ROOSTER	• 1933 • 1993	• Clever • Quick-witted • Tender-hearted

NEGATIVE TRAITS

Roosters can be demanding, expecting others to listen while they speak and then becoming agitated if they are not heeded. Sometimes vain or boastful, Roosters like to brag about their achievements, crowing like their namesakes. They can be perfectionists who will criticize anything they believe does not meet their standards.

ROMANCE OUTLOOK

When Roosters fall in love, they become very caring. This tenderness often makes their partners grow infatuated with them. They are good communicators but not when it comes to romance; they have to let

The Rooster is the 10th of the Chinese zodiac animals.

Mercury is the ruling planet of the Rooster.

their behavior do the talking. This sign finds refuge and contentment in the family setting, and their potential mates should be forewarned that they believe the more family members the better.

Best Matches

Roosters and Dragons form the most compatible pair, with Roosters willing to support the Dragons and back them up; meanwhile Dragons' accomplishments make Roosters proud. Roosters and Snakes can discuss the secrets of life and pursue dreams together. Ox's honesty and conservativeness meshes with the Rooster personality. The least successful pairings are Rabbit, Dog, and other Roosters, which should be obvious . . . there just can't be two centers of attention in one relationship.

CAREER OUTLOOK

Roosters do not really care about making money. They earn it and quickly spend it. Still, they take

their jobs very seriously and usually make good career choices. Their communication skills allow them to shine in interactive positions. They have a strong sense or self-respect and rarely rely on others to get things done. Roosters should consider working as a police officer, diplomat, athlete, cosmetologist, intelligence agent, speech writer, teacher, actor/actress, politician, diplomat, tour guide, or fashion designer.

ROOSTER at a Glance

MANDARIN NAME
Jī

YEARS
1933, 1945, 1957, 1969, 1981, 1993, 2005, 2017, 2029

RULING PLANET
Mercury

POLARITY
Yin

LUCKY NUMBERS
5, 7, 8

LUCKY DAYS
4th and 26th of lunar month

LUCKY DIRECTIONS
East, southeast, south

SEASON
Autumn

COLOR
- Gold
- Brown
- Yellow

GEMSTONE
Citrine

FLOWER
Cockscomb

WESTERN COUNTERPART
Virgo

YEAR of the DOG

Those born in the Year of the Dog are extroverts who are loyal and lively.

This is an upstanding sign that values justice and sincerity and is popular as a supportive friend who dispenses good advice. Dogs tend to be happy individuals who are active at sports. They don't chase the almighty dollar and so are more relaxed than most at work and at home. This inner peace makes them resistant to illnesses.

POSITIVE TRAITS

Dogs are loyal, amiable, and industrious. Men born in Dog years tend to be no-nonsense and genuine individuals; they are usually energetic, though somewhat pessimistic. They are deeply attached to

ELEMENTS	YEARS	TRAITS
WOOD DOG	• 1934 • 1994	• Reliable • Considerate • Understanding
FIRE DOG	• 1934 • 1994	• Intelligent • Hardworking • Genuine
EARTH DOG	• 1934 • 1994	• Communicative • Attentive • Responsible
METAL DOG	• 1910 • 1970	• Conservative • Desirable • Self-confident
WATER DOG	• 1922 • 1982	• Brave • Responsible • Sweet-natured

their families, to the point that any stubbornness in their character disappears when they are dealing with those they love. Women are naturally cautious, giving their trust only sparingly, and are highly protective of their families. They enjoy any activities that bring them outdoors and into nature.

NEGATIVE TRAITS

Unlike their animal namesakes, which can convey a message to their human by just the expression in their eyes, those born under the Dog sign are not great communicators. Often nervous or worried on the inside, Dogs still tend to stick to their decisions no

The Dog is the 11th of the Chinese zodiac animals.

Venus is the ruling planet of the Dog.

CAREER OUTLOOK

Faithful, obedient Dogs often do well at service jobs. They make valuable and valued employees who typically give their all. Easy to get along with, they often help share the workload. During heavy work periods, they need to make sure to get enough rest. Potential career paths might include police officer, scientist, defense attorney, judge, hospitality worker, event planner, nurse, EMT, counselor, interior designer, professor, political aide, priest, and sales clerk.

matter what. Men can be very opinionated and quick to correct others. Women are often openly indifferent toward those they don't like.

ROMANCE OUTLOOK

Dogs have trouble giving their hearts away, and they can take longer than other signs to open up emotionally, even with someone they are attracted to. Yet once they trust the other person enough to commit, they will become completely faithful and loyal. Even if they suffer a lot of emotional ups and downs, devotion is their watchword.

Best Matches

Those born under the Dog sign pair up best with Rabbits; all the other signs can be somewhat problematic for romance. Dogs matched with other Dogs may first think they have found the perfect complement, but when faced with their equally high standards, the couple will need to work out how to relax and be comfortable together. The worst pairings are with Dragon, Goat, and Rooster.

DOG at a Glance

MANDARIN NAME
GŎU

YEARS
1934, 1946, 1958, 1970, 1982, 1994, 2006, 2018, 2030

RULING PLANET
Venus

POLARITY
Yang

LUCKY NUMBERS
3, 4, 9

LUCKY DAYS
7th and 28th of lunar month

LUCKY DIRECTIONS
East, southeast, south

SEASON
Autumn

COLOR
- Red
- Green
- Purple

GEMSTONE
Diamond

FLOWER
Rose

WESTERN COUNTERPART
Libra

YEAR of the PIG

Those born in the Year of the Pig are upright souls who are diligent and sincere.

In China pigs are revered for their calm demeanor and as symbols of luck, wealth, and prosperity. Those born under the Pig sign are known for their diligence, compassion, and generosity. Ultra-responsible, they keep their eyes on the goal and never flag, no matter what the obstacles. Even though they rarely seek help from others, they are quick to volunteer to lend a hand.

POSITIVE TRAITS

Pigs are kind-hearted, even-tempered, and very loyal. They are gallant, never seeking to harm others. They project a calm appearance that reflects their steady natures, but they may occasionally be impetuous.

ELEMENTS	YEARS	TRAITS
WOOD PIG	• 1935 • 1995	• Sweet-natured • Attractive • Easy-going
FIRE PIG	• 1947 • 2007	• Ambitious • Persevering • Clever
EARTH PIG	• 1959 • 2019	• Communicative • Popular • Punctual
METAL PIG	• 1971 • 2031	• Open-minded • Amiable • Helpful
WATER PIG	• 1923 • 1983	• Ambitious • Independent • Serious

NEGATIVE TRAITS

Because they are so straightforward themselves, Pigs rarely suspect trickery and so are easily taken advantage of. They believe that money is very important and can buy peace of mind. They may shower a love object with gifts as proof of their feelings. Pigs can sometimes be slow-witted or hesitant, or, conversely, hot-headed and rash.

ROMANCE OUTLOOK

Pig signs in love are usually sensitive, refined, and affectionate, with an almost old-fashioned attitude about what to expect from a romance. Their courtship

The Pig is the 12th of the Chinese zodiac animals.

Pluto is the ruling planet of the Pig.

CAREER OUTLOOK

Pigs have great concentration and stay calm in a crisis. They work well in groups and are accustomed to relying on others. Many enjoy working with animals and nature, as well as in public service and in medical or creative fields. They should stay away from competitive jobs that require strict schedules. Some career options include veterinarian, forester, engineer, civil servant, police officer, doctor, livestock breeder, professor, artist, singer, dancer, and HR counselor.

can be defined as sweet rather than sensual, and they show their attraction by caring actions, not sexy moves. Men of this sign speak of craving a passionate marriage, yet they often act shy, thinking it will attract the partner they have chosen. Women born under this sign may act fragile or passive during courtship, but their real thoughts are often veiled.

Best Matches

The optimum pairings for Pigs are Goats, Tigers, and Rabbits. These signs are attracted to one another and, most important, know how to please the other. As a married couple they admire each other's merits and are willing to work hard for the family. The worst matches for this sign are Monkeys and Snakes. At the most these couples are polite to each other but lack the deep connection that a lifelong union requires. A match between two Pig signs will probably be quite compatible and sensual, but they run the risk of becoming so fixated on each other, and on pleasing their partner, that the outer world fades away. They can also get into a criticism-countercriticism loop that is dangerous to their harmony.

PIG at a Glance

MANDARIN NAME ZHŪ	**LUCKY DIRECTIONS** Southeast, northeast
YEARS 1935, 1947, 1959, 1971, 1983, 1995, 2007, 2019, 2031	**SEASON** Winter
RULING PLANET Pluto	**COLOR** • Gold • Gray • Yellow
POLARITY Yin	**GEMSTONE** Ruby
LUCKY NUMBERS 2, 5, 8	**FLOWER** Hydrangea
LUCKY DAYS 17th and 24th of lunar month	**WESTERN COUNTERPART** Scorpio

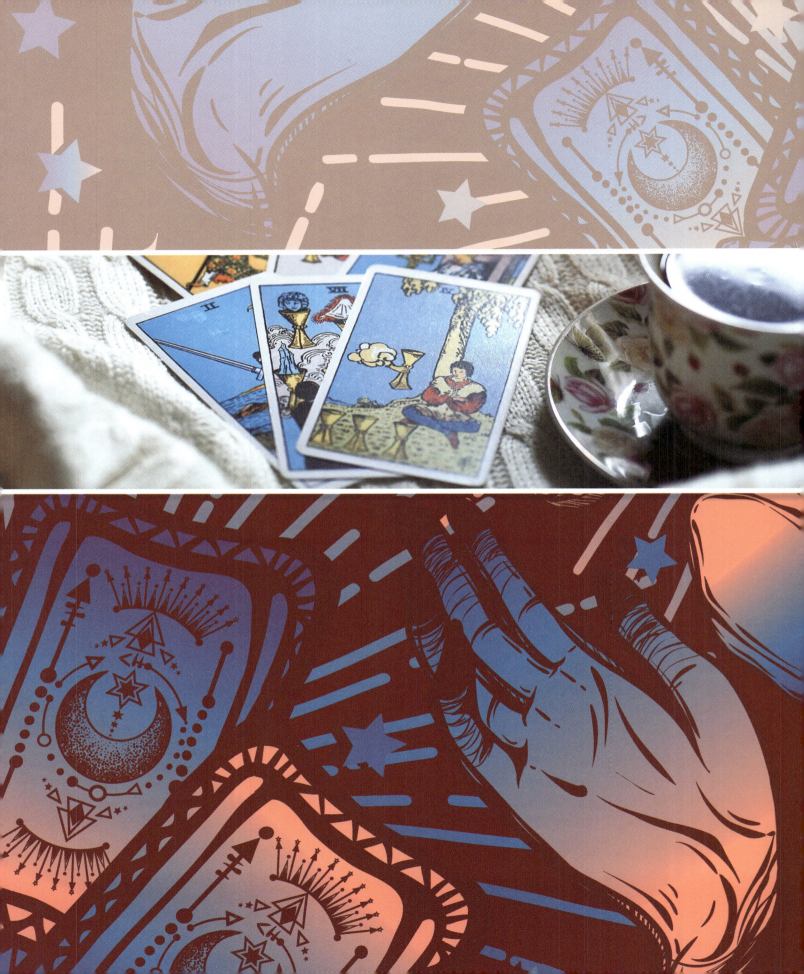

C·H·A·P·T·E·R 2

CARTOMANCY and the
ART of the TAROT

DIVINING with CARTOMANCY

This divination method uses a standard deck of playing cards to foretell the future.

You merely need a deck of playing cards to tell a fortune. Formally called cartomancy, this practice appeared in Europe in the 14th century, not long after cards themselves were introduced on the Continent. Practitioners of cartomancy are generally known as cartomancers or card readers.

METHODS

Layouts for cartomancy using a standard 52-card deck range from pulling a single card to a more complicated spread using 21 cards. You can also use the same layouts as you would with a tarot deck, which include a significator for the querent. You can also augment the 52-card deck with a Joker or read with a French-style 32-card piquet deck, which includes the aces of each suit, the face cards, and the sevens through to the tens.

The JOKER

If you choose to include a Joker in your reading, only add one. The Joker, which corresponds to the Fool in the tarot deck, has some of the same meanings in the regular deck of playing cards. It is truly a "wild card," and when it appears in a reading, it means that something unexpected and uncontrolled can occur—the querent should expect a surprise.

The Significator

In cartomancy (as well as the tarot), the significator is a card that stands for the querent. Traditionally, a King represents a mature male, a Queen a mature female, and a Jack stands for young people of either gender. Each of the face, or court, cards has also traditionally been associated with a person's coloring—the Hearts standing in for those with sandy, dark blond, or light brown hair and brown, blue, or hazel eyes; the Clubs for those with medium or dark brown hair and brown, blue, or hazel eyes; the Diamonds for those with red or light blond hair with blue, green, or gray eyes; and the Spades for those with dark brown to black hair and dark brown eyes. A more modern approach places greater emphasis on the temperaments of the suits, which might better match the querent's true nature rather than their outward appearance.

Quick Guide: Common Significators

KING OF HEARTS

Fair-haired, mature man
- Generous
- Good-natured, but can be rash
- Amorous
- Passionate
- Hasty

QUEEN OF HEARTS

Fair-haired mature woman
- Faithful
- Affectionate
- Amiable
- Mild-mannered
- Honest

JACK OF HEARTS

Fair-haired young person
- Good-tempered
- Learned
- Lucky
- Adventurous
- Starry-eyed

KING OF CLUBS

Medium-to-dark-haired mature man
- Honest
- Affectionate
- Humane
- Upright
- Steadfast

QUEEN OF CLUBS

Medium-to-dark-haired woman
- Charming
- Confident
- Tender
- Quick-tempered
- Attractive

JACK OF CLUBS

Medium-to-dark-haired young person
- Reliable
- Open
- Sincere
- Caring

KING OF DIAMONDS

Red-to-auburn-haired mature man
- Stubborn
- Dignified
- Quick to anger
- Vengeful
- Cunning

QUEEN OF DIAMONDS

Red-to-auburn-haired woman
- Flirty
- Sociable
- Talkative
- Gossipy
- Hedonistic

JACK OF DIAMONDS

Red-to-auburn-haired young person
- Stubborn
- Hot-headed
- Tattle-tale
- Fickle

KING OF SPADES

Dark-haired mature man
- Ambitious
- Authoritative
- Learned
- Proud
- Successful
- Passionate

QUEEN OF SPADES

Dark-haired woman
- Open
- Mercurial
- Changeable
- Learned
- Easily flattered

JACK OF SPADES

Dark-haired young person
- Well-meaning
- Obliging, but can be self-absorbed
- Critical
- Hot-tempered

Temperaments of the Suits

Each suit represents a certain temperament. Keep these in mind as you read the cards as a general guideline to the overall feel of the cards selected, especially when choosing the querent's significator.

- *Hearts* Affectionate, home-loving, genial, social, hospitable, sympathetic; also can be somewhat shy
- *Clubs* Intuitive, constant, reliable, upright, cheerful, friendly, intellectual, eloquent, persuasive
- *Diamonds* Outgoing, breezy, optimistic, inspiring, ambitious, buoyant; also can be impatient
- *Spades* Reserved, cool, introverted, logical, self-contained, steadfast; also can be melancholy or easily discouraged

READING THE CARDS

As with the temperament of the querent, the suits are also indicators of other aspects of the reading, and a preponderance of one suit can indicate aspects of the question the querent is posing.

- *Hearts* Emotional – mostly signify love, invitations, and good friends
- *Clubs* Achievement – mostly indicate happiness and good business arrangements
- *Diamonds* Material – mostly concern finances
- *Spades* Challenges – mostly portend annoyances, sickness, or worry

The Spreads

The single-card method can be used whenever you want to evaluate how your day is going or to get a quick answer to a question. You simply concentrate on your question while well shuffling the deck, and then draw a single card.

Other methods include the Three-Card Spread, the Nine-Card Spread, the Magic Square, the Horseshoe Spreads, the Pyramid Spread, the Celestial Circle, and the Classic Fortune-Telling Spread.

DIVINATORY MEANINGS

Various meanings have been ascribed to the individual cards in different countries and times, but there is a general feel to each of the cards that transcends these differences. Note too, that their meanings, unlike in the tarot, remain the same whether upright or reversed.

♥ The Suit of Hearts

- *Ace* Feasting, pleasure, happiness, the home, love, friendship, joy, the start of a romance
- *King* A good-natured man, affectionate, but can be hot and hasty, rash in his undertakings, and very amorous
- *Queen* A woman of fair complexion, faithful, trustworthy, and affectionate
- *Jack* A person of no particular sex, but always the closest friend or nearest relation of the querent
- *Ten* A good heart, good fortune
- *Nine* Wealth, grandeur, and high esteem
- *Eight* Drinking, feasting, visits, and visitors
- *Seven* A fickle and unfaithful person
- *Six* A generous, open and credulous disposition, easily imposed on, but a friend of the distressed
- *Five* A wavering and unsettled disposition; also jealousy
- *Four* A late marriage; change or a journey.
- *Three* Imprudence that greatly contributes to querent experiencing much ill will from others
- *Two* Extraordinary good future and success

♣ The Suit of Clubs

- *Ace* Great wealth, much prosperity; also peace and tranquility of mind
- *King* A humane, upright, and affectionate man; faithful, honest, open, generous

Opposite: The Fortune-Teller *by French artist Frédéric Bazille was painted circa 1869. In this period, card reading was mainly a pastime of women and girls.*

- *Queen* A tender, mild woman; also attractive, helpful, honest, self-confident
- *Jack* An open, sincere, and good friend
- *Ten* Speedy wealth, travel
- *Nine* Obstinacy; also new romance
- *Eight* A covetous person; also danger, recklessness, jealousy, spite
- *Seven* Brilliant fortune, exquisite bliss, but beware of the opposite sex, from these alone can misfortune be experienced
- *Six* A lucrative partnership
- *Five* Marriage to a person who will improve your circumstances; also help from a spouse
- *Four* Inconstancy and change
- *Three* Wealthy marriages
- *Two* Opposition or disappointment

♦ The Suit of Diamonds

- *Ace* A letter; a ring or gift
- *King* A man of fiery temper, continued anger, seeking revenge, and obstinate in his resolutions
- *Queen* A flirt, sophisticated, witty, fond of company
- *Jack* A youth who will look more to his own interest than yours; also opinionated, argumentative
- *Ten* A country spouse, with wealth and many children; also a purse of gold
- *Nine* A surprise about money
- *Eight* Unhappy late marriage; also uncertain finances
- *Seven* Waste of goods and losses; also surprising news or gifts
- *Six* An early marriage and widowhood, but beware a second marriage; also a reconciliation
- *Five* Success in enterprises; also good children

- *Four* Vexation and annoyance; also an inheritance, improving finances
- *Three* Quarrels, possible lawsuits, and domestic disagreements, family strife
- *Two* Early love, but you will meet with great opposition

♣ Suit of Spades

- *Ace* Emotional upheaval, tumultuous love affair
- *King* An ambitious and successful man
- *Queen* A woman who will be corrupted by the rich of both sexes; also a widow
- *Jack* An immature young person, well-meaning, but unreliable
- *Ten* Worry, misfortune, bad news
- *Nine* Terrible luck, dangerous sickness, loss of fortune, calamity; also family quarrels

- *Eight* Opposition from friends, disappointment, thwarted plans
- *Seven* Loss of a valuable friend; also warning of other sorrows
- *Six* Very little interpretation of your success
- *Five* Good luck in the choice of your companion for life; also bad temper and interference
- *Four* Worries, sickness, troubles
- *Three* Good fortune in marriage; also an inconstant partner, faithlessness
- *Two* Scandal, deceit, separation

You can tell fortunes with any deck of playing cards, but there are many beautiful vintage and hand-drawn designs available to choose from.

The Fortune-Teller *by Mikhail Vrubel, painted in 1895, depicts what appears to be a Romany card reader. Although few people took cartomancy seriously in this period, there was a hidden world of women— mostly older—who managed to eke out a living by reading cards.*

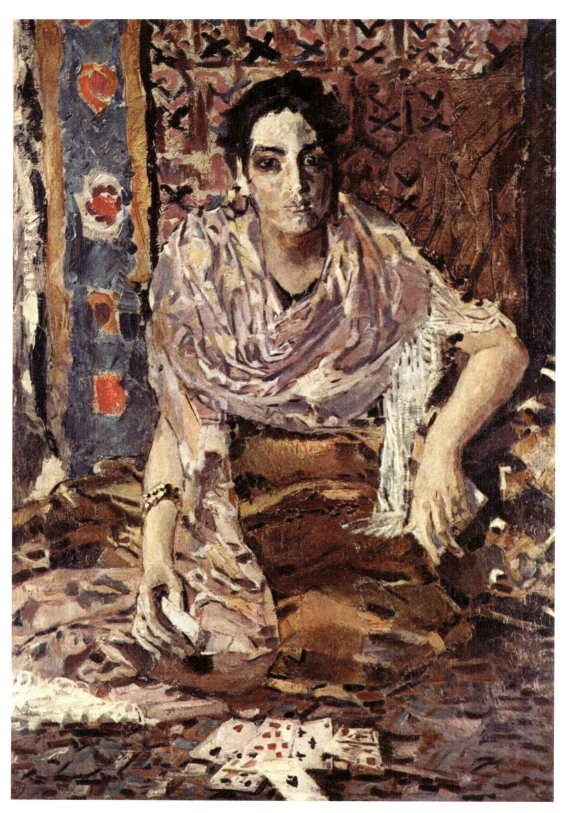

QUICK GUIDE: Common Spreads

THREE-CARD SPREAD

This spread gives a bit more depth to the querent's question than the single-card reading.

1. Shuffle the deck, concentrating on your question.
2. Lay out the cards in a row from left to right.
3. Read in order.

1
THE PAST

2
THE PRESENT

3
THE FUTURE

NINE-CARD SPREAD

This spread gives a bit more depth to the querent's question than the Three-Card Spread.

1. Shuffle the deck, concentrating on your question.
2. Lay out the cards in 3 rows across and 3 down.
3. Read in order.

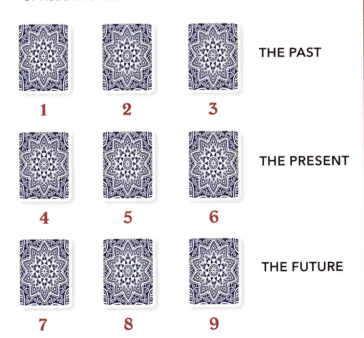

THE PAST — 1 2 3

THE PRESENT — 4 5 6

THE FUTURE — 7 8 9

CLASSIC FORTUNE-TELLER'S SPREAD

Often called the Gypsy Spread or the Romany Spread, this layout is known as one for the experts, demanding experience and great skill. This spread works whether you or the querent are just looking for a general overview of a situation or there are several interconnected issues. With its free-form nature, it leaves much to the interpretation of the reader.

1. Shuffle the deck, concentrating on the querent's question or the situation at hand.
2. From left to right, lay three rows of seven cards.
3. Read the cards, combining them into a cohesive and meaningful narrative.

• Column 1 (cards 1, 8, and 15) – The self
• Column 2 (cards 2, 9, and 16) – Surroundings
• Column 3 (cards 3, 10, and 17) – Hopes and dreams
• Column 4 (cards 4, 11, and 18) – Known Factors
• Column 5 (cards 5, 12, and 19) – Hidden destiny
• Column 6 (cards 6, 13, and 20) – Short-term future
• Column 7 (cards 7, 14, and 21) – The outcome

1 2 3 4 5 6 7
THE PAST

8 9 10 11 12 13 14
THE PRESENT

15 16 17 18 19 20 21
THE FUTURE

PYRAMID SPREAD

There are many variations of the Pyramid Spread. It is a very flexible layout, and it gives a good general reading.

1. Have the querent shuffle the deck, concentrating on their question.
2. Spread out all cards face down in a fan shape.
3. Select 10 cards from the spread.
4. Place the cards face up in the order shown.
5. Read in order.

- Card 1 – Overall influence
- Cards 2, 3 – Action
- Cards 4, 5, 6 – Underlying forces
- Cards 7, 8, 9, 10 – The outcome

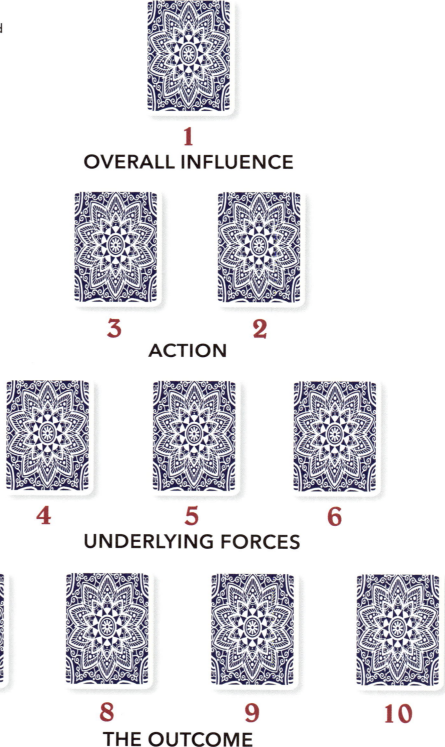

1

OVERALL INFLUENCE

3　　　　　**2**

ACTION

4　　　**5**　　　**6**

UNDERLYING FORCES

7　　**8**　　**9**　　**10**

THE OUTCOME

**1 or
1, 8, 15**

**7 or
7, 14, 21**

**2 or
2, 9, 16**

**6 or
6, 13, 20**

**3 or
3, 10, 17**

**5 or
5, 12, 19**

**4 or
4, 11, 18**

THE HORSESHOE SPREADS

Seven-Card Horseshoe Spread

The 7-card version of the Horseshoe Spread is a good choice when your querent has a specific question, such as whether to move, change jobs, or get married.

1. Have the querent shuffle the deck, concentrating on their question.
2. Lay out the cards face up in a horseshoe pattern, starting at the top left-hand corner, working down to the 4th card and then pack up to the 7th.
3. Read in order.

- Card 1 – Past influences
- Card 2 – Choices and alternatives
- Card 3 – Stability or instability of situation
- Card 4 – Challenges
- Card 5 – Help or hindrances
- Card 6 – Who are friends or foes
- Card 7 – The outcome

Twenty-One-Card Horseshoe Spread

This 21-card version of a Horseshoe spread works better for giving an overview of the querent's life.

1. Have the querent shuffle the deck, concentrating on their question.
2. Lay out the cards face up in a horseshoe pattern, starting at the top left-hand corner, working down to the 4th card and then pack up to the 7th (as you would for the basic Horseshoe).
3. Lay the 8th card on top of the 1st, and work your way down and up to the 14th card.
4. Place the 15th card over the 8th, and repeat the process, until you've place the 21st card.
5. Read in order.

- Cards 1, 8, 15 – The past situation
- Cards 2, 9, 16 – The present situation
- Cards 3, 10, 17 – The near future
- Cards 4, 11, 18 – Unexpected developments
- Cards 5, 12, 19 – Other people's influence
- Cards 6, 13, 20 – Obstacles and opposition
- Cards 7, 14, 21 – The outcome

MAGIC SQUARE SPREAD

This spread will give the querent a good reading of their psychological state in regards to their question.

1. Choose a significator, and place it to one side.
2. Have the querent shuffle the remainder of the deck, concentrating on their question.
3. When shuffled, take four cards from the top of the deck, and place them in the order shown. The 5th card is the significator.
4. Taking from the top of the deck, lay out the 6th, 7th, 8th, and 9th cards as shown below.
5. Read in order.

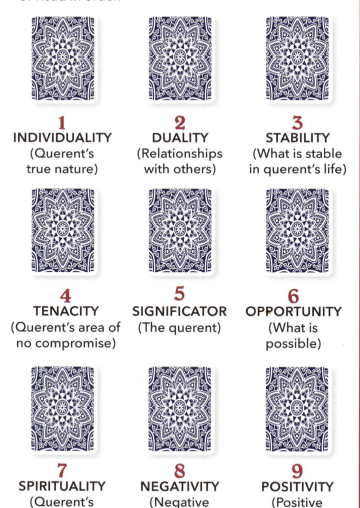

1
INDIVIDUALITY
(Querent's true nature)

2
DUALITY
(Relationships with others)

3
STABILITY
(What is stable in querent's life)

4
TENACITY
(Querent's area of no compromise)

5
SIGNIFICATOR
(The querent)

6
OPPORTUNITY
(What is possible)

7
SPIRITUALITY
(Querent's spiritual life)

8
NEGATIVITY
(Negative influences)

9
POSITIVITY
(Positive influences)

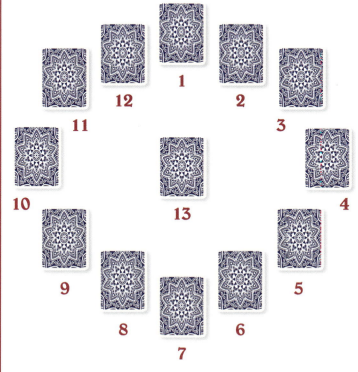

CELESTIAL CIRCLE

This 13-card spread should be done only once a year, with each card representing a calendar month.

1. Have the querent shuffle the deck, concentrating on the year ahead.
2. Spread out all card face down in a fan shape.
3. Select 13 cards from the spread.
4. Place the first 12 cards face up in the order they were selected, starting at the center top and working clockwise.
5. Place the 13th card in the center.
6. Read in order, as months of the year, with the first card as the current month.
7. The 13th card is the overall forecast for the year. Read this card by suit alone.

- Heart – Happiness
- Diamond – Success
- Club – Accomplishment
- Spade – Discord

The SUITS of PLAYING CARDS

Playing cards, as well as the Minor Arcana of tarot, are divided into suits, with each having the court cards and the pip, or numerical, cards from ace to 10. The contemporary standard sets include Hearts, Clubs, Diamonds, and Spades. The earliest suit system in Europe was the Latin, which used Coins, Clubs, Cups, and Swords. During the 15th-century, German-speaking manufacturers devised new sets, depicting Hearts, Bells, Acorns, and Leaves. Swiss-Germans used Roses, Bells, Acorns, and Shields. The French suits—Clovers (or clubs), Tiles or Diamonds), Hearts, and Pikes (or Spades)—were inspired by the German suits. Italian and Spanish suits follow the Latin suits of Coins, Clubs, Cups, and Swords.

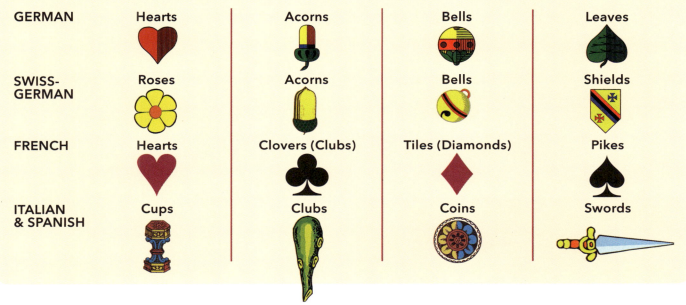

GERMAN	Hearts	Acorns	Bells	Leaves
SWISS-GERMAN	Roses	Acorns	Bells	Shields
FRENCH	Hearts	Clovers (Clubs)	Tiles (Diamonds)	Pikes
ITALIAN & SPANISH	Cups	Clubs	Coins	Swords

READING the TAROT

The tarot is a form a cartomancy that uses a specialized deck designed for divination.

The tarot has a long and storied history, but many sources trace the genesis of tarot-like illustrated cards to the first documented packs recorded between 1440 and 1450 in Italy.

Among ancient cards that are mentioned in connection with the tarot, there are the Mantegna Tarocchi, also known as the Tarocchi Cards or Baldini Cards, by two different unknown artists. There seems to be no record that they were used for the purposes of a game, whether of chance or skill.

Later, tarot cards were made to play games, but evidence of a tarot deck used for cartomancy dates to about 1750 when rudimentary divinatory meanings were assigned to the cards of the Tarocco Bolognese. This was a 62-card Italian-suited deck. By the 1780s, the use of tarot decks had become popular in Paris during the 1780s, using the Tarot of Marseilles. In 1789, the French occultist Etteilla issued the first tarot deck specifically designed for divination. Etteilla, the pseudonym of Jean-Baptiste Alliette, became the first professional tarot occultist in history to make his living by cartomancy. He also published his thoughts on the correspondences between the tarot and astrology, ideas that persist to this day.

These days, the tarot continues to thrive as a popular form of divination, whether one is a true believer in fortune-telling or if reading for amusement.

COMPOSITION OF THE DECK

A modern tarot deck consists of 78 cards, which are divided into two distinct parts: the 22 cards of the Major Arcana and the 56 pip cards of the Minor Arcana. The terms *Major Arcana* and *Minor Arcana* were first used by French author Jean-Baptiste Pitois in the late 19th century.

This painting, created in the late 1600s, depicts Prince Francesco Antelminelli Castracani Fibbia (1360–1419) with a deck of the Tarocchino Bolognese. Despite the presence of these cards, actual tarot cards were not invented until two decades after the prince's death.

The Major Arcana has captured the interest of many an artist, and some tarot decks exist primarily as artwork, containing only the 22 cards of the Major Arcana. Many of these variations are based on the Rider-Waite deck; other common decks are the Tarot of Marseilles and the Thoth deck painted by Lady Frieda Harris, according to instructions from famed occultist Aleister Crowley.

Insight Easily the most recognizable tarot deck, the Rider-Waite was originally published in 1909. Illustrator Pamela Colman Smith drew the images from the instructions of academic and mystic A. E. Waite, and the cards were originally published by the Rider Company. This deck has inspired numerous variants and imitations.

METHODS

As with cartomancy using a standard deck of playing cards, divination using a tarot deck can be as simple as pulling a single card or as complicated as one of the more involved spreads, such as the Celtic Cross. Many tarot spreads will designate one of the cards as a Significator for the querent.

The Significator

The significator is a card that stands for the querent. One long-used method is to simply designate The Magician for a male seeker and The High Priestess for a female seeker. Another traditional method uses the court cards. In tarot, a King traditionally represents an older, mature male, a Queen a female, a Knight stands for a young man, and the Page a youth or child of either gender. As with general cartomancy, each of the court cards has also traditionally been associated with a person's coloring, although the meanings are a bit different.

- *Cups* Blonde hair, blue eyes, fair skin
- *Wands* Red hair, ruddy complexion, blue, or green eyes
- *Pentacles* Dark hair, dark eyes, dark complexion
- *Swords* Brown hair, medium complexion, brown, hazel, or gray eyes

You should not, however, be bound by physical description, which can be very limiting and lump people with very different personalities into one group by ethnic phenotype. A more modern approach is to select a Significator that matches the querent's personality, rather than their appearance.

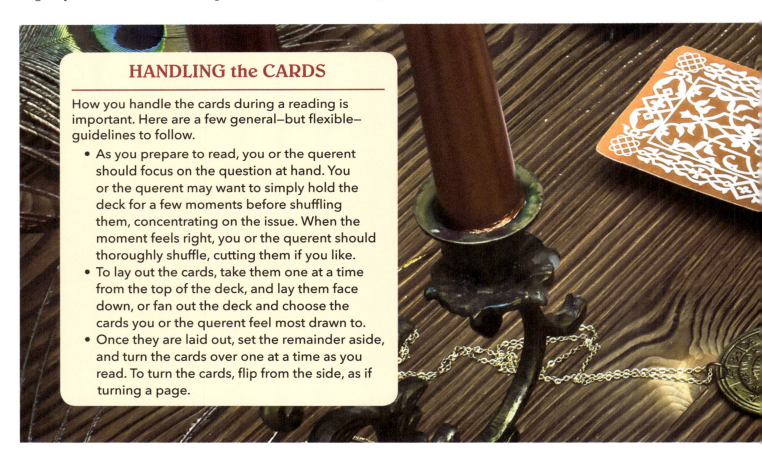

HANDLING the CARDS

How you handle the cards during a reading is important. Here are a few general—but flexible—guidelines to follow.

- As you prepare to read, you or the querent should focus on the question at hand. You or the querent may want to simply hold the deck for a few moments before shuffling them, concentrating on the issue. When the moment feels right, you or the querent should thoroughly shuffle, cutting them if you like.
- To lay out the cards, take them one at a time from the top of the deck, and lay them face down, or fan out the deck and choose the cards you or the querent feel most drawn to.
- Once they are laid out, set the remainder aside, and turn the cards over one at a time as you read. To turn the cards, flip from the side, as if turning a page.

- *King of Cups* Individuals who are self-assured—they are caring, creative, spiritual, big-hearted, and warm.
- *Queen of Cups* Individuals who follow their heart—they are sweet, empathetic, intuitive, compassionate, and sensitive.
- *Knight of Cups* Individuals who stand out from the crowd—they are charming, moody, dependent, romantic, and idealistic.
- *Page of Cups* Individuals who may still be immature—they are dreamy, sensitive, innocent, filled with deep emotion, and dramatic.
- *King of Wands* Individuals who are innovative and prove to be leaders—they are passionate, brave, energetic, and funny.
- *Queen of Wands* Individuals who make good friends—they are independent, easily excited, feisty, determined, passionate, and sincere.

- *Knight of Wands* Individuals who are energetic and enthusiastic—they can be reckless or impulsive.
- *Page of Wands* Individuals keen to learn and discover new things—they are imaginative, adventurous, mischievous, and bold.
- *King of Pentacles* Individuals who are traditionalists—they are hard-working providers, generous, stable, and family-oriented.
- *Queen of Pentacles* Individuals who set priorities and balance work and home life—they are patient, nurturing, practical, traditional, and conservative,.
- *Knight of Pentacles* Individuals who are hard-working—they are responsible, finance and career driven, and can be workaholics.
- *Page of Pentacles* Individuals who have a yet-unfulfilled promise—they studious, diligent, quiet, perfectionistic, and focused.

Tarot cards often include the symbols of the zodiac signs in their designs. In this set, the Ace of Cups shows the symbols of the water signs, the Ace of Wands show the fire signs, the Ace of Pentacles, the earth signs, and the Ace of Swords show the symbols of the air signs.

You can also can also determine the suit of the significator based on its affinity to the water, fire, earth, and air signs of the zodiac.

- *Cups* Water signs: Cancer, Scorpio, Pisces
- *Wands* Fire signs: Aries, Leo, Sagittarius
- *Pentacles* Earth signs: Taurus, Virgo, Capricorn
- *Swords* Air signs: Gemini, Libra, Aquarius

READING THE CARDS

As with the temperament of the querent, the suits are also indicators of other aspects of the reading, and a preponderance of one suit can indicate aspects of the question the querent is posing.

- *Cups* Love, family, or relationships
- *Wands* Work or business
- *Pentacles* Finance or health
- *Swords* Strife or quarrels

The Spreads

As when reading the future with standard playing cards, you can use a single-card method whenever you want to evaluate how your day is going or to get a quick answer to a question. You simply concentrate on your question while thoroughly shuffling the deck, and then draw a single card.

Other methods include the Three-Card Spread, the Five-Card Spread and its variations, and the Celtic Cross. You can also tailor a layout to reflect the kind of question, whether it is about romance, career, or just the general state of affairs. The choice is wide, with hundreds of spreads and their variants out there; the following pages highlight just a few.

- *King of Swords* Individuals who are intellectual—they are rational, communicative, disciplined, distant, cautious, and aloof.
- *Queen of Swords* Individuals who are mysterious—they are intelligent, guarded, sharp, seductive, careful, and reserved and can be cold and distant
- *Knight of Swords* Individuals who are aggressive—they are ambitious, often manipulative, and controlling.
- *Page of Swords* Individuals who are sly and cunning—they are filled with anxious, nervous, bright, chatty, and curious.

STORING YOUR CARDS

By their very nature tarot cards are fragile. Made of laminated paper, they can begin to show signs of wear from repeated use, and the oils from your hands can stain them. To prevent damage, you want to properly store your cards in a protective case or cover. You can use their original packaging or a specially designed tarot box. For easy portability, you can wrap them in a scarf or place them in a tarot pouch. If you favor a scarf or pouch, choose one made of natural fabric, such as silk or linen. There are many beautiful styles of pouches available, or you can easily make one yourself.

QUICK GUIDE: Common Spreads

THREE-CARD SPREAD

This simple spread is a great way for beginners to hone their reading skills. The three cards give a sense of the past, present, and future perspective on any situation.

1. Shuffle the deck, concentrating on your question.
2. Lay out the cards in a row from left to right.
3. Read in order.

1	**2**	**3**
THE PAST	THE PRESENT	THE FUTURE

EVERYDAY SPREAD

Another three-card spread, this one is perfect to give yourself a reading every day. It is a great one to do for yourself at the start of your day.

1. Shuffle the deck, concentrating on the day ahead.
2. Lay out the cards in a row from left to right.
3. Read in order.

- Card 1 – Represents you at the moment you pull the card.
- Card 2 – The crossing card tells you what you will encounter that day.
- Card 3 – The outcome card tells you how to effectively handle the day's conflicts.

FIVE-CARD SPREAD

A five-card tarot spread is not only easy to master, but it is also versatile enough to give insight into a variety of questions. You can also adapt this layout to answer questions about specific themes, such as an existing relationship or finding new love.

1. Shuffle the deck, concentrating on your question.
2. Lay out the cards in the order shown below.
3. Read in order.

GENERAL READING

- Card 1 – Preconceived Ideas
- Card 2 – The Present
- Card 3 – The Unexpected
- Card 4 – The Near Future
- Card 5 – The Distant Future

RELATIONSHIP CROSS

- Card 1 – Querent's place in the relationship
- Card 2 – Partner's place in the relationship
- Card 3 – Foundations of the relationship
- Card 4 – Present state of the relationship
- Card 5 – Likely outcome

5

1   **4**   **2**

3

FIVE-CARD FINDING LOVE CROSS

This variation of the Five-Card Spread gives the querent insight in how to find love. It is most often used for issues of romance, but it can be read for questions concerning love of self and self-confidence.

1. Shuffle the deck, concentrating on your question.
2. Lay out the cards in the order shown below.
3. Read in order.

- Card 1 – Current issues in querent's love life
- Card 2 – Past relationships/influences
- Card 3 – Issues to address to allow love in
- Card 4 – Areas to develop to allow love in
- Card 5 – The likely outcome

FIVE-CARD MONEY SPREAD

If you or your querent has a question about finances, try this spread to divine a path forward.

1. Shuffle the deck, concentrating on your question.
2. Lay out the cards in the order shown below.
3. Read in order.

- Card 1 – The current financial situation
- Card 2 – Whether money is coming
- Card 3 – Financial opportunities
- Card 4 – What might be of financial benefit
- Card 5 – The likely outcome

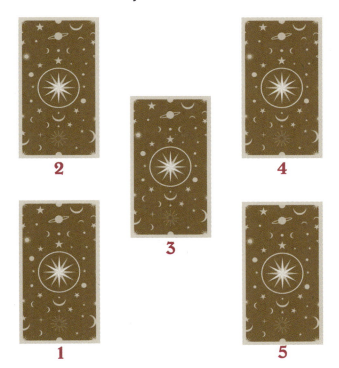

Insight For the best reading, a question should be as specific as possible. Ask, what am I holding on to, or what do I need to let go of? What opportunities lie before me? What do I need to pay attention to today? Be sure to concentrate on the question while holding and shuffling the cards.

BIRTHDAY SPREAD

This is a fun spread to do on your birthday to prepare for the year ahead. It also makes a perfect gift for someone else.

1. Shuffle the deck, concentrating on your question.
2. Lay out the cards in a row from left to right.
3. Read in order.

1
THE YEAR
BEHIND YOU

2
WHAT YOU
NEED TO
LEAVE
BEHIND YOU

3
A GIFT TO YOU

4
WHAT YOU
NEED TO
EMBRACE
THIS YEAR

5
THE YEAR
AHEAD

WITCH'S LADDER SPREAD

This six-card spread is meant for when you or the querent is starting a new journey. It can be a literal journey or travel, but it can also be a journey toward a set goal, such as a new job or a new course of study. It is for when you have a destination in mind and need to chart a path to it. This spread will help you create a plan to reach that destination or achieve that goal.

1. Shuffle the deck, concentrating on your destination or goal.
2. Lay out the cards in a row from left to right.
3. Read in order.

5

4

3

2

1

- Card 1 – Currents values
- Card 2 – Currently resources
- Card 3 – A mentor
- Card 4 – An important area for growth
- Card 5 – A first concrete step to take to start the journey to the destination or goal

NEW YEAR'S CIRCLE

This 13-card spread should be done only once a year, with each card representing a calendar month, along with one to summarize the entire year.

1. Have the querent shuffle the deck, concentrating on the year ahead.
2. Spread out all card face down in a fan shape.
3. Select 13 cards from the spread.
4. Place the first 12 cards face up in the order they were selected, starting at nine o'clock position, and working clockwise.
5. Place the 13th card in the center.
6. Read in order, as months of the year, with the first card as the current month.
7. The 13th card is the year's overall forecast.

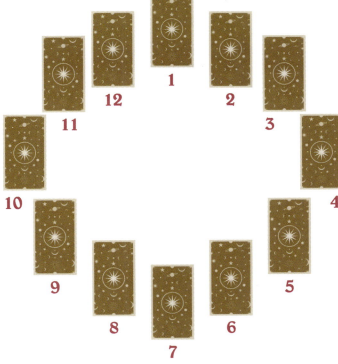

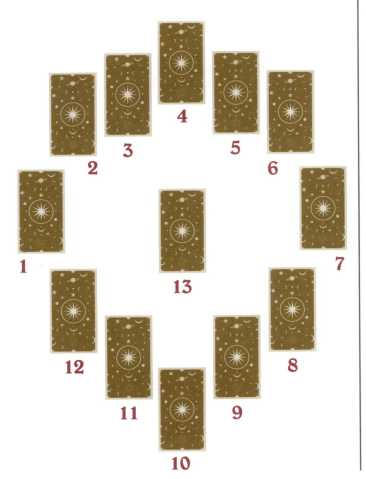

ZODIAC CIRCLE

This 12-card uses the signs of the zodiac, assigning qualities to each one.

1. Have the querent shuffle the deck, concentrating on the year ahead.
2. Spread out all card face down in a fan shape.
3. Select 12 cards from the spread, and place the first 12 cards face up in the order shown at left.
4. Place the 13th card in the center.
5. Read in order.

- Card 1 – Aries: Personality
- Card 2 – Taurus: Financial
- Card 3 – Gemini: Communication
- Card 4 – Cancer: Home
- Card 5 – Leo: Leisure
- Card 6 – Virgo: Career
- Card 7 – Libra: Relationships
- Card 8 – Scorpio: Hidden
- Card 9 – Sagittarius: Culture
- Card 10 – Capricorn: Achievements
- Card 10 – Aquarius: Social
- Card 111 – Pisces: Subconscious

THE CELTIC CROSS

One of the most commonly seen spreads in a tarot reading is the Celtic Cross. This mode of divination is the most suitable for obtaining an answer to a definite question. There are several variants of this layout, with slight differences in the order of the cards and what they might signify.

1. To use the traditional layout, first select a significator to represent the person or matter about which the inquiry is made. Place it on the table, face upward. If the significator cannot be said to face either way, you must decide before beginning the reading which side the image will face.
2. Shuffle and cut the rest of the pack three times, keeping the faces of the cards downward.

The first five cards will form the cross of the spread.

3. Turn up the top or first card of the deck, cover the significator with it, and say: "This covers you." This card gives the influence that is affecting the person or matter generally, the atmosphere of it in which the other currents work.
4. Turn up the second card, and lay it across the first, and say: "This crosses you." It shows the nature of the obstacles in the matter. If it is a favorable card, the opposing forces will not be serious, or it may indicate that something good in itself will not be productive of good in the particular connection.
5. Turn up the third card, place it above the significator, and say: "This crowns you." It represents the querent's aim or ideal in the matter, and points to the best that can be achieved under the circumstances, but that which has not yet been made actual.

6. Turn up the fourth card, place it below the significator, and say: "This is beneath you." It shows the foundation or basis of the matter, that which has already passed into actuality and that the significator has made his own.
7. Turn up the fifth card, place it to the side of the significator from which the image is facing away, and say: "This is behind you." It gives the influence that is just passed, or is now passing away.
8. Turn up the sixth card, place it on the side that the significator is facing, and say: "This is before you." It shows the influence that is coming into action and will operate in the near future.

The next four cards are turned up in succession and placed one above the other in a line, on the right hand side of the cross you have made with the other cards.

9. Turn up the seventh card. It signifies the querent's question—whether it concerns a person or a thing—and shows the querent's position or attitude in the circumstances.
10. Turn up the eighth card. It signifies the querent's house, their environment, and the tendencies that have an effect on the matter—for instance, their position in life, the influence of immediate friends, and so forth.
11. Turn up the ninth card. It gives the querent's hopes or fears in the matter.
12. Turn up the tenth. It is what will come, the final result, the culmination brought about by the influences shown by the other cards. It is on this card that you should especially concentrate your intuitive faculties. It should embody whatever you may have divined from the other cards on the table, including the significator itself.

Insight As tempting as it may be to dive right into the Celtic Cross, it does take practice to read all the elements so that they tell a coherent story. Study the meanings of both the Major and Minor Arcana until you can get a sense of their meanings without constantly checking a reference book. While it works best to answer a concrete question, it flexible enough to use even when you don't have a particular question to ask and just want to get a general feel of a situation.

TRADITIONAL CELTIC CROSS SPREAD

The Significator
Card 1 – What covers them
Card 2 – What crosses them
Card 3 – What crowns them
Card 4 – What is beneath them
Card 5 – What is behind them*
Card 6 – What is before them*
Card 7 – The querent
Card 8 – Their house
Card 9 – Their hopes or fears
Card 10 – What will come

3
POSSIBILITIES
What
crowns them

10
LONG-TERM
OUTCOME

6*
THE PRESENT
What is before them

SIGNIFICATOR
The querent

5*
THE PAST
What is behind them

9
HOPES AND FEARS

1
QUESTION AT HAND
What covers them

2
OBSTACLES OR
CHALLENGES
What crosses them

8
INTERNAL
INFLUENCES

4
THE
RECENT
PAST
What is
beneath them

* Note that Cards 5 and 6 can switch places, depending on the direction the significator faces.

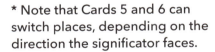

7
SELF-
PERCEPTION

The MAJOR ARCANA

Also known as the Greater Arcana, these are the most recognizable cards in the tarot deck.

The Major Arcana, meaning "greater secrets", are also called the trump cards. This group consists of 22 cards. Cards from The Magician to The World are numbered in Roman numerals from I to XXI. The Fool is the only unnumbered card, although it is sometimes placed at the beginning of the deck marked as 0, or at the end as XXII. Neither placement is more valid than the other.

IMAGERY OF THE MAJOR ARCANA

Each card of the Major Arcana depicts a scene rich with symbolic elements, with almost all featuring a figure or several figures. Most contemporary decks number the cards and include the name of the card, although some will only have pictures. Despite the wide variation in designs, almost all tarot decks evoke the same symbolism. A few might also switch the places of certain cards; for instance, earlier decks numbered Strength (or Fortitude) as XI and Justice as VIII. After the influential Rider-Waite deck switched their positions to make them better fit the astrological correspondences worked out by the Hermetic Order of the Golden Dawn, Strength, with its depiction of a lion, was moved to the 8th position to correspond with the zodiac sign Leo the Lion, and Justice was moved the 11th position to correspond with Libra the Scales.

A selection of cards from the influential and stunning Aleister Crowley Thoth deck, including The Hermit, The Wheel of Fortune, Justice, and Strength.

THE MAJOR ARCANA IN A READING

A Major Arcana card can set the scene for an entire reading, with the other cards in the array relating back to that card's essential meaning, working with it to draw a picture of the situation.

These cards call on the querent to reflect on the overarching themes that are currently dominating their present situation. A preponderance of upright Major Arcana card points to the querent experiencing life-changing events with long-term consequences, and they give hints of what the correct course will be. If the cards are reversed, however, it reminds the querent that they need to learn their lessons before they can begin to truly move forward.

You can also use a Major Arcana card as a significator, basing your selection on the tone or topic of the querent's overriding question.

- *The Fool* New beginnings
- *The Magician* New enterprises
- *The High Priestess* Spiritual growth
- *The Empress* Parenthood and nurturing
- *The Emperor* Business and career
- *The Hierophant* Other people's values
- *The Lovers* Romance and love
- *The Chariot* Achievements
- *Justice* Law and morals
- *The Hermit* Self-discovery
- *The Wheel of Fortune* Luck and fortune
- *Strength* Courage and strength
- *The Hanged Man* Health or sacrifices
- *Death* Life-changing decisions
- *Temperance* Peace and happiness
- *The Devil* Addictions and obsessions
- *The Tower* Sudden shocks
- *The Star* Hope and wishes
- *The Moon* Uncertain issues
- *The Sun* Holidays and family
- *Judgment* Calling and destiny
- *The World* Travel

The Magician (Le Magicien ou le Bateleur)

Above and left: Justice (La Justice) and Death (La Mort) from the Grand Etteilla tarot deck. This deck was published by H. Pussey in Paris, circa 1890, following the designs of the French occultist Etteilla, who produced the first tarot deck specifically designed for divination.

QUICK GUIDE: The MAJOR ARCANA

ZERO. THE FOOL

A youth setting out on a journey

INTERPRETATION
Upright: Idealism, new beginnings, travel, adventure, innocence, youth, freedom, originality, spontaneity; can also mean lack of commitment, foolishness, folly, carelessness, mania, extravagance
Reversed: Apathy, negligence, absence, stupidity, distraction, irrationality

I. THE MAGICIAN

A figure in the robe of a magician; also called the Magus, Magician, or Juggler

INTERPRETATION
Upright: Skill, diplomacy, logic, intellect, address, willpower, subtlety; sickness, pain, loss, disaster, snares of enemies, self-confidence, will; can be the querent
Reversed: Illusions, trickery, mental disease, disgrace, disquiet

II. THE HIGH PRIESTESS

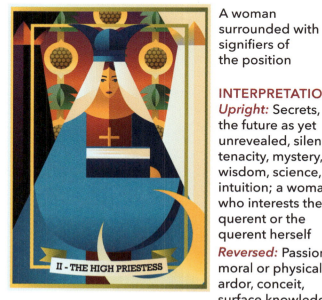

A woman surrounded with signifiers of the position

INTERPRETATION
Upright: Secrets, the future as yet unrevealed, silence, tenacity, mystery, wisdom, science, intuition; a woman who interests the querent or the querent herself
Reversed: Passion, moral or physical ardor, conceit, surface knowledge, repressed feelings

III. THE EMPRESS

A stately woman of royal aspect sits on her throne

INTERPRETATION
Upright: Nature, fertility, action, initiative, maternity clandestine, the unknown, also difficulty, doubt, ignorance
Reversed: Light, truth, the unraveling of involved matters, rejoicing; can also mean vacillation dependence, nosiness, smothering

IV. THE EMPEROR

A stoic ruler figure sitting upright on his throne

INTERPRETATION

Upright: Stability, structure, power, protection, control, realization, a great person, aid, reason, conviction; also authority and will

Reversed: Benevolence, credit, compassion; can also mean coldness, tyranny, confusion to enemies, obstruction, immaturity

V. THE HIEROPHANT

A mature man in papal insignia

INTERPRETATION

Upright: Ethics, tradition, morality, conformity, marriage, alliance, captivity, servitude; can also mean mercy and goodness; inspiration; a man to whom the querent has recourse

Reversed: Society, concord, new approaches; can also mean rebellion, weakness

VI. THE LOVERS

A man and woman protected and blessed by an angel above

INTERPRETATION

Upright: Love, attraction, partners, union, beauty, trials overcome

Reversed: Failure, foolish designs, imbalance, disharmony; can also mean frustrated marriage and contrarieties of all kinds

VII. THE CHARIOT

A figure in a chariot driven by a black and a white sphinx

INTERPRETATION

Upright: Control, direction, succor, providence, willpower; also war, triumph, presumption, vengeance, trouble

Reversed: Lack of direction or control, riot, quarrel, dispute, litigation, defeat

VIII. STRENGTH

A gentle woman calmly holds a lion; also called Fortitude

INTERPRETATION

Upright: Action, courage, inner strength, compassion, focus, power, energy, magnanimity; also complete success and honors

Reversed: Doubt, despotism, abuse of power, weakness, discord, even disgrace

IX. THE HERMIT

A figure stands holding a staff and lamp, often alone on a mountaintop

INTERPRETATION

Upright: Truth, prudence, circumspection, contemplation; also dissimulation, roguery, corruption

Reversed: Fear, isolation, loneliness, concealment, disguise, policy, unreasoned caution, loss of way

X. WHEEL OF FORTUNE

A giant wheel, covered in esoteric symbols surrounded by an angel, eagle, bull and lion

INTERPRETATION

Upright: Change, destiny, fortune, success, elevation, luck, felicity

Reversed: Bad luck, lack of control, increase, abundance, superfluity

XI. JUSTICE

A woman sits holding scales in her left hand and a double-edged sword in her right

INTERPRETATION

Upright: Truth, clarity, equity, rightness, probity, executive, triumph of the deserving side in law

Reversed: Bias, bigotry, legal complications, dishonesty, unaccountability, unfairness

XII. THE HANGED MAN

A man suspended upside-down, hanging by his foot from the living world tree

INTERPRETATION

Upright: Wisdom, circumspection, discernment, release, trials, sacrifice, intuition, divination, prophecy
Reversed: Fear of sacrifice, needless sacrifice, selfishness, stalling, the crowd, body politic

XIII. DEATH

A skeleton in armor holding a black flag and riding a horse

INTERPRETATION

Upright: End of cycle, change, beginnings, metamorphosis; can also mean mortality, destruction, loss of a benefactor or marriage prospect, corruption
Reversed: Fear of change, inertia, stagnation, sleep, lethargy, petrifaction, hope destroyed

XIV. TEMPERANCE

A winged figure with one foot in water and the other on land mixing the waters of two cups

INTERPRETATION

Upright:: Patience, moderation, economy, frugality, management, accommodation
Reversed: Disunion, unfortunate combinations, competing interests, imbalance, extremes, recklessness, hastiness

XV. THE DEVIL

A horned satyr with bat wings and an inverted pentagram on his forehead

INTERPRETATION

Upright: Disaster, sudden upheaval, broken pride, ravage, violence, vehemence, extraordinary efforts, force, fatality, that which is predestined
Reversed: Evil fatality, weakness, pettiness, blindness, extremes

XVI. THE TOWER

A lightning bolt strikes a tower, setting it ablaze; people are jumping out the windows

INTERPRETATION
Upright: Misery, distress, indigence, adversity, calamity, disgrace, deception, ruin, unforeseen catastrophe
Reversed: The same in a lesser degree; also oppression, imprisonment, tyranny

XVII. THE STAR

Beneath a star, a woman kneels at the edge of a small pond pouring water from two jugs

INTERPRETATION
Upright: Hope, faith, bright prospects, rejuvenation; can also mean loss, theft, privation, abandonment
Reversed: Arrogance, haughtiness, insecurity, impotence, faithlessness, discouragement

XVIII. THE MOON

Beneath the Moon, a wolf and a dog howl as a crayfish crawls from the water between them

INTERPRETATION
Upright: The unconscious, illusions, intuition; can also mean enemies, danger, calumny, darkness, terror, deception, occult forces, error
Reversed: Fear, confusion, instability, inconstancy, silence, lesser degrees of deception and error

XIX. THE SUN

Beneath the Sun, a naked child plays joyfully riding a white horse and surrounded by flowers

INTERPRETATION
Upright: Joy, material happiness, fortunate marriage, contentment, success, celebration, positivity
Reversed: The same in a lesser degree; negativity, depression, sadness

XX. THE LAST JUDGMENT

Women, men, and children rise from the grave to respond to Gabriel's trumpet call

INTERPRETATION
Upright: Change of position, reflection, reckoning, awakening, renewal, outcome
Reversed: Weakness, pusillanimity, simplicity, doubt, self-loathing; also deliberation, decision, sentence

XXI. THE WORLD

A dancing figure at the center holding a wand in each hand and surrounded by a wreath

INTERPRETATION
Upright: Assured success, completion, fulfillment, wholeness, harmony recompense, voyage, route, emigration, flight, change of place
Reversed: Inertia, fixity, stagnation, permanence, lack of closure, emptiness

A tarot reader turns a card, contemplating its relation to the querent's question and the other cards of the spread.

The MINOR ARCANA

The Minor Arcana correspond with the cards of a traditional 52-card deck, with the addition of the Page in the set of court cards.

The Minor Arcana, meaning "lesser secrets" consists of 56 cards. They are similar to a standard deck of playing cards and are divided into four suits of 14 cards each. There are 10 numbered cards and four court, or face, cards. The court cards are the King, Queen, Knight (or Jack), and Page in each of the four tarot suits.

Despite the name, the Minor Arcana have a major impact on a reading. These cards tell querents what is happening in their lives, reflecting the ups and downs of daily experience, and how these events are affecting them. They offer insight into their present situation and what steps may be needed to achieve their goals. They are, however, somewhat ephemeral. Reflecting daily experience means they can change, depending on actions querents might take.

THE MINOR ARCANA SUITS

The traditional Italian Tarot suits are Swords, Batons, Coins, and Cups, but most modern decks call the Batons suit Wands, Rods, or Staves, while the Coins suit is called Pentacles. Their significance is determined by the reader, the querent, and the spread, but the suits do reflect temperaments and attitudes and have somewhat standard divinatory meanings,

- *Cups* Represent feelings, emotions, intuition, and creativity. A preponderance of Cups cards might appear when a querent's question relates to romance and relationships.

- *Wands* Represent passion, energy, and motivation. A preponderance of Wands cards might appear when a querent's question relates to spirituality and larger issues of their purpose in life.
- *Pentacles* Represent work, finances, and material possession. A preponderance of Pentacles cards might appear when a querent's question relates to their career or finances.
- *Swords* Represent thoughts, words, and actions. A preponderance of Swords cards might appear when a querent's question relates to decision-making or communication.

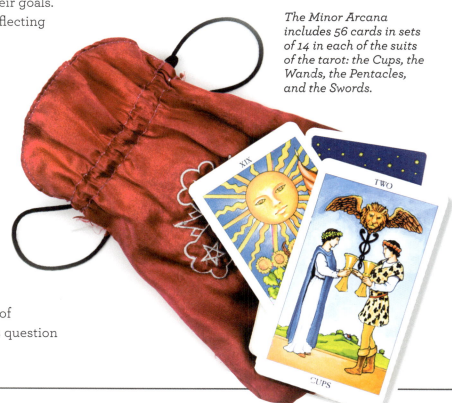

The Minor Arcana includes 56 cards in sets of 14 in each of the suits of the tarot: the Cups, the Wands, the Pentacles, and the Swords.

DIVINATORY MEANINGS

The meanings ascribed to the individual cards can vary slightly from source to source, but there is a general feel to each of the cards that transcends these differences.

THE SUIT OF CUPS

King A mature, fair-haired man sits on a throne holding a cup in his right hand and a scepter in his left. A man who is "all heart," and appreciates the finer things in life, such as music and art; also warm-hearted and kind, successful in business, law, or science; responsible, rational, intelligent.

- *Upright:* Emotional balance, compassion, diplomacy
- *Reversed:* Dishonesty, double-dealing, injustice, scandal, considerable loss

Queen A mature, fair-haired woman holds an ornate lidded cup or chalice. She is described as a model of virtue, purer of heart than most, a loving mother, and a loyal friend.

- *Upright:* Honesty, devotion, loving intelligence, happiness, pleasure; also a good mother
- *Reversed:* An untrustworthy woman, vice, dishonor

Knight A fair-haired young man, graceful, but not warlike, rides sedately wearing a winged helmet, referring to those higher graces of the imagination; a dreamer.

- *Upright:* A visit from a friend, who will bring unexpected money to the querent, an arrival, advances, proposition, invitation, incitement
- *Reversed:* Trickery, artifice, subtlety, swindling, duplicity, fraud

QUEEN of CUPS.

Page A fair-haired young man contemplates a fish rising from a cup to look at him; the pictures of the mind taking form; he is studious, but unfortunate in love.

- *Upright:* A young person to whom the querent will be connected might be impelled to render service to the querent; a studious youth; news, message; application, reflection, meditation; also these things directed to business
- *Reversed:* Taste, inclination, attachment, seduction, deception, artifice; also obstacles of all kinds

PAGE of CUPS.

Ten A man and woman joyfully gaze up at 10 cups in a rainbow; 2 children dance near them.

- *Upright:* Contentment, repose of the entire heart; the perfection of that state; also perfection of human love and friendship if with several picture cards
- *Reversed:* Sorrow; also a serious quarrel

Nine A man who has feasted to his heart's content, with cups of wine on the arched counter behind him, seeming to indicate that the future is also assured.

- *Upright:* Concord, contentment; also victory, success, advantage; satisfaction for the querent
- *Reversed:* Mistakes, disappointment, underachievement; also loyalty, liberty

Eight A man of dejected aspect is deserting the cups of his felicity, enterprise, undertaking, or previous concern.
- *Upright:* The decline of a matter, or that a matter that has been thought to be important is really of slight consequence—either for good or evil
- *Reversed:* Great joy, happiness, feasting

Seven Strange chalices of vision, but the images are more especially those of the fantastic spirit.
- *Upright:* Fair child; idea, design, resolve, movement.
- *Reversed:* A period of clarity after a time of confusion, long-held dreams or ambitions are being overturned, either for good or ill; also success, if accompanied by the Three of Cups

Six Children in a garden of an old house, their cups filled with flowers; a figure, which appears to be an older person, walks away from the children.
- *Upright:* A card of the past and of pleasant memories, happiness, enjoyment, but coming rather from the past; things that have vanished
- *Reversed:* The future, renewal, that which will come to pass presently; also new relations, new knowledge, new environment; also inheritance to fall in quickly

> **Insight** If your reading turns up mostly cards of the Minor Arcana, it points to the conclusion that the question at hand might not have a lasting influence. The issue is one that will pass, but they present the querent with the opportunity to learn from the experience.

Five A dark, cloaked figure, looking sideways at three prone cups; two others stand upright behind him; a bridge is in the background, leading to a small keep.
- *Upright:* It is a card of loss, but something remains; three have been taken, but two are left; also inheritance, patrimony, transmission, but not corresponding to expectations
- *Reversed:* News, alliances, affinity, consanguinity, ancestry, return, false projects, also return of some long-lost relative

Four A young man sits under a tree and contemplates three cups set on the grass before him; an arm issuing from a cloud offers him another cup; his expression is one of discontent with his environment.
- *Upright:* Contrarieties, weariness, disgust, aversion, imaginary vexations, as if the wine of this world had caused satiety only; another wine, as if a fairy gift, is now offered the wastrel, but he sees no consolation therein; also a card of blended pleasure
- *Reversed:* Novelty, new instruction, new relations, presentiment

Three Three young women in a garden dance with cups uplifted, as if joyfully pledging one another.
- *Upright:* A bountiful conclusion of a matter, perfection and merriment, victory, fulfillment, solace, healing
- *Reversed:* Consolation, cure, end of business, expedition, dispatch, achievement, end; also physical excess

Two A young man and woman pledge each other, and above their cups rises the Caduceus of Hermes; a lion's head appears between the great wings.

- *Upright:* Love, passion, friendship, affinity, union, concord, sympathy, the interrelation of the sexes; also wealth and honor
- *Reversed:* Passion

Ace

A hand issues from a cloud, holding in its palm a cup, from which four streams are pouring; in the water beneath are water lilies, and a dove, bearing in its bill a cross-marked communion wafer, descends to place the wafer in the cup; dew is falling on all sides.

- *Upright:* Inflexible will, unalterable law
- *Reversed:* Unexpected change of position

THE SUIT OF SWORDS

King A mature man holds a double-edged sword that points upward in his right hand while sitting on a throne decorated with butterflies; he possesses sound intellectual understanding and reasoning and is strong-hearted, decisive, and intellectually oriented.

- *Upright:* Law, reason, power, command, authority, militant intelligence, authority, discipline, integrity, morality, serious, high standards, strictness
- *Reversed:* Cruelty, perversity, barbarity, perfidy, evil intention; also a caution to put an end to a ruinous lawsuit

Queen A mature woman wearing a crown of butterflies sits on a throne holding a double-edged sword that points upward in her right hand while

extending her left; her countenance is severe but chastened, suggesting familiarity with sorrow. She is often thought to represent a widow.

- *Upright:* Widowhood, female sadness and embarrassment, absence, sterility, mourning, privation, separation
- *Reversed:* Malice, bigotry, artifice, prudery deceit; also a bad woman, with ill-will towards the querent

Knight A young man rides a white horse whose harnesses are decorated with images of birds and butterflies, as is the knight's cape. He rides in full course, as if scattering his enemies, resembling a prototypical hero of romantic chivalry; overall purity and intellectual energy motivates him.

- *Upright:* Heroic action; also someone brave, assertive, direct, impatient, intellectual, daring, focused, perfectionist, ambitious
- *Reversed:* Imprudence, incapacity, extravagance

Page A lithe, active figure holds a sword upright in both hands, while walking swiftly as he passes over rugged land and under stormy clouds; he is alert, as if an expected enemy might appear at any moment.

- *Upright:* Authority, overseeing, vigilance, spying, examination; also an indiscreet person will pry into the querent's secrets
- *Reversed:* The more negative side of its upright qualities; what is unforeseen, unprepared state; sickness; also astonishing news

Ten A figure lies prostrate, pierced by swords.
- *Upright:* Pain, affliction, tears, sadness, desolation; if followed by Ace and King, imprisonment; also unfaithful friends
- *Reversed:* Advantage, profit, success, favor, but none of these are permanent; also power and authority

Nine A woman seated on her couch in lamentation, with nine swords over her; she is as one who knows no sorrow that is like hers. A card of utter desolation.
- *Upright:* Death, failure, miscarriage, delay, deception, disappointment, despair
- *Reversed:* Imprisonment, suspicion, doubt, reasonable fear, shame

Eight A woman, bound and blindfolded with the swords of the card about her. It is a card of temporary durance, rather than of irretrievable bondage.
- *Upright:* Bad news, violent chagrin, crisis, censure, power in trammels, conflict, calumny; also sickness
- *Reversed:* Disquiet, difficulty, opposition, accident, treachery; what is unforeseen; fatality; also departure of a relative

Seven A man is in the act of rapidly carrying away five swords; the two others of the card remain stuck in the ground.
- *Upright:* Design, attempt, wish, hope, confidence; also quarreling, a plan that may fail, annoyance; can also be a good card, promising a country life after a competence has been secured
- *Reversed:* Counsel, instruction, slander, babbling, also good advice, probably neglected

Six A ferryman carries passengers in his punt to the farther shore; his course is smooth, the freight light, so that the work is not beyond his strength.
- *Upright:* A pleasant voyage, journey by water, route, way, envoy, expediency
- *Reversed:* Declaration, confession, publicity, a proposal of love; also an unfavorable lawsuit

Five A disdainful man looks after two retreating and dejected figures whose swords lie upon the ground. He is the master in possession of the field, carrying two other swords on his left shoulder, and a third is in his right hand, pointing to the earth.
- *Upright:* Degradation, destruction, revocation, infamy, dishonor, an attack on the fortune or well-being of the querent
- *Reversed:* Sorrow, mourning

Four The effigy of a knight in the attitude of prayer lies at full length upon his tomb.
- *Upright:* Vigilance, retreat, solitude, hermit's repose, exile, tomb and coffin
- *Reversed:* A certain success following wise administration, circumspection, economy, avarice, precaution, testament

Three Three swords pierce a heart with clouds and rain behind.
- *Upright:* Removal, absence, delay, division, rupture, dispersion; also the flight of her lover
- *Reversed:* Mental alienation, error, loss, distraction, disorder, confusion; also a meeting with one whom the querent has compromised

Two A blindfolded female figure balances two swords upon her shoulders.
- *Upright:* Conformity and the equipoise that it suggests, courage, friendship, concord in a state of arms; also tenderness, affection, intimacy, as well as gifts for a woman or influential protection for a man in search of help
- *Reversed:* Imposture, falsehood, duplicity, disloyalty

Ace A hand issues from a cloud, grasping a sword, the point of which is encircled by a crown.
- *Upright:* Triumph, the excessive degree in everything, conquest, triumph of force; can mean great prosperity or great misery
- *Reversed:* The more negative side of its upright qualities; broken marriage due to querent's own actions

THE SUIT OF WANDS

King A mature man sits on a throne decorated with a lion and a salamander, holding in his right hand a blossoming wand to represent creativity and passion; he is ardent, lithe, animated, impassioned, and noble.
- *Upright:* Generally favorable; may signify a good marriage. Signifies honesty and may mean news concerning an unexpected heritage to fall in before very long
- *Reversed:* Advice that should be followed

Queen A woman in golden attire sits on a throne decorated with lions, holding a blossoming wand in her right hand and sunflower in her left, while a black cat sits at her feet; she is friendly, a countrywoman, generally married, honest, and conscientious; more magnetic than the corresponding King.
- *Upright:* A good harvest, which may be taken in several senses. If the card beside her signifies a man, she is well disposed towards him; if a woman, she is interested in the querent. Also, love of money, or a certain success in business
- *Reversed:* Good-will towards the querent, but without the opportunity to exercise it

Knight A young man sits astride a rearing horse holding a holding a blossoming wand in his right hand; he appears ready for battle, but is straight-forward.
- *Upright:* A bad card; alienation; also departure, absence, flight, emigration.

KING of WANDS

- *Reversed:* Division, discord; also marriage, but probably frustrated

Page A young man stands in the act of proclamation holding a blossoming staff taller than himself; he is adventurous, ambitious, energetic, active, and skilled.
- *Upright:* Faithfulness, a lover, an envoy, a postman; also young man of family in search of a partner
- *Reversed:* Bad news; also instability and indecision

Ten A man oppressed by the weight of the 10 staves that he is carrying.
- *Upright:* Oppression, also difficulties and contradictions, if near a good card
- *Reversed:* Contrarieties, difficulties, intrigues, and their analogies

Nine The figure leans upon his staff and has an expectant look, as if he is awaiting an enemy. Behind are eight other staves—erect, in orderly disposition, like a palisade.
- *Upright:* Generally speaking, a bad card. Signifies strength in opposition
- *Reversed:* Obstacles, adversity, calamity

Eight A flight of wands through an open country; but they draw to the term of their course.
- *Upright:* Swiftness, activity in undertakings, hope
- *Reversed:* Arrows of jealousy, internal dispute, stingings of conscience, quarrels; also domestic disputes for a married person

Seven
A young man on a craggy eminence brandishing a staff; six other staves are raised toward him from below.
- *Upright:* Valor success; on the intellectual plane, it signifies discussion, wordy strife; in business, it is negotiations, war of trade, barter, competition
- *Reversed:* Perplexity, embarrassments, anxiety; also a caution against indecision

Six A laureled horseman bears one staff adorned with a laurel crown; footmen with staves are at his side.
- *Upright:* Triumph, hope
- *Reversed:* Apprehension, fear, treachery, disloyalty

Five A posse of youths brandish staves, as if in sport or strife, mimicking warfare.
- *Upright:* Imitation, a sham fight, also the strenuous competition and struggle of the search after riches and fortune; also success in financial speculation
- *Reversed:* Litigation, disputes, trickery, contradiction

Four A garland is suspended from the four great staves planted in the foreground; two female figures uplift nosegays; at their side is a bridge over a moat, leading to an old manorial house.
- *Upright:* Country life, haven of refuge, repose, concord, harmony, prosperity, peace
- *Reversed:* Meaning remains unaltered: prosperity, increase, felicity, beauty, embellishment, unexpected good fortune

Three A calm, stately personage, with his back turned, looking from a cliff's edge at ships passing over the sea. Three staves are planted in the ground, and he leans slightly on one of them.
- *Upright:* A very good card; collaboration will favor business endeavors. Also strength, enterprise, effort, trade, commerce, discovery
- *Reversed:* End of troubles, suspension or cessation of adversity, toil, or disappointment

Two A tall man looks from a battlemented roof over sea and shore; he holds a globe in his right hand, while a staff in his left rests on the battlement; another staff is fixed in a ring.
- *Upright:* A contradictory card; may mean riches, fortune, magnificence; can also mean physical suffering, disease, chagrin, sadness, mortification
- *Reversed:* Surprise, wonder, enchantment, emotion; also trouble, fear

Ace A hand issuing from a cloud grasps a stout wand or club.
- *Upright:* Creation, invention, enterprise, the powers that result in these; principle, beginning, source; birth, family, origin; the starting point of enterprises; can also mean money, fortune, inheritance
- *Reversed:* Calamities of all kinds, a fall, decadence, ruin, perdition, to perish; also a certain clouded joy

THE SUIT OF PENTACLES.
King A dark man dressed in dark robes sits on a throne embellished with carvings of bulls, which represent his connection to the astrological sign of Taurus, and the grapes and vines that adorn his robe symbolize wealth and abundance. In his right hand, he holds a scepter, and, in his left, he holds a golden coin, symbolic of his material influence. He is often thought to be a merchant, master, or professor.
- *Upright:* Valor, intelligence, logic, business, mathematical gifts
- *Reversed:* Vice, weakness, perversity, peril, also an old and vicious man

Queen A dark woman in robes of gold, whose qualities might be summed up in the idea of greatness of soul; she has also the serious cast of intelligence, and she contemplates upon her symbol and may see worlds therein.

- *Upright:* Opulence, generosity, magnificence, security, liberty, also a Dark woman, presents from a rich relative
- *Reversed:* Suspicion, suspense, fear, mistrust, illness

Knight A dark young man sits astride a slow, enduring, heavy horse, exhibiting his symbol, but does not look therein; he is stubborn or hard-working, serious, or set in his ways.

- *Upright:* Utility, serviceableness, interest, responsibility, rectitude, a useful man, seriousness, useful discoveries
- *Reversed:* Inertia, idleness, repose of that kind, stagnation; also placidity, discouragement, carelessness, also a brave man out of employment

Page A dark youth looks intently at the pentacle that hovers over his raised hands, insensible of that which is around him; he is a student.

- *Upright:* Application, study, scholarship, reflection; also news, messages and the bringer thereof; also rule, management
- *Reversed:* Prodigality, dissipation, liberality, luxury, unfavorable news

Ten A man and woman beneath an archway that gives entrance to a house and domain; they are accompanied by a child, who with a hand on one of the dogs, looks curiously at two dogs accosting an ancient figure seated in the foreground.

- *Upright:* Gain, riches; family matters, archives, extraction, the abode of a family

- *Reversed:* Chance, fatality, loss, robbery, games of hazard; sometimes gifts, dowry, pension

Nine A woman with a bird perched on her wrist stands amid a great abundance of grapevines in the garden of a manorial house, which testifies to material well-being.
- *Upright:* Prudence, safety, success, accomplishment, certitude, discernment; also prompt fulfillment of what is presaged by neighboring cards
- *Reversed:* Vain hopes, deception, a voided project, bad faith

Eight An artist in stone sits at his work, which he exhibits in the form of trophies.
- *Upright:* Work, employment, commission, craftsmanship, skill in craft and business, perhaps in the preparatory stage

- *Reversed:* Voided ambition, vanity, cupidity, exaction, usury; also the possession of skill, in the sense of the ingenious mind turned to cunning and intrigue

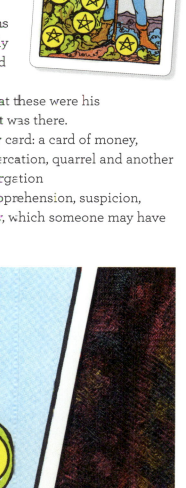

Seven A young man leans on his staff, looking intently at seven pentacles attached to a clump of greenery on his right; one would say that these were his treasures and that his heart was there.
- *Upright:* A contradictory card: a card of money, business, barter; also altercation, quarrel and another innocence, ingenuity, purgation
- *Reversed:* Impatience, apprehension, suspicion, anxiety regarding money, which someone may have proposed to lend to you

Six A dignified man in the guise of a merchant weighs money in a pair of scales and distributes it to the needy and distressed, which may be testimony to his own success in life, as well as the goodness of his heart.
- *Upright:* Presents, gifts, gratification; also the need for attention, vigilance; now is the accepted time, present prosperity
- *Reversed:* Desire, cupidity, envy, jealousy, illusion; also a check on the querent's ambition

Five Two weary beggars pass a lighted stained-glass window as they trudge through a snowstorm.
- *Upright:* A card of material trouble above all; also love and lovers—wife, husband, friend, mistress; also concordance, affinities
- *Reversed:* Disorder, chaos, ruin, discord, profligacy, troubles in love

Four A crowned figure with a pentacle over his crown clasps another pentacle with hands and arms, and two pentacles are under his feet, symbolizing that he holds on to that which he has.
- *Upright:* The surety of possessions, cleaving to that which one has, gift, legacy, inheritance
- *Reversed:* Observation, hindrances, suspense, opposition, delay

Three A sculptor at his work in a monastery; compare with the Eight of Pentacles; here the apprentice or amateur has received his reward and is now at work in earnest.
- *Upright:* Mastery, trade, skilled labor; also nobility, aristocracy, renown, glory
- *Reversed:* Mediocrity, in work and otherwise, puerility, pettiness, weakness

Two A young man dancing with a pentacle in either hand, and they are joined by an endless cord that is like the number 8 reversed.

- *Upright:* A card of gaiety, recreation and its connections, troubles are more imaginary than real; also news and messages in writing, as obstacles, agitation, trouble, embroilment
- *Reversed:* Bad omen, ignorance, injustice, enforced gaiety, simulated enjoyment, literal sense, handwriting, composition, letters of exchange

Ace A hand issuing from a cloud holds up a pentacle.
- *Upright:* The most favorable of all cards: perfect contentment, felicity, ecstasy; also speedy intelligence; gold
- *Reversed:* The evil side of wealth, bad intelligence; also great riches

C·H·A·P·T·E·R 3
PALMISTRY, CHIROLOGY,
and the ART of CHIROMANCY

READING the HANDS

Chiromancy teaches how to read both character and destiny in the lines and marks of the hand.

Palm-reading is as ancient as astrology, and though it likely originated in India, the practice appears all over the world, with variations according to culture. Palmistry and chirology properly refer only to a judgment formed from what appears in the palm of the hand, while chiromancy (from the Greek words *cheir*, a "hand," and *manteia*, "divination") signifies the revelations made by the hand, taken as a whole. In chiromancy the hand represents a natural horoscope. Chiromancy can indicate what planets have been powerful at the time of a querent's birth and what their effect will be over that person's life and can help find the dates of the principal events of the life.

Modern palmistry traces its roots to the nineteenth-century. Leading figures include the Irish William John Warner, known as Cheiro. Cheiro, who studied palmistry under gurus in India, set up a practice in London that drew famous clients from around the world. He published several books on palmistry, as well as ones on astrology and numerology. British Edward Heron-Allen published several works on the subject, and his 1883 book, *Palmistry – A Manual of Cheirosophy,* is still in print.

Those who practice chiromancy and palmistry are commonly called chirologists, hand readers, palmists, or palm readers.

METHOD

To begin a palm-reading, you start with a basic evaluation of the querent's hand, usually their dominant hand. The dominant hand is thought to represent the conscious mind, while the other the subconscious, and in some traditions hereditary or family traits. A general evaluation of the hand's size, its skin texture, flexibility, and overall shape can often tell you if your querent possesses traits such as earthiness, imagination, idealism, practicality, and the like. You can also look at the fingers, fingernails, fingerprints, and patterns of the palms.

The various lines of the hands are next evaluated, including the major lines, such as the Heart Line, the Head Line, and the Life Line (in that order), and then the mounts or fleshy bumps on the palm, such as the Mount of Venus or the Mount of Jupiter.

Each area of the palm and fingers is related to a god or goddess, and the features of that area indicate the nature of the corresponding aspect of the querent. For example, characteristics of the ring finger are tied to art, music, aesthetics, fame, wealth, and harmony.

As you come to study the traits associated with the various aspects of the hand, you will be better able to discern a cohesive pattern.

To do a palm-reading, your major focus will be on the lines and mounts of the palm. Not every mount or line will appear in every hand, but three lines—the Heart Line, the Head Line, and the Life Line—are found in a clearer or fainter degree on all hands, even if they vary in their relative position.

Opposite: A palmistry chart illustrates the major lines of the hand and also the planets that correspond with the fingers. Each planet has certain qualities associated with it.

PALMISTRY

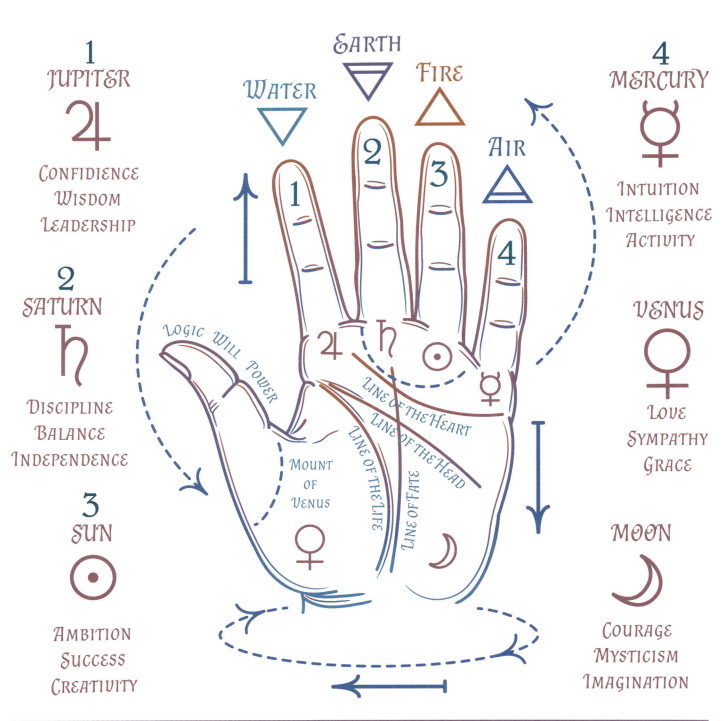

1 JUPITER ♃
CONFIDENCE
WISDOM
LEADERSHIP

2 SATURN ♄
DISCIPLINE
BALANCE
INDEPENDENCE

3 SUN ☉
AMBITION
SUCCESS
CREATIVITY

4 MERCURY ☿
INTUITION
INTELLIGENCE
ACTIVITY

VENUS ♀
LOVE
SYMPATHY
GRACE

MOON ☾
COURAGE
MYSTICISM
IMAGINATION

WATER ▽
EARTH ▽
FIRE △
AIR △

LOGIC WILL POWER
LINE OF THE HEART
LINE OF THE HEAD
LINE OF THE LIFE
LINE OF FATE
MOUNT OF VENUS

QUALITIES of the HANDS

There are numerous attributes of the hands, including shape, texture, and size, that can tell a reader much about a querent.

Before a closer reading of the lines of the palm, readers often evaluate various qualities of the hand, including its overall shape, the relative size of the palm and length of the fingers, the color and texture of the skin and fingernails, and the prominence of the knuckles.

In most schools of palmistry, the shape of the hand corresponds with one of the classical elements: earth, fire, air, and water. This correspondence will indicate character traits based on the qualities of those elements, which are taken from astrology. This allows for some subtle nuances; for instance, your querent might be a fiery Sagittarius, but the shape of their hand will tell you that they also possess some of the sensitive traits of a water sign.

- *Earth hands* Broad, square palms and fingers. The length of the palm from wrist to the bottom of the fingers and the length of the fingers is about equal. Signifies a practical, logical, and grounded individual. They can, however, be stuck in the present moment, which keeps them from successfully planning for the long term to achieve their goals.
- *Air hands* Square or rectangular palms with long fingers and sometimes protruding knuckles, and low-set thumbs. Signifies an intellectually curious, analytical, and communicative individual. They can, however, be easily distracted and when unstimulated are anxious or edgy.

Earth Hand
Broad, square palm, square fingers
- Realistic
- Down-to-earth
- Pragmatic

Air Hand
Square or rectangular palm, long fingers
- Adaptive
- Curious
- Eloquent

Fire Hand
Square or rectangular palm, short fingers
- Fiery
- Restless
- Warm-hearted

Water Hand
Long, oval palm, long, conical fingers
- Sensitive
- Emotional
- Empathetic

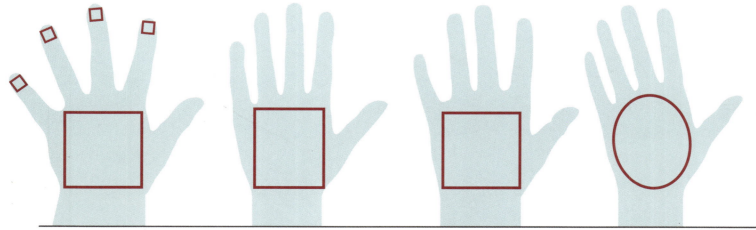

- *Fire hands* Square or rectangular palm and short fingers. The length of the palm from wrist to the bottom of the fingers is usually greater than the length of the fingers. Signifies a passionate, confident, and industrious individual. They can, however, be so focused on themselves that they lack tact and empathy.

- *Water hands* Long, sometimes oval-shaped palm, with long, conical fingers. The length of the palm from wrist to the bottom of the fingers is usually less than the width across the widest part of the palm and usually equal to the length of the fingers. Signifies an intuitive, compassionate, and imaginative individual. They can, however, be extremely sensitive.

QUICK GUIDE: OTHER HAND SHAPES

Conical
Long palm, pointed fingers
- Imaginative
- Ambitious
- Beauty-loving

Elementary or Basic
Broad palm, short fingers
- Hard-working
- Down-to-earth
- Pragmatic

Philosophical or Thinking
Broad palm, saucer-like fingertips
- Logical
- Introverted
- Thoughtful

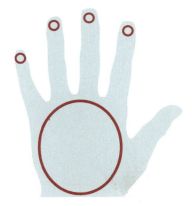

Practical or Square
Square palm, blunt fingers
- Organized
- Persistent
- Skeptical

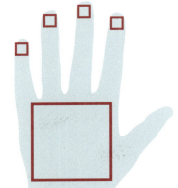

Psychic or Intuitive
Long delicate hand, pointed fingers
- Idealistic
- Emotional
- Opinionated

Spatulate
Broad palm, spatulate fingers
- Energetic
- Inquisitive
- Enthusiastic

QUALITIES of the FINGERS

There are numerous attributes of the fingers, including their shape and length, that can tell a reader much about a querent.

An examination of the fingers is a common part of palmistry. In general, people with short fingers are quicker, more impulsive, and have more intuition than those with long fingers. Those with long fingers have much love of detail—often to a worrying extent; they are inquisitive and somewhat distrustful.

LENGTH, PROPORTIONS, AND SHAPE

The relative lengths of the three divisions of the fingers are also indicators of three separate influences—the soul, the mind, and the body.

- *First division longest* Fingers that have the first division (that containing the nail) longest, show high aspirations and power of veneration—the soul.
- *Second division longest* Fingers with the second division longest indicate intellectual force—the mind.
- *Third division longest* Fingers having the lowest division longest show a love of material pleasure—the body.

The shapes and relative proportions of the fingers to the palm modify the indications given by the lines and mounts, so it is necessary to consider these qualities.

- *Fingers longer than the palm with pointed tips* An expression of the Moon, this configuration shows idealism. People with these fingers

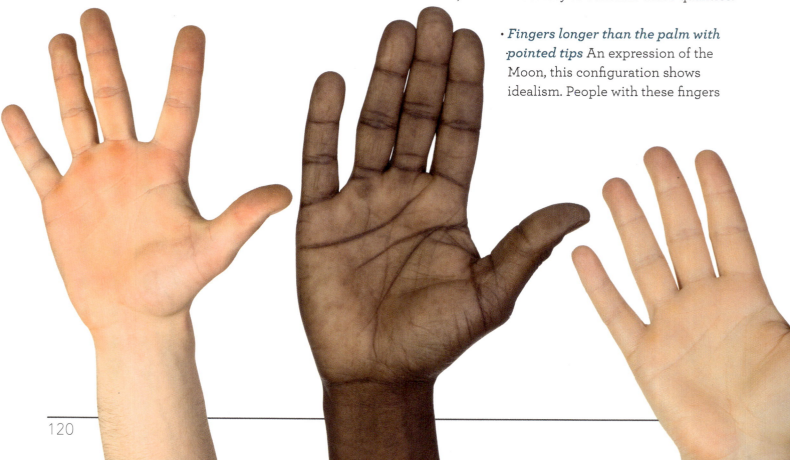

see everything in the golden light of imagination and find happiness in dreams of intangible beauty. Poetical expression (ethereal, not passionate) is their natural language. They are drawn to the spiritualistic side of all things and have a tendency to believe in omens, occult literature, and the supernatural. People with these fingers are often young at heart.

- *Fingers the same length as the palm with slightly pointed tips* These show refinement, elegant taste, and a love of art—these are the fingers of those born under the dominant influence of the Sun.
- *Fingers the same length as the palm, but fleshy at base and square at tips* These show practicality, family affection, love of animals, good judgment, respect for the world's opinion, and appreciation of material comfort. These fingers show the strong influence of Jupiter.

Long fingers, knotty at the joints with square tips These show reasoning power and taste for science and reason. Persons with these tend to stay away from the mystical or spiritual and instead study history, jurisprudence, mathematics, and the exact sciences. They are naturally clever at calculation and have much sense of order. Such fingers show the influence of Saturn.

- *Fingers shorter than the palm with spatulated tips* These show sensuality in love and materialism in all things. Persons with these tend to be energetic, love sports, and possess a great deal of courage. Such fingers indicate the influence of Mars at birth.
- *Fingers shorter than the palm with very pointed tips and thick at the base* These show self-indulgence and love of luxury, along with a certain refinement of taste. Persons with such fingers are very sensuous and are ardently pursue material pleasures. Such fingers are often seen in the hands of singers of both sexes.

Adults show a wide range of sizes, with the lengths and proportions of their fingers varying greatly.

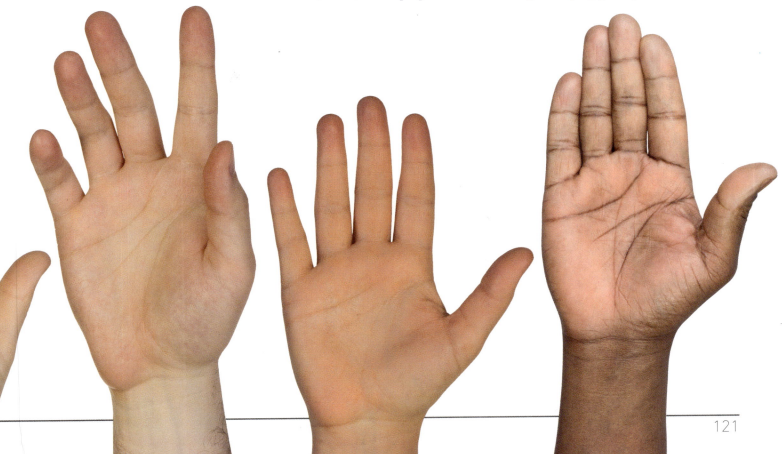

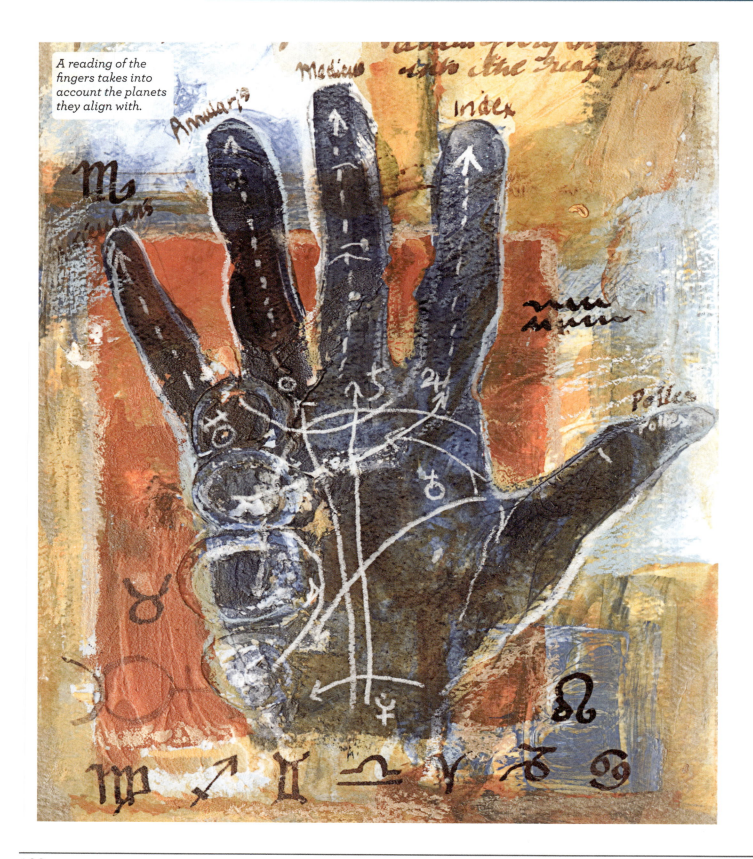

A reading of the fingers takes into account the planets they align with.

- *Fingers slender and longer than the palm with spatulate tips* These indicate versatility, wit, and intuitive perception. Such fingers show the dominant influence of Mercury.

THE FINGERTIPS

Various types of fingertips are often seen in the same hand, which shows that several planets have much the same amount of influence.

- *Finger of Jupiter* ♃ Pointed gives idealistic religious feeling and a sense of honor; square shows reasoning power; spatulate, energy and impulse.
- *Finger of Saturn* ♄ Pointed mitigates the melancholy given by the planet and shows callousness and frivolity; square indicates prudence, love of agriculture, and mechanical genius; spatulate betokens sadness and superstition.
- *Finger of Sun* ☉ Pointed shows idealism and artistic tastes; square reveals realism in art and a love of wealth; spatulate gives a spirit of adventure, especially when it is as long as the first finger. If the third finger is longer than the first and spatulate it indicates love of risk.
- *Finger of Mercury* ☿ Pointed shows intuition, eloquence, and talent for languages; square denotes logic, facility of expression, science and love of research; spatulate gives movement and vivacity.
- *Thumb* Pointed gives impressionability; square a decided but not obstinate will. The thumb bending outward shows generosity and impulse and, when much bent inwards toward the palm, avarice and reticence.

THE THUMB

The joints of the thumb each represent certain aspects of a querent's nature.

- *First joint* The one nearest the nail represents will. When short, it indicates want of will—a character very impressionable and therefore easily led. When long, it indicates great power of will and therefore force of character.
- *Second joint* This represents logic, judgment and reason. If this joint is long these qualities exist in excess and, if it is short, they are wanting in both.
- *Third joint* The joint outside the Mount of Venus represents the power that love will have on the character. If long and thick it implies the existence of strong passion; if short and flat a cold disposition.

FINGER DIVISIONS

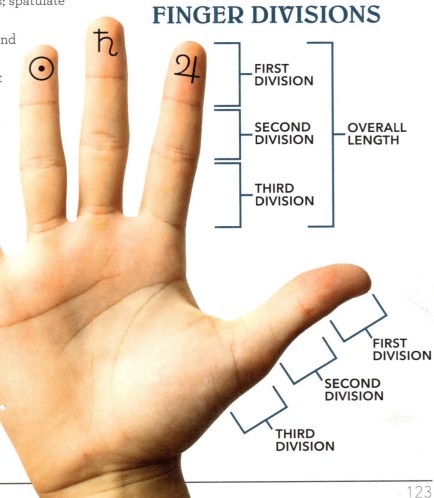

FIRST DIVISION

SECOND DIVISION

THIRD DIVISION

OVERALL LENGTH

FIRST DIVISION

SECOND DIVISION

THIRD DIVISION

The MOUNTS of the PALM

Each hand is unique, but there are several principal mounts of the hand that are traditionally used to read the palms.

The fleshy lumps of the palm, made of muscle, skin and fat, reflect the querent's personality. These mounts of the palm, which can be more or less developed, lie at the base of each finger. Each mount corresponds with one of the planets or other heavenly body, which influence your querent to varying degrees, according to its development, along with the signs or marks found upon it. Each finger corresponds to a planet or the Sun.

The ancients gave to each finger the name of one of the planets, as follows.

- *First finger* Represents Jupiter; the mount at its base being called the Mount of Jupiter.
- *Second finger* Represents Saturn; the mount at its root being the Mount of Saturn.
- *Third finger* Represents the Sun; the mount below being the Mount of the Sun.
- *Fourth finger* Represents Mercury; the mount at its base being called the Mount of Mercury.
- *Thumb* Represents Venus; the root of the thumb is called the Mount of Venus.

The Moon is represented by the Mount of Moon, which lies at the lower part of the palm on the opposite side of the hand to the thumb. Although no finger is dedicated to Mars, it is twice represented in the hand: along the side of the palm by the Mount of Mars, and in the palm, between the Life Line and the Head Line, which is called the Plain of Mars.

The definition or prominence of each mount will give you clues to how strongly they act upon your querent. When these mounts are well in their places

and clearly but not too strongly defined, they give the qualities of the planet they represent. When any mount is not well marked, or even, as frequently happens, is quite deficient, the corresponding qualities are lessened or diminished. Mounts that are not only ill-defined but also represented by a cavity indicate the existence of qualities that are the reverse of those indicated by the mount. Very strong development denotes an excess of the qualities given by the mount.

The mounts are often irregularly placed. If one should lean towards another, it absorbs some of the qualities of the mount that it invades.

A couple consult a palm reader near the Keesaragutta Temple in India. Palmistry is practiced around the world, including by the Hindu Brahmins, and it is also indirectly referenced in the Bible.

A palm reader analyzes the lines and mounts of the querent's hand.

QUICK GUIDE: The MOUNTS of the PALM

♃ Mount of Jupiter

Position: Root of the first finger
Related to: Confidence, wisdom, and leadership

- *High and firm* – Natural leader, intelligent, ambitious
- *High and spongy* – Vain, proud, over-indulgent, superstitious, domineering
- *Low* – Kind, more interested in respect than wealth
- *Missing* – Low self-respect, coldness, selfishness

☿ Mount of Mercury

Position: Root of the fourth finger
Related to: Intuition, intelligence, and activity

- *High* – Clever, crafty, competitive
- *Low* – Impractical, insincere, inventive
- *Missing* – Tends to be poor

♄ Mount of Saturn

Position: Root of the second finger
Related to: Discipline, balance, and independence

- *High and firm* – Responsible, hard-working, aloof, gloomy
- *High and spongy* – Morbid
- *Low* – Faith in fate
- *Missing* – Disorganized, superficial, un-self-aware

♀ Mount of Venus

Position: Formed by the root of the thumb
Related to: Love, sympathy, and grace

- *High* – Affectionate, sympathetic
- *Low* – Overindulgent, promiscuous
- *Missing* – Solitary, highly critical

☉ Mount of Sun

Position: Root of the third finger.
Related to: Ambition, success, happiness, and creativity

- *High and firm* – Adaptable, outgoing, self-confident, quick-tempered
- *High and spongy* – Proud, smooth-tongued, extravagant
- *Low* – Interested in beauty, practical, lack imagination
- *Missing* – Ordinary, indecisive

☾ Mount of Moon

Position: Base of palm, on the little finger side of the hand
Related to: Imagination, creativity, and emotion

- *High* – Lovers of nature and beauty, imaginative, religious
- *Low* – Imaginative, emotional
- *Missing* – Hard-hearted, materialistic, pessimistic

♂ Mounts of Mars

MARS POSITIVE (INNER/LOWER MARS)

Position: Near crook of thumb

Related to: Courage and adventure

- *Well-developed* – Courageous, healthy and adventurous
- *Overdeveloped* – Aggressive, argumentative, hot-tempered
- *Low* – Difficulty standing up to others

MARS NEGATIVE (OUTER/UPPER MARS)

Position: Below little finger

Related to: Self-control, perseverance, and endurance

- *Well-developed* – Strong-willed
- *Overdeveloped* – Lacking in courage, easily manipulated
- *Low* – Struggles through difficulties

PLAIN OF MARS

Position: Center of palm

Related to: Temperament and relations with others

- *Firm* – Makes use of the qualities of the Heart, Head and Destiny Lines
- *Spongy* – Easily influenced, low-energy, life of challenges

♆ Mount of Neptune

Position: Base of palm, at center

Related to: Leadership, self-worth, organization, and authority

- *High and firm* – natural leader, intelligent, ambitious
- *High and spongy* – vain, proud, over-indulgent, superstition, domineering
- *Low* – kind, more interested in respect than wealth
- *Missing* – low self-respect, coldness, selfishness

Insight To begin your reading, identify which mount on your querent's palm is the most dominant one. It is the characteristics associated with this mount that most clearly defines the personality of your querent. Having more than one dominant mount is considered lucky. When you notice two prominent mounts, you can be assure this querent will be confident, ambitious, and driven. If no mount stands out, look for a lack of self confidence.

MOUNT OF JUPITER

The Mount of Jupiter, which is immediately under the index finger, indicates how your querent perceives the world and how they want to be viewed by others.

A high and firm mount that is normally elevated and prominent can indicate a spiritual and compassionate individual who looks to help others and even when faced with difficulty will maintain a positive attitude.

If it appears overdeveloped and higher than the other mounts, your querent may tend to be domineering, self-centered, and lacking in compassion.

A low, less-defined mount will appear on a querent who is kind and more interested in the good opinion of others rather than the accumulation of wealth or status symbols. If the mount is flat or missing, your querent might be selfish, have little self-esteem, and lack ambition.

MOUNT OF SATURN

The Mount of Saturn is found immediately beneath the second finger, which the ancients assigned to Saturn, the planet of Fatality. Its influence is one of extremes—giving extreme misfortune or extreme good fortune, according to the development of the mount and the signs and lines to be seen upon it, along with the course of the Fate Line, or Saturnian Line. The Mount of Saturn indicates patience, duty, responsibility, and modesty. Those born under the influence of Saturn are timid lovers of solitude but are very persistent in their affections when they do love someone.

If the mount is high and firm and normally elevated and prominent, your querent will most likely be friendly and independent, with an easy-going attitude.

A palm reader can study the general qualities of a querent's hand before beginning the session.

If it appears overdeveloped and higher than the other mounts, your querent may be a taciturn individual who can be stubborn to a fault, prone to depression, cynical, and often very shy, keeping themselves isolated from others.

If the mount is flat or missing, your querent might be disorganized, superficial, and lacking in self-awareness.

MOUNT OF SUN

The Mount of Sun, also known as the Mount of Apollo, is placed at the root of the third finger and lies on the upper part of the Heart Line. It indicates a querent's level of self-assurance, compassion, and success.

A high and firm mount that is normally elevated and prominent can indicate that your querent has a love of art, music, and literature, and they are mostly likely lively and outgoing, someone who wants to stand out in a crowd.

PALMISTRY and the ZODIAC

Palmistry charts often include the astrological symbols because the signs of the zodiac are also represented on the hand.

- Aries begins the astrological year; it is placed at the base, close to the Mount of Venus.
- Taurus is on the Mount of Venus; Gemini is at the base of the Mount of Jupiter. These represent the spring of the life, and are placed near Venus, which represents happiness.
- Cancer, Leo, and Virgo represent the second age, which is given to production; these appear on the finger of Jupiter.
- Libra, Scorpio, and Sagittarius represent the third age when a person enjoys what they have accomplished. They appear are on the third finger, that of the Sun.
- Capricorn is beneath the Mount of Sun, Aquarius is on the upper part of the Mount of Moon, and Pisces lies at the base.

If it appears overdeveloped and higher than the other mounts, your querent make be extravagant, frivolous, and a bit too fond of attention. They can also be quick to temper, which can place strain on their relationships.

If it is flat or unpronounced, your querent might be a rather dull, colorless individual and not very outgoing. These individuals often have difficulty making sound decisions.

MOUNT OF MERCURY

The Mount of Mercury is found at the base of the fourth finger and is an indicator of financial acumen, practicality, verbal sharpness, and adaptability.

A high and firm mount that is normally elevated and prominent can indicate intelligence, success in science or occult studies, industriousness of mind and body, shrewdness, and eloquence. This individual has many interests, is flexible, and is a good communicator who is adept at reading other people.

If it appears overdeveloped and higher than the other mounts, your querent probably tends to talk too much and can be impudent and given to falsehood, all too willing to lie when they think it benefits them. This individual might also be greedy and materialistic.

If it is flat or unpronounced, your querent might be shy and have difficulty communicating verbally. They also have difficulty with finances.

MOUNT OF VENUS

The Mount of Venus is located on the part of the palm that is at the base of the thumb. It is an indicator of love, affection, and passion.

A high and firm mount that is normally elevated and prominent can indicate an appreciation for beauty, an interest in music, and a passion for the arts. These individuals are often attractive, and they tend to be influential and are staunch friends.

If it appears overdeveloped and higher than the other mounts, your querent may be prone to overindulgence and promiscuity. They tend to seek instant gratification.

If it is flat or unpronounced, your querent might be a loner, with little connection to family or friends. These individuals often face hardship and can suffer from illness. They tend to be highly critical of others and are not impressed by physical beauty.

MOUNT OF MOON

The Mount of Moon, also known as the Mount of Luna, is located on the base of the palm on the little finger side of the hand. It is an indicator of intuition, creativity and, a lively, vivid imagination.

A palm reader's shingle advertises her services at Santa Barbara Pier, California.

A high and firm mount that is normally elevated and prominent can indicate a creative or artistic person. This is a compassionate, helpful individual who can be somewhat dreamy and sentimental. A lover of nature and the ocean, as well as solitude, they can be gently melancholic. They can be highly intuitive and even possess psychic abilities

If it appears overdeveloped and higher than the other mounts, your querent might wallow in morbid melancholy and caprice. They are prone to let their imagination run wild and have difficulty grounding themself in reality, content to live in a fantasy world.

If it is flat, your querent might still possess imagination, but keeps it to themself. They might also be devoid of imagination and enthusiasm become closed individuals, pessimistic and deep in their own thoughts.

MOUNTS OF MARS

The Mounts of Mars are located in three areas of the palm: the inner part of the palm, the outer part, and the center plain. The Inner and Outer mounts tend to be similar, and these are what most palm readers focus on.

Mars Positive

Mars Positive, also known as the Mount of Inner Mars or the Mount of Lower Mars, lies below the little finger between the Head Line and the Heart Line. It is an indicator of temperament.

A well-developed mount indicates courage, ardor, and resolution. This is a well-balanced and healthy individual.

If it appears overdeveloped, look for a stubborn, defiant individual with a tendency towards aggression.

If it is flat or missing, your querent is likely timid and indecisive. The absence of the mount indicates cowardice and the want of self-command.

Mars Negative

Mars Negative, also known as the Mount of Outer Mars or the Mount of Upper Mars or indicates enthusiasm or aggression, as well as self-control and endurance.

A well-developed mount indicates a steady, persevering individual, who may be fearless, unless it involves money, when they prefer to avoid risk.

If it appears overly developed, your querent is likely a quick-tempered individual, who can be overindulgent, egotistical, and argumentative. They may lack courage and stay in negative situations that they could avoid.

If it is flat, low, or missing, your querent likely lacks endurance, self-esteem, and motivation. They can be impetuous and will have trouble expressing true feelings and tend to withdraw into themselves during times of uncertainty.

Plain of Mars

The Plain of Mars, also known as the Middle Mars Plain, is located in the center of the palm.

An undefined Plain of Mars shows a highly self-centered person, who can also display temper tantrums.

A thick, well-developed mount indicates a high-energy, sociable individual. Usually upbeat, they do tend to rebellion and can disregard the feelings of others.

If there is a dip, they are likely calm and patient.

MOUNT OF NEPTUNE

The Mount of Neptune is located on the palm below the Head Line and above the Mount of Moon. It is closely tied to artistic, musical, and creative ability.

Balanced, prominent development of the mount gives the querent the potential to becomes an eminent musician, poet, or a writer.

If the mount leans toward the Mount of Moon, the standards of the querent are lowered, and they may be antisocial. If it leans toward the Mount of Venus, the querent many be socially irresponsible.

If it appears overdeveloped and higher than the other mounts, your querent might have a difficult life and family troubles.

If it is low or missing, the querent will lack artistic, musical, or other creative talent.

The LINES of the PALM

The lines of the palm are the heart of palmistry, mapping our potential future.

The lines that cross every palm are said to chart the querent's destiny. The largest line, which encircles the thumb, is called the Life Line. Its length, color, and evenness—or the reverse—indicate the length of a person's life. It also indicates the illnesses and accidents that might menace that life running its course. The

HEART LINE

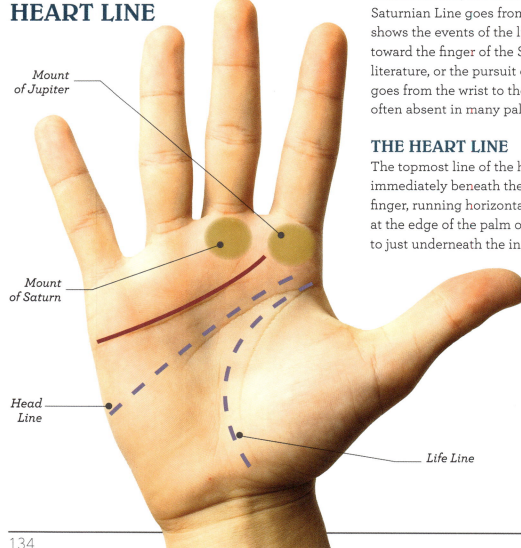

Mount of Jupiter

Mount of Saturn

Head Line

Life Line

line immediately above it, crossing the palm of the hand, is the Head Line, which a reader uses to judge the intellectual powers of a querent. Above it is the Heart Line, from which you can form an opinion of the strength of affection—or the want of it—in the querent.

The lines that are not found in every palm are the Saturnian Line, the Sun Line, and the Health Line. The Saturnian Line goes from the wrist to the finger and shows the events of the life. The Sun Line, which goes toward the finger of the Sun, indicates success in art, literature, or the pursuit of riches. The Health Line goes from the wrist to the finger of Mercury and is often absent in many palms.

THE HEART LINE

The topmost line of the hand, the Heart Line is placed immediately beneath the mounts at the root of each finger, running horizontally across the palm. It begins at the edge of the palm on the pinkie side and extends to just underneath the index or middle finger. It is as its name suggests, it is the heart of the querent, giving insights into their relationships, emotions, and potential for personal growth. In general, the deeper the heart line, the deeper an individual's capacity to give and receive love. Reading the Heart Line can help you guide a querent to do what is best to protect their hearts and to

QUICK GUIDE: HEART LINE and HEAD LINE SAMPLE READINGS

Heart Line starts at Mount of Jupiter

- A romantic individual, who is idealistic, but can be calculating

Heart Line starts between Jupiter and Saturn

- A happy realistic individual, who is well-balanced

Heart Line starts at Mount of Saturn

- A self-centered individual, with a strong sex drive

Head Line Horizontal

- A down-to-earth realist, who is practical and a good organizer

Head Line Chained

- An disorganized individual; a bit of an unfocused scatterbrain

Head Line Diagonal

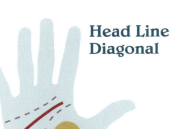

- A self-expressive individual, who can well plan the future

make the most of their potential for positive, beneficial relationships. This line is the first a palm reader evaluates, noting the following attributes.

- *Clear, straight, and well-colored* When rising in the Mount of Jupiter and extending to the outer edge of the hand, this kind of line signifies a good heart capable of strong affection. If, instead of commencing on the Mount of Jupiter, it take its rise at the Mount of Saturn, then the love will be of a more sensual nature. If it stretches across the whole of the hand, it may indicate a passionate and blind devotion in affection.

- *Chained* When the line appears in the form of the links of a chain instead of in one clear line, it indicates inconstancy and indecision—a tendency towards a series of crushes rather than serious affection. If it goes around to the percussion of the hand it indicates jealousy.
- *Drooping* A line drooping toward the Head Line and touching is a sign of coldness
- *Pale and wide* This kind of line is an indication of coldness of temperament.
- *Red punctures* These indicate frequent heartbreak.
- *White spots* These show the persons who have deeply loved the querent.

- *Deep red color* This indicates an obsessive love.
- *Solomon's Ring* When, at its starting point, the Heart Line turns around the base of the Mount of Jupiter somewhat in the form of a circle, it indicates an aptitude for the occult sciences.
- *Bi-forked or branched* If, at the starting point, the line is bi-forked, and one branch of the fork rises towards the Mount of Jupiter, it indicates great happiness, but if the other branch stops between the finger of Jupiter and that of Saturn, it is merely negative happiness or lack of unhappiness—a life passed without great misfortunes.

HEAD LINE

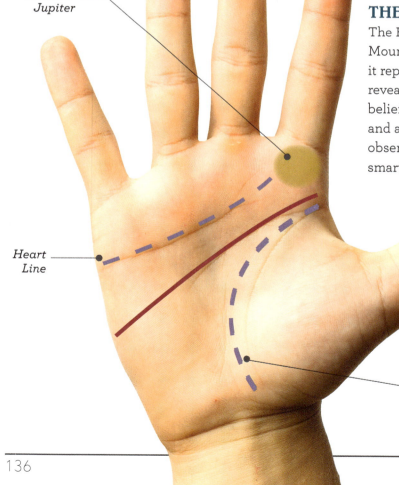

Mount of Jupiter

Heart Line

Life Line

- *Broken in several places* This means inconstancy, both in love and friendship.
  - If the breaks are seen immediately beneath the Mount of Saturn, it indicates a tragic end to love.
  - If beneath the Mount of the Sun, it means an end to love due to pride.
  - If between the Mount of Saturn and the Mount of the Sun, the heartbreak is due to folly.
  - If between the Mounts of Apollo and Mercury, it is heartbreak from greed.
  - If the break occurs immediately beneath the Mount of Mercury, caprice ends love.
- *Absent* A missing Heart Line (which is rare) indicates an iron will and a tendency toward cruelty, unless the Ring of Venus is deep and goes toward the Mount of Mercury, in which case it would take the place of the Heart Line.

THE HEAD LINE

The Head Line rises between the Life Line and the Mount of Jupiter. Also known as the Wisdom Line, it represents all things related to mental capacity, revealing intelligence, intuition, self-control, wisdom, beliefs, and attitudes, as well as level of creativity and ability to remember. It is the second line usually observed by a reader. It is not a measurement of how smart an individual is, but more a gauge of the scope of their intellectual life. The shorter the head line, the more focused and narrow their interests; whereas a longer head line indicates an individual with broad and varied interests. Other attributes to look for are as follows.

- *Long and clear* This denotes sound judgment, a good memory, and masterly intellect.

- *Pale-colored and wide* A want of intelligence.
- *Drooping* A long line that droops toward the Mount of Moon signifies excessive idealism. If it rises towards other mounts it reflects qualities of those mounts.
  - If it rises beneath the Mount of Mercury, the intellect will be employed successfully in affairs or on the stage.
  - If towards the Sun, the intellect will be engaged in art and literature.

- *Separate* When the Head Line is not joined to the Life Line at its starting point, it indicates self-confidence, but also and impulsiveness, jealousy, and a tendency to exaggerate of facts. It also gives audacity and enthusiasm.
- *White spots* These indicate as many successes in literary pursuits as there are spots to be seen.
- *Doubled* Two lines, though rare, is sign of fortune by inheritance or legacy.

In Caravaggio's Good Luck, a well-dressed young man looks pleased at the fortune he is receiving from a palm reader. Painted in the late 16th century, it also shows that the woman is removing the young man's ring.

THE LIFE LINE

The Life Line, the one that leaps to most minds when you say, "palmistry," is an often-misunderstood line. The ancient chiromancists divided the Life Line into 10 compartments, each representing 10 years of life. This enabled them to predict at what date in the life the illnesses or dangers indicated by the form or color of the line would be likely to happen. In an age when death often came far earlier for most people than it does today, many of their interpretations are rather morbid predictions of doom. A more modern approach to chiromancy reads the Life Line as an indicator of a person's vitality system. In other words, not how many days they live, but how well they live their days.

New interpretations also focus on how the Life Line lets a reader evaluate a querent's connection to their family, friends, and loved ones. In this system, a short line does not equate with an early death, but rather an independent life or a lack of groundedness. Your querent might enjoy that independence, or they may want to find ways to connect to others who can ground them.

When reading, keep a few general statements about the Life Line in mind. A line rising in the Mount of Jupiter, instead of starting from the side of the hand (which is rare) indicates a life of successful ambition, honors, and celebrity—qualities given by the influence of Jupiter. A line very far from the Heart Line indicates a life without love. Other notable attributes include the following.

- *Long and well-formed* A long, well-formed, slightly colored line indicates well-balanced individual with robust health, stamina, vitality.
- *Long and deep* If deep, expect a smooth path in life.
- *Short and deep* A short and deep line indicates the ability to overcome physical problems.
- *Short and shallow* Expect an individual easily influenced by other people.
- *Faint* Indicates a low-energy individual, with little taste for adventure.
- *Broken* A broken line on one hand but a continuous line on the other points to a serious illness from which they will quickly recover. It can also mean an unexpected change. A break in the line on both hands can signify a serious illness. A break near the wrist area can indicate early-childhood problems.

LIFE LINE

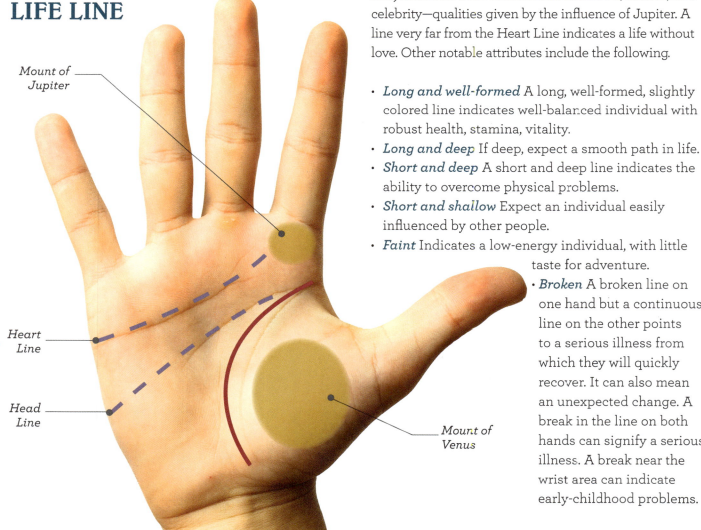

Mount of Jupiter

Heart Line

Head Line

Mount of Venus

- *Forked* A forked line generally indicates a redirection or scattered and split energies.
  - If the line is bi-forked near the wrist, expect a new direction very late in life.
  - If it leads to the Mount of Jupiter, expect success and recognition.
  - If it leads to the Mount of Moon, expect long-distance travel.

- *Chained* A chained line indicates a life path with many directions.
- *Doubled* A double line, sometimes called the Line of Mars, indicates a person of great stamina surrounded by positive energies. It can mean a true partner is out there or could indicate a double life.
- *Absent* An absent line indicates a high-strung, nervous individual.

QUICK GUIDE: LIFE LINE SAMPLE READINGS

Long and Deep

- A healthy individual with stamina, vitality, and energy

Short and Deep

- A tenacious individual, who is a survivor

Short and Thin

- An sharp, intuitive individual, prepared for anything

Broken

- A sudden change will occur in this individual's life path

Curved under Mount of Venus

- A calm, stable individual, who thinks before acting

Curved toward Mount of Moon

- An impetuous individual, who acts before thinking

Insight Ethical and compassionate practices are key when you read someone's palm, especially as you are learning the art of palmistry. It is not your job to instill fear or panic. Never predict mortality—keep in mind that a palm reading is about your querent's journey through life. Concentrate instead on how the Life Line reveals experiences, vitality, and zest. Its depth suggests the richness of those experiences, while the length reveals the influence of others on your querent's path through life.

THE FATE LINE

Also called the Saturnian Line or the Destiny Line, the Fate Line is a vertical crease in the center of the palm that emanates at the wrist and travels upward toward the fingers that is present in some, but not all, hands. Our hands change over our lives, and this is a line that can develop over time. Despite its name, it does not reveal an individual's ultimate fate or destiny, but instead indicates the degree external forces beyond their control will affect their life. It can tell a reader how much ambition, determination, and focus a querent is exerting to improve and control their life.

FATE LINE

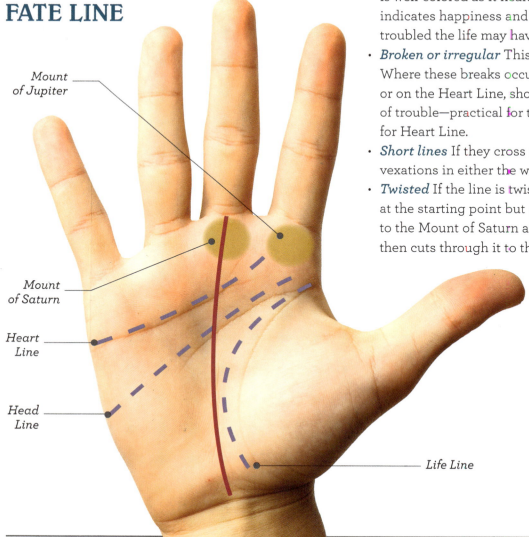

Mount of Jupiter

Mount of Saturn

Heart Line

Head Line

Life Line

- *Direct line* If the line starts from the wrist, exactly below the finger of Saturn, and goes in a direct line to it, cutting through the mount, but stopping at the root of the finger, it is a sign of a life of extreme happiness.
- *Angled line* If the line goes toward the Mount of Jupiter, it is a sign happiness is the result of a marriage bringing both love and financial security and love.
- *Shortened* If the line stops short at the Head Line, it points to misfortune in affairs through a false calculation.
- *Straight and well-colored at termination* If the line is well-colored as it nears the Finger of Saturn, it indicates happiness and success in old age, however troubled the life may have been before.
- *Broken or irregular* This indicates trouble and worry. Where these breaks occur, whether on the Head Line or on the Heart Line, shows if the kind of trouble—practical for the Head Line and romantic for Heart Line.
- *Short lines* If they cross the Fate Line, they indicate vexations in either the work or in love matters.
- *Twisted* If the line is twisted in a sort of spiral at the starting point but goes in a clear, direct line to the Mount of Saturn at the upper part of it, and then cuts through it to the root of the finger without penetrating beyond, it indicates a troubled and anxious youth, followed by riches and good fortune in middle age. If the twisted line continues and crosses the Head Line and the Heart Line, the troubles will continue until very late in life, and the good fortune will only manifest very near the close of life.

THE SUN LINE

Also called Apollo's Line, the Sun Line is the vertical crease farthest toward the pinkie side of the palm, taking its rise either in the Life Line or from the Mount of Moon, and, ascending, it traces a furrow in the Mount of Sun, but stops at the root of the finger. It can vary greatly in length, depth, and position, and it reflects the querent's public image and when they might achieve success or even fame. A Sun Line intersecting or running parallel to the Fate Line indicates success or notoriety that comes from external influences outside of an individual's control. If these two lines sit far from each other, success will be in the individual's control. Those with a Sun Line, even if they are not artists by profession, will have artistic tastes, an eye for color, an ear for music, or a perception of beauty in form or in language. Many interpretations of the line focus on the arts, as the following examples show.

- *Straight and well defined* This kind of line signifies the potential for celebrity in literature or art, whether in poetry, painting, sculpture, or music. The mount decides in some measure which branch of art is preferred; with Venus large, it would probably be music or painting. The Moon much developed signifies poetry or literature. Where the line only begins in the Heart Line, the artistic feeling is only appreciative, not productive, but when it rises as low as the Mount of the Moon, it signifies creative power.
- *Subdivided* If the line subdivides into several lines, it indicates a tendency to cultivate several branches of art, which prevents the success in any one of them,

and it can signify a dilettante or patron of the arts rather than the artist themself.

- *Barred* If the line is barred by several transverse lines in its upward course, there are probably obstacles to the career of art, but if the line continues and marks a single deep furrow in the mount until it reaches the root of the finger, these obstacles will, in the end, be conquered and artistic success will eventually be attained.
- *Elevated* If the line begins above the Head Line, the deep line at its close only means riches after 50 and has nothing to do with art.

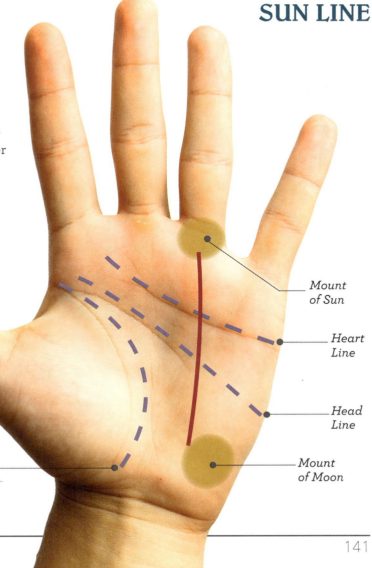

SUN LINE

Mount of Sun

Heart Line

Head Line

Mount of Moon

Life Line

THE HEALTH LINE

The Health Line, or, as it is sometimes called, the Liver Line, takes its rise at the wrist, near the Life Line, and mounts in the direction of the Mount of Mercury. The Health Line sometimes takes a curved form on one hand only, tracing a sort of half-circle from the Mount of Moon to the Mount of Mercury. In this case it is called the Presentiment Line and indicates vivid intuition, especially if Mercury is strong in the querent's influence. When the Health Line on both hands takes this form, it indicates mediumistic powers and powerful second sight. It is also a general indicator of one's health as a whole. This line does not occur in all

HEALTH LINE

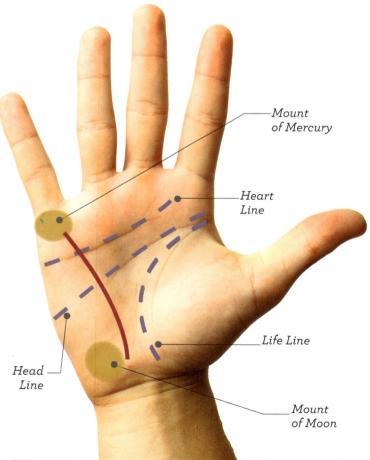

Mount of Mercury

Heart Line

Life Line

Head Line

Mount of Moon

CHANCE LINES

These are lines that are sometimes—but only rarely—seen on any hand. Even so, a chance lines can tell a lot about a querent. Here are just a few.

- *Two lines* When two starting from the Mount of Venus join with a star on the Plain of Mars, it indicates two loves carried on at once and both having a disastrous issue.
- *Square* A square with spots at all four corners placed on the Mount of the Sun shows danger by fire with preservation.
- *Line from Mars to Sun* A line from the Mount of Mars going to the Mount of Sun indicates love of glory, desire to attain distinction in life. This is an individual who loves a large audience.
- *Circle* A circle on the Heart Line beneath the finger of Mercury denotes the person as likely to cause—though unwittingly—the death of someone much loved.
- *Star* This indicates something beyond our own power of action.

hands, but its appearance doesn't mean a querent is doomed to disease or distress, but rather it can alert a querent to potential health risks and vulnerabilities so they can work to stave off any issues. Its appearance is said to correlate with certain areas of the body that might be affected.

- *Well-colored and unbroken* This denotes good health and great power of memory; also success in business pursuits.
- *Starts from Life Line* This indicates hearing issues.
- *Wavy* This is associated the digestive system and indicates gastrointestinal issues and also liver or bladder malfunctioning.
- *Crossed* A line crossed by many short ones indicates poor general health or an accident-prone individual.
- *Forked at its close* If it is broken or forked before it reaches the mount, it indicates severe health issues in later years.

- *Broken* This kind of line is also associated with digestive health.
- *Partnered* The Health Line is sometimes, but rarely, accompanied by another line called the Milky

Way; when the Milky Way line commences side by side with the Health Line and mounts with it in an unbroken line, toward the finger of Mercury, it signifies a long life of uninterrupted happiness.

QUICK GUIDE: COMMON MARKS of the PALM

BRANCHED LINES	DOUBLES LINES	ISLANDS	TRANSVERSE LINES
NEGATIVE	NEGATIVE	NEGATIVE	NEGATIVE
CHAINED LINES	DOWNWARD LINES	SPOTS	TRIANGLES
NEGATIVE	POSITIVE	POSITIVE	POSITIVE
CIRCLES	FORKED LINES	SQUARES	WAVY LINES
POSITIVE/NEGATIVE	POSITIVE	POSITIVE	POSITIVE/NEGATIVE
CROSSES	GRILLS	STARS	UPWARD LINES
NEGATIVE	NEGATIVE	POSITIVE	POSITIVE

OTHER FREQUENTLY OCCURRING LINES

There are three other lines that can be seen in most hands. The relative proportions of these three lines to one another is influenced by the three different worlds they represent. In reading the hand, each line must be judged with reference to the others, and the hand must be considered in all its bearings before an opinion on the tendencies it indicates can be arrived at with any degree of correctness.

The Ring of Venus

Also called the Girdle of Venus, this line seems to enclose, as in an island, the Mounts of Saturn and Sun.

- *Fully developed* This signifies unbridled passion when, in conjunction with it, the Mount of Venus is strongly developed and marked with crossway lines.

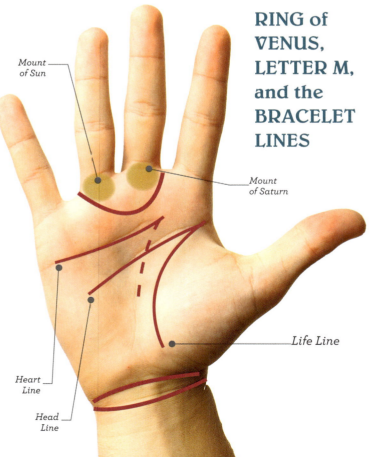

Mount of Sun

Mount of Saturn

RING of VENUS, LETTER M, and the BRACELET LINES

Life Line

Heart Line

Head Line

- *Broken at its center* If, with the signs mentioned above, it is strongly marked, yet broken at its center in both hands, it is a sign of eccentric and depraved passion. Still, there are always modifications of these bad signs, and a very good Head Line would bring reason to bear upon passion.
- *Traversed by fine lines* When the ring is seen on a hand where both the planets Venus and the Moon are strongly indicated and where it is traversed by innumerable fine lines, it is a true sign of an hysterical temperament.
- *Ascending* Sometimes the ring ascends and loses itself on the Mount of Mercury, leaving one end of the semicircle open, which mitigates, in some sort, the terribly strong passions indicated by this mark, but if the semicircle, after extending itself to the Mount of Mercury, closes itself at the root of the finger, would indicate a terrible and absorbing power of passion, which would not hesitate at any means to secure its end.

The Letter M

The letter M, formed more or less regularly in every hand by the Life, Head, and Heart Lines, represents the three worlds—the material, the natural, and the divine.

- *The first* The Life Line represents the material world, or world of sense. It surrounds love and generation, as represented by the thumb, which is sacred to Venus, but the Mount of Venus may either degenerate love to vice or perfect it to tenderness. With high instincts the Mount of Venus is a good quality, because without it, all the other passions are hard and selfish.
- *The second* The Head Line stretches across the natural world, and it traverses the Plain and the Mount of Mars, which represent the struggle of love and reason in existence. The Plain and Mount of Mars both mean a struggle: the Mount is the struggle of resistance, and the Plain the struggle of aggression.

The letter M is present at the center of the palm in nearly everyone's hand, with the lines often varying in depth and color.

- *The third* The Heart Line encloses the divine world, for it surrounds the mounts, which represent religion (Jupiter), fate (Saturn), art (the Sun), and science (Mercury).

The Bracelet Lines

Also called the Wrist Lines, these trace across the base of the palm at the wrist. This is a sign of long life.

- *Three lines* If there are three of these lines, as is sometimes seen, it forms the triple bracelet. These lines are said to indicate 30 years of life each, and the three lines form what is called the magic bracelet, indicating long life, health, and financial ease.

- *Three irregular lines* If the Bracelet Lines are formed irregularly, like the links of a chain, it indicates a long life of labor, but acquiring ease and competency at its close.
- *Cross* If a cross appears in the center of the wrist, it indicates a rich heritage at the close of life.
- *Ascending* When lines start upward from the triple bracelet and ascend towards the Mount of the Moon, they denote as many travels by land as there are lines. When these travel lines go as high as the Head and Heart Lines, they denote journeys during which some person is met who influences either the fortunes or the affections, according to whether the line stops at the Head or Heart.

C·H·A·P·T·E·R 4

READING the TEA LEAVES
and COFFEE GROUNDS

READING the CUP

Reading the Cup, the art of interpreting the patterns of leftover tea leaves in a cup of tea, is essentially a domestic form of fortune-telling that can be practiced at home.

Tea leaf–reading has a long history, which most likely began in Asia. As soon as tea was introduced to the Western world in the seventeenth century, the practice also took off. It continued to grow in popularity in the Victorian era, and it remains popular in the British Isles and the Middle East.

The art of reading tea leaves, formally known as tasseography or tasseomancy and Reading the Cup or tea leaf–reading more informally, can be done by anyone who masters a few simple rules. It takes no more than a cup of tea and the leaves left in the bottom after the tea had been drunk. With the requisite knowledge and some skill and intuition, anyone can learn to tell a fortune in a tea cup.

Tea-leaf reading can tell an immediate fortune, dealing with the events of the hour or the succeeding 24 hours, or up to a year ahead. You can therefore consult the tea leaves once a day and foresee many of the minor happenings of life with considerable accuracy, according to your skill in discerning the symbols and the intuition required to interpret them. The forthcoming events are those which cast their shadows, so to speak, within the circle of the cup. Practice and the study of the signification of the various symbols is all that is necessary in order to become proficient and to tell your own fortune and that of your friends, whether you consult the tea leaves seriously or just for fun.

STRIKE an AVERAGE

A tea-leaf reader must learn to balance the bad and good, the lucky and unlucky symbols, and strike an average. For example, a large bouquet of flowers, which is a fortunate sign, would outweigh in importance one or two tiny crosses, which signify some small delay in the realization of success; whereas one large cross in a prominent position would be a warning of disaster that would be little, if at all, mitigated by the presence of small isolated flowers, however lucky individually these may be. Symbols that stand out clearly and distinctly are of more importance than those that are difficult to discern amid cloudlike masses of shapeless leaves. When clouds obscure or surround a lucky sign, they weaken its force, and vice versa.

METHOD

The ritual to be observed is very simple.

- Start with a traditional tea cup, white or very pale-colored so that the patterns are easiest to read.
- Put a pinch of loose-leaf tea into the cup, preferably a black tea, such as oolong, and pour hot water on top of the leaves. Allow the leaves to steep for approximately three minutes.
- The querent then sips the tea while reflecting upon any questions they hope to have answered. During this procedure they should concentrate upon their future destiny and will the symbols to form under the guidance of their hand and arm to correctly represent the future. They should drink until only about half teaspoonful of tea remains in the cup.
- The querent then takes the cup by the handle in the left hand, rim upwards, and turns it three times

clockwise (from left to right) in one fairly rapid swinging movement. This should allow some of the tea leaves to swish up the sides of the cup, while the rest stick to the bottom.

- They then very slowly and carefully invert it over the saucer and leave it there for a minute, so as to permit of all the liquid to drain away.
- To begin the reading, you should then carefully flip the cup right-side up, taking it gently in hand to avoid disturbing the patterns. If this simple

ritual has been correctly carried out, the tea leaves, whether many or few, will be found distributed about the bottom and sides of the cup. The fortune may be equally well told whether there are many leaves or few, but of course there must be some.

- The handle of the cup is akin to the "house" in divination by cards. From this fixed point, judgment is made as to events approaching the house: journeys away from home, messages or visitors to be expected, relative distance, and so forth.

A reader explains the meaning of the shapes found in a querent's tea cup.

- The bottom of the cup represents the remoter future, the sides concern events not so far distant, and matters symbolized near the rim are those that may be expected to occur quickly. The nearer the symbols are to the handle in all three cases, the nearer to fulfillment will be the events foretold.

THE READING

The interior of the tea cup will exhibit the leaves scattered apparently in a fortuitous and accidental manner, but really in accordance with the muscular action of the left arm as controlled by the mind of the querent. These scattered leaves will form lines and circles of dots or small leaves and dust combined with stems, and groups of leaves in larger or smaller patches, apparently in meaningless confusion.

Carefully study the shapes and figures formed inside the cup, viewing them from different positions, so that their meaning becomes clear. It is not very easy at first to see what the shapes really are, but after looking

The CUP

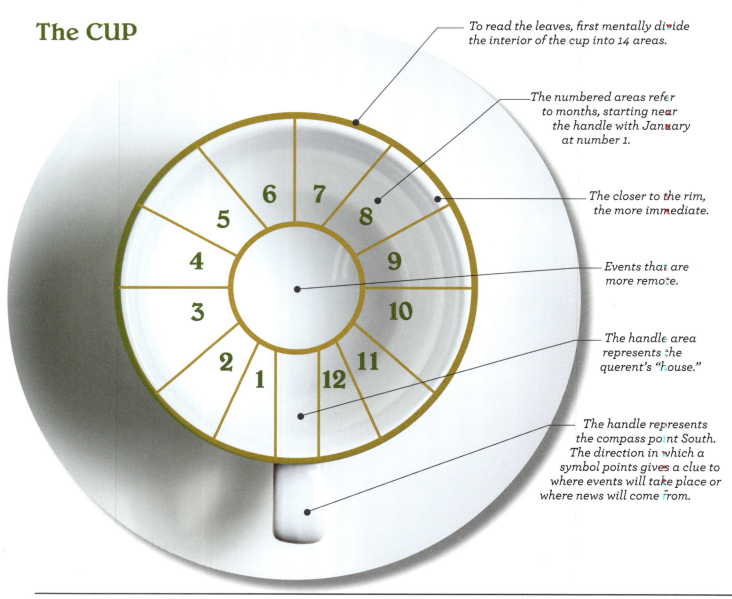

To read the leaves, first mentally divide the interior of the cup into 14 areas.

The numbered areas refer to months, starting near the handle with January at number 1.

The closer to the rim, the more immediate.

Events that are more remote.

The handle area represents the querent's "house."

The handle represents the compass point South. The direction in which a symbol points gives a clue to where events will take place or where news will come from.

at them carefully they become plainer. The different shapes and figures in the cup must be taken together in a general reading. Bad indications will be balanced by good ones; some good ones will be strengthened by others, and so on.

UNDERSTANDING THE SYMBOLS

As you become more practiced, you will recognize some fairly close resemblances between the groups formed by the leaves and various natural or artificial objects. You will learn the representations of such things as trees, animals, birds, anchors, crowns, flowers, as well as simpler shapes such as squares, triangles, and crosses. Each of these possesses, as a symbol, some fortunate or unfortunate signification. Such signs may be either large or small, and you should use their size to judge their relative importance. For example, supposing the symbol observed indicates the receipt of a legacy: if the symbol is small it would mean that the inheritance would be small; if large it would be more substantial.

Letters of the Alphabet

Keep an eye out too for isolated leaves or groups of a few leaves or stems that form letters of the alphabet or numbers. The meanings of these letters and numbers must be sought in conjunction with other signs. If a small square or oblong leaf is seen near a letter L or if a number of very small dots form such a square or oblong, it indicates that a letter, email, or parcel will be received from somebody whose surname (not first name) begins with an L. If the combined symbol appears near the handle and near the rim of the cup, the letter is close at hand; if in the bottom there will be delay in its receipt. If the sign of a letter is accompanied by the appearance of a bird flying towards the house, it means the communication is incoming; if flying away from the house the communication will be outgoing (from the querent). Flying birds always indicate news of some sort.

Directional Cues

Again, the dust in the tea and the smaller leaves and stems frequently form lines of dots. These signify a journey, and their extent and direction show its length and the point of the compass toward which it will extend. The handle of the cup is considered due south.

Numbers

Numerals may indicate the number of days, or if in connection with a number of small dots grouped around the sign of a letter, may indicate a present or a legacy. The numeral can indicate the number of presents to be expected or the amount of the legacy coming. Dots surrounding a symbol always indicate money coming in some form or other, according to the nature of the symbol.

Common Symbols

Although included in alphabetical order in the list that follows, there are certain figures and symbols that so commonly occur and bear such definite interpretation that it is advisable to pay special attention to them. Certain ones are invariably signs of approaching good fortune; certain others threaten ill luck. Good omens include triangles, stars, clover leaves, anchors, trees, garlands and flowers, bridges or arches, and crowns. Bad omens include coffins, clouds, crosses, serpents, rats and mice and some wild beasts, hourglasses, umbrellas, church steeples, swords and guns, ravens, owls, and monkeys.

QUICK GUIDE: SIGNIFICATIONS of TEA SYMBOLS

Abbey Future ease and freedom from worry.

Acorn Improvement in health, continued health, strength, and good fortune.

Aircraft Long journey; a rise in social position.

Anchor A lucky sign; success in business and constancy in love; if cloudy, the reverse.

Angel Good news, especially good fortune in love.

Apes Secret enemies.

Apple Long life; if bitten into, temptation.

Apple tree Change for the better.

Arch A journey abroad.

Arrow Point down, bad news; up, good news.

Ass Misfortune overcome by patience; or a legacy.

Axe Difficulties overcome.

Baby Fretting and small worries.

Bag A trap; if open, escape, from a trap.

Balloon A celebration or party soon.

Basket An addition to the family; a treat, award, compliment, recognition.

Bat Fruitless journeys or tasks.

Bear A long period of travel.

Beasts Misfortune.

Bell Announcement; the nearer the top, the better.

Bird A lucky sign; good news if flying, if at rest a fortunate journey.

Boat A friend will visit.

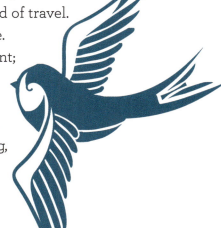

Book If open, good news; if closed, hidden secrets.

Bottle Drunkenness, temptations offered.

Bouquet One of the luckiest of symbols; staunch friends, success, a happy marriage.

Bridge A favorable journey.

Broom A new home; a thorough house-cleaning.

Building A removal.

Bull Slander by some enemy.

Bush A secret friend or secret opportunities.

Butterfly Success and pleasure.

Camel A burden that must be patiently borne.

Candle Help from others.

Cannon Good fortune.

Car Approaching wealth, visits from friends.

Castle Unexpected fortune.

Cat Difficulties caused by treachery.

Chain An early marriage; if broken, trouble in store.

Chair An addition to the family; a guest is coming.

Church A legacy.

Circle Money or presents.

Clock Better health if medical help is sought soon.

Clouds Serious trouble; if surrounded by dots, financial success.

Clover A very lucky sign; happiness and prosperity. At the top, it will come quickly. As it nears the bottom, it will mean more or less distant.

Coffin Long sickness or sign of death of a near relation or close friend.

Comet Misfortune and trouble.

Compass A sign of traveling as a profession.

Cow A prosperous sign.

Cross A sign of trouble and delay or even death.

Crown Success and honor.

Cup Reward of merit; if overturned, justified criticism toward you.

Dagger Favors from friends; danger from self or others; beware injury.

Deer Quarrels, disputes; failure in trade.

Dog Faithful friends, if at top of cup; in middle of cup, they are untrustworthy; at the bottom means secret enemies.

Donkey A legacy long awaited.

Door Opportunities arise through an odd event.

Dove A lucky symbol; progress in prosperity and affection.

Dragon Great and sudden changes.

Duck Increase of wealth by trade.

Eagle Success by soaring over obstacles.

Egg If unbroken, success; if broken, failure.

Elephant A lucky sign; good health.

Eye Look sharp; be cautious; also, you may be psychic.

Face A change is coming, it may be a setback.

Falcon A persistent enemy.

Fan Flirtation.

Feather Insincerity, undependability, lack of focus.

Fence Limitations, minor setbacks, easily mended.

Ferret Active enemies.

Finger Extra emphasis on whatever it points to.

Fire At top, achievement; at bottom, danger, haste.

Fish Good news from abroad; if surrounded by dots, emigration or foreign travel.

Flag Danger from wounds inflicted by an enemy.

Flowers Good fortune, success; a happy marriage.

Fly Domestic annoyances.

Fox Treachery by a trusted friend.

Frog Success in love and commerce.

Fruit Prosperity, a successful outcome to labor.

Gallows A sign of good luck.

Gate Opportunity, future success beckons.

Glass A cocktail glass means dissatisfaction with life; a water glass, integrity and temperance.

Goat A sign of enemies; beware stubborn people.

Goose Happiness; a successful venture or undertaking.

Grapes Good health, fertility, happiness; inebriation.

Grasshopper A close friend will become a soldier.

Greyhound Good fortune by strenuous exertion.

Gun Discord and slander.

Hammer Triumph over adversity.

Hand Read in conjunction with neighboring symbols and according to where it points.

Hare A long journey or the return of an absent friend. Also speedy and fortunate marriage.

Harp Marriage, success in love.

Hat Success in life.

Hawk An enemy.

Heart Pleasures to come; if surrounded by dots, through money; if accompanied by a ring, through marriage.

Heavenly bodies (Sun, Moon, and stars) happiness and success.

Hen Increase in riches or an addition to the family.

Horse Galloping, good news; head only, a lover.

Horseshoe A very lucky omen, a winning bet, good fortune.

Hourglass Imminent peril.

House Success in business; security and safety.

Human figures Judge according to what they appear to be doing. They are generally good and denote love and marriage.

Insect Minor problems require immediate attention.

Ivy Honor and happiness through faithful friends.

Jackal A mischief maker of no account.

Jewels Gifts of some kind will be offered to you.

Jockey Successful speculation.

Jug Good health.

Kangaroo A rival in business or in love.

Kettle Death; minor illness.

Key Money, prosperity, understanding.

Kite A lengthy voyage; travel leading to honor and dignity.

Knife A warning of disaster through quarrels.

Ladder Travel; job promotion, a rise in life, advancement.

Lamp At top, a feast; at side, secrets revealed.

Leaf Change in health: up, better; down, worse.

Leopard Emigration with subsequent success.

Letters Shown by square or oblong tea-leaves, signifies news. Initials near will show surnames of writers; if accompanied by dots they will contain money; if unclouded, good; but if fixed about by clouds, bad news or loss of money.

Lily (or fleur-de-lis) At top of cup, health and happiness; at bottom, anger and strife.

Lines Journeys and their direction, read in conjunction with other signs of travel; wavy lines denote troublesome journeys or losses therein.

Lion Greatness through powerful friends.

Lock Overwhelming obstacles.

Logs (timber) Business success.

Lynx Danger of divorce or break off of an engagement or relationship.

Man A visitor arriving. If the arm is held out, he brings a present.

Man Near handle, a visitor; elsewhere, a pen-pal.

Mermaid Misfortune, especially to seafaring persons.

Monkey The querent will be deceived in love.

Moon (crescent) Prosperity and fortune; a change in plans.

Mountain Powerful friends; many mountains, equally powerful enemies.

Mouse Danger of poverty through theft or swindling.

Mushroom At top, country life; at bottom, growth.

Nail Injustice, unfairness, unfair punishment.

Necklace Whole, admirers; broken, losing a lover.

Needle Recognition, admiration.

Nest Save your money; take care of your home.

Numbers Depends on symbols in conjunction with them.

Oak Very lucky; long life, good health, profitable business, and a happy marriage.

Oblong figures Family or business squabbles.

Octopus Danger.

Ostrich Travel abroad.

Owl An evil omen, indicative of sickness, poverty, disgrace, a warning against commencing any new enterprise. If the querent is in love, they will be deceived.

Palm tree Good luck; success in any undertaking.

Parrot Foreign travel for a lengthy period.

Peacock Success and the acquisition of property; also a happy marriage.

Pear Great wealth and improved social position; success in business.

Pedestrian Good news; an important appointment.

Pheasant A legacy.

Pig Good and bad luck mixed: a faithful lover but envious friends.

Pigeon Important news if flying; if at rest, domestic bliss and wealth acquired in business.

Pine tree Continuous happiness.

Pipe Reconciliation of a broken friendship.

Pistol Disaster.

Plow A struggle ahead; hard going.

Purse At top, profit; at bottom, loss.

Question mark Doubt or disappointment.

Rabbit Fair success in a city or large town.

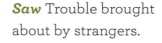

Rainbow The most difficult time is now over.

Rake Watch details lest you stumble.

Rat Losses through an enemy's actions.

Raven Death for the aged; disappointment in love, divorce, failure in business, and trouble generally.

Reptile Quarrels.

Rider Good news from overseas regarding finances or inheritance.

Rifle Discord and strife.

Ring Marriage; if a letter is near it, this is the initial of the future spouse. If clouds are nearby, an unhappy marriage; if all is clear, the contrary. A ring right at the bottom means the wedding will not take place.

Rooster Much prosperity.

Rose Good fortune and happiness; popularity; romance.

Saw Trouble brought about by strangers.

Scales A lawsuit; balanced, justice; unbalanced, injustice.

Scissors Quarrels; illness; separation of lovers.

Serpent Spiteful enemies; bad luck; illness.

Shark Danger of death.

Sheep Success, prosperity.

Shell Good news from over the sea.

Ship Successful journey.

Shoe Hard work leads to a change for the better.

Sickle Illness, sorrow, and pain.

Snake A bad omen. Great caution is needed to ward off misfortune.

Spider Money coming to the querent.

Spoon Generosity.

Square Comfort and peace are on their way.

Squirrel Save up now for future times of want.

Stairs Orderly progress leads to eventual success.

Star A lucky sign; if surrounded by dots foretells great wealth; health, happiness, hope; absolute success.

Steeple Bad luck.

Straight line A very pleasant journey; peace, happiness, and long life.

Sun Joy, success, power, children, well-being.

Swallow A journey with a pleasant ending.

Swan Good luck and a happy marriage.

Sword Dispute, quarrels between lovers; a broken sword, victory of an enemy.

Table A social enjoyable gathering.

Teardrops Sorrow and tears.

Tent Travel you are not well prepared for.

Thimble Changes at home; a need for mending.

Toad Deceit and unexpected enemies.

Tortoise Criticism, usually beneficial.

Tower Disappointment and possible ruin.

Tree A lucky sign; prosperity and happiness; surrounded by dots, a fortune in the country.

Triangle Good luck and unexpected legacies.

Trident Success and honors in the navy.

Turtle Slow progress; a sluggard is near to you.

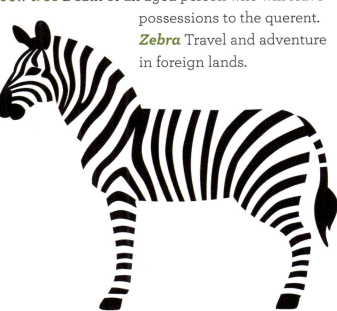

Twisted figures Disturbances and vexation; grievances if there are many such figures.

Umbrella Annoyance and trouble.

Unicorn Scandal.

Vase A friend needs your help.

Violin A self-centered person.

Volcano Harmful and emotional words may erupt.

Vulture Bitter foes.

Wagon Approaching poverty.

Wasp A rival in romance.

Wavy line If long and waved, denote losses and vexations. The number and weight determine their importance.

Wheel If whole, good fortune; if broken, loss.

Windmill Success in a venturous enterprise.

Wings Messages from Heaven.

Wolf Beware of jealous intrigues.

Woman Pleasure and happiness; if accompanied by dots, wealth or children. Several women indicate scandal.

Wood A speedy marriage.

Worm Secret foes.

Yacht Pleasure and happiness.

Yew tree Death of an aged person who will leave possessions to the querent.

Zebra Travel and adventure in foreign lands.

QUICK GUIDE: SAMPLE READINGS

Principal Symbols

1. Hammer
2. A letter approaching the house, accompanied by dots
3. Hat
4. Initials Y and J, accompanied by small cross

INTERPRETATION

- A letter is approaching the querent containing a considerable sum of money, as it is surrounded by dots.
- The future, shown by the bottom of the cup, is not clear, and betokens adversities; but the presence of the hammer there denotes triumph over these, a sign confirmed by the hat on the side.
- The querent will be annoyed by somebody whose name begins with J, and assisted by one bearing the initial Y.

Principal Symbols

1. Large tree
2. Anchor
3. Bird flying high toward handle
4. Small cross in bottom
5. Letter sign close to handle
6. Triangle
7. Initial L with letter sign
8. Initial C

INTERPRETATION

- A letter containing good news (shown by bird flying toward the handle and the triangle) may be expected immediately. If from a lover, the anchor on the side shows they are constant and prosperous.
- The tree indicates happiness and prosperity.
- A letter will be received from someone whose initial is L.
- In the bottom of the cup there are signs of minor vexations or delays in connection with someone whose name begins with C.

Principal Symbols

1. Crescent moon
2. Bird flying
3. Triangles
4. Flag
5. Initial A in conjunction with sign of letter in official envelope
6. Other initials, H and two Ls

INTERPRETATION

- The crescent moon on the side shows prosperity and fortune as the result of a journey denoted by the lines.
- The number of triangles in conjunction with the initial H indicates the name begins with that letter, and, being near the rim, at no great distance of time.
- The bird flying towards and near the handle, accompanied by a triangle and a long envelope, denotes good news from an official source. The flag gives warning of some danger from an enemy.

Principal Symbols

1. Large tree
2. Lily
3. Butterfly
4. Line of dots leading east to a building
5. Initials N and C

INTERPRETATION

- The querent is about to journey eastward to some large building or institution, shown by the figure at the end of the straight line of dots.
- There is some confusion in his or her affairs caused by too much indulgence in pleasure and gaiety, denoted by the butterfly on side approaching handle involved in obscure groups of leaves.
- The tree and the lily in the bottom of the cup are, however, signs of eventual success, probably through the assistance of some person whose name begins with an N.

The COFFEE READER

Telling fortunes from the patterns left in a coffee cup or saucer is an entertaining method of tasseography.

Coffee-reading is the practice of telling fortunes by interpreting the pattern of the coffee grounds left in a cup or on the saucer. A popular pastime in the Balkans and Turkey, this form of tasseography originated in Turkey in the 16th century. It is also commonly practiced in Greece, Russia, and countries of the Middle East. It is much like reading tea leaves, but the interpretations of the patterns can vary in some cases. As with reading tea leaves, it just takes some practice and a careful study of the significations of the various symbols. Keep in mind that it is not customary to read your own cup. Practice with friends or family, and they can also practice on you.

It is customary to place a ring on top of the overturned cup when the querent's issue is about love or relationships.

METHOD

The ritual to be observed is very simple.

- Start by preparing a strong Turkish coffee.
- Pour the coffee into a small cup with a saucer and a white or very pale interior.
- The querent then sips the coffee from one side of the cup while reflecting upon any questions they hope to have answered. During this procedure they should concentrate upon their question or wish. Some traditions call for drinking the coffee in a set number of sips, typically one, three, or five, leaving a single sip in the cup.
- With the last sip, the querent makes a wish, and then takes the saucer and places it tightly over the cup.
- Still focusing on their question or issue, they then hold the saucer-covered cup at chest level and swirl them three times in a clockwise direction to loosen and spread the sediment inside.
- They should then flip the cup and saucer and set it down so the grounds can run down the cup onto the saucer, leaving patterns that you can interpret.
- The querent should then pass you the cup and saucer. If the question at hand is about relationships, place a ring on the bottom of the cup. If the question at hand is about money, place a coin on the bottom of the cup.
- Let the cup sit for 5 to 10 minutes so that it cools and drains completely and the grounds have time to settle into their final patterns.
- When the cup is cooled, gently separate the cup from the saucer, letting any excess grounds and sediment slide out from the handle-side of the cup.

A reader carefully lifts the overturned cup from the saucer to reveal the grounds and sediment.

THE READING

Once you have separated the cup and saucer it is time to begin the reading. The first thing to note is how the excess grounds fall.

- *Big chunks of grounds* Big chunks falling on the saucer is a good sign, traditionally reading as if troubles and worries are on the wane.
- *A pile of grounds* A pile points to money on its way.
- *A stuck cup* If the cup and saucer stick together, take it as a sign that the querent's wish is coming true.

READING the SAUCER

To also read the saucer, swirl it until the sediments are in an even layer. Then tilt the saucer vertically, so that a drop falls. If it makes a long trail, the querent's wish will come true; a short one means it won't. You can then interpret the shapes on the saucer as you would those of the cup.

Holding the cup, you then look for shapes and symbols inside the cup. The shapes will tell you about the querent questions or wishes, but there are aspects to keep in mind. Its size is a clue to a symbol's importance, with a larger one having a greater impact than a smaller one.

Readers also divide the cup various ways. Decide before you begin which you prefer and which will best answer your querent's question.

UNDERSTANDING THE SYMBOLS

To read the symbols, you must take them as a group, weaving a story that takes in the relative impacts of each. There are general categories to keep in mind.

- *Letters of alphabet* Often interpreted as the initial of someone's name or a place name.
- *Numbers* These can represent dates, time, or age.
- *Clustered specks* These may indicate movement.
- *Lines* If clear they show that plans must lead to a specific goal; if wavy, they indicate uncertainty.
- *Faint or poorly outlined* This can signify indecision or obstacles.
- *Objects* Often the meaning is clear—a coin means money or a fence means obstacles. A boat or airplane may indicate a journey The meanings of the symbols can vary from culture to culture, but use the following quick guide for inspiration.

You can include both the shapes in the sediment and the negative spaces they leave in your reading.

Quick Guide: DIVIDING the CUP

Five Sections

In this, as you hold the cup by the handle with the rim facing straight in front of you, mentally divide the interior into five sections.

- Front rim area – Money matters
- Left area – The present
- Bottom cup area – Home and family matters
- Right area – The future
- Handle area – Matters of the heart

Four Sections

In this, as you hold the cup by the handle with the rim facing straight in front of you, draw an imaginary line running parallel to the handle from rim to rim and then another perpendicular one bisecting it at the middle.

- Right of vertical axis – Positive events
- Left of vertical axis – Negative events
- Above horizontal axis – Events in the near future
- Below horizontal axis – Events in the far-off future

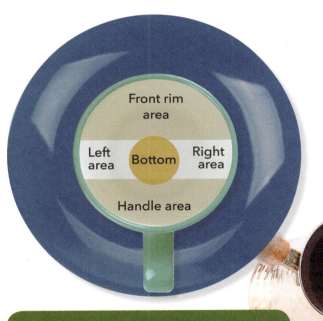

Insight Turkish coffee is a rich and thick style that is not filtered. Instead the coffee beans are ground extremely fine to a flour consistency and become part of the drink that leaves sediment in a cup. Turkish coffee is traditionally served in *fincans*, small espresso- or demitasse-sized cups. *Demitasse*, French for "half cup," refers to its size in relation to a regular coffee cup. It holds about 2 to 3 fluid ounces (60 to 90 milliliters).

Three Sections

Divides the cup horizontally in thirds.

- Top – Future
- Middle – Present
- Bottom – Past

Two Sections

Draw an imaginary line running parallel to the handle from rim to rim.

- To the left of the line – Past and near present; positive.
- To the right of the line – Future events; negative

QUICK GUIDE: SIGNIFICATIONS of COFFEE SYMBOLS

Airplane A trip; also need to get away.

Alligator Use caution in new business ventures.

Almond Good fortune at home or at work.

Anchor Good fortune if clear and well-formed; if unclear.

Angel Protection; also good news.

Apple Fertility and creativity.

Arch Money coming in from business matters.

Ball Upward mobility.

Basket Need to walk around an obstacle.

Bat Friendship; also a long healthy life.

Beetle Avoid quarrels with friends.

Bird Good news.

Bread Nurture your hopes and dreams.

Bridge A major decision soon to be faced.

Cake Fulfillment of desires.

Camel Difficulties and worries.

Camera Someone is attracted to you.

Canoe Isolated and loneliness.

Cat Argument with a friend.

Coin Money is on the way.

Comet A neighborhood problem.

Crown An inheritance or legacy.

Devil Danger, bad news.

Diamonds Marriage proposal; also money and material wealth.

Dog True friendship.

Dress Successful plan.

Drum Success from great talent.

Eagle Nothing is impossible.

Elephant Help from friends or family.

Eyeglasses Need to recognize true situation.

Fence Obstacles.

Fire Passion or lust.

Fish Career achievement

Flag Danger at home or business.

Flower Happiness.

Fork Possible quarrel.

Garland A happy marriage; also an invitation to a wedding.

Genie lamp Your wish will be granted.

Gondola An idle love life.

Harp Traditional romance.

Hat Someone will come into your life but not stay for long.

Haystack Foundation for a prosperous future.

Heart Whole, love; if broken or misshapen, broken-hearted

Ice cream cone An opportunity to help a child.

Insects Need for more truth in all relationships.

Island Isolation.

Jellyfish A false friend or co-worker.

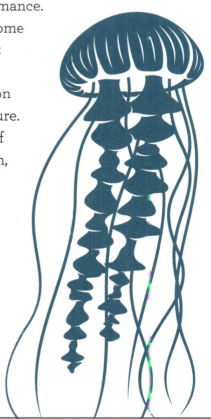

Jewelry Great fortune.

Jug You are taking better care of your body.

Kangaroo An irresponsible lover.

Kite A restless soul.

Knife Break up with a friend.

Knot Worry over small matters.

Ladder A slow climb to achieve your goals.

Leaf Good health and robust living.

Lemon Jealousy toward others.

Monkey Manipulation by clever people.

Monster A lurking fear.

Moon If full, love; crescent, prosperity.

Mountain Obstacles.

Mouse Trouble through a friend or business associate.

Nest Pregnancy.

Obelisk You must stand alone.

Package A surprise is heading your way.

Padlock A feeling of not having many choices.

Puppy A party.

Pyramid Successful dreams.

Quail An untruthful friend or acquaintance.

Question mark A question.

Rainbow Good fortune.

Raven/crow Bad News.

Ring Marriage, new love; if broken divorce or break-up.

Road Creative opportunities.

Scissors False friends.

See-Saw A short-term relationship.

Sheep Careful planning pays off.

Ship A business opportunity.

Snake A serious decision is ahead.

Spider Financial success.

Square Happy marriage, new home

Tambourine Inconstancy in a relationship.

Tassel Company is coming.

Tiger Find your inner strength.

Umbrella Shelter from obstacles or avoidance of financial woes.

Unicorn Daydreams and plans may materialize.

Vase A secret will be revealed.

Violin An exciting, whirlwind romance.

Volcano Loss of control.

Whale A small legacy or bit of money.

Wolf Strength and courage.

Xylophone A very talented individual comes into your life.

Yarn/string Overworked.

Zebra Relax, and learn to enjoy your friends.

Zeppelin Good things can happen.

C·H·A·P·T·E·R 5
CRYSTAL GAZING and the
ART of READING STONES

CRYSTAL BALL GAZING

Crystal gazing is truly an art that takes not only dedicated practice, but also an innate gift.

Crystallomancy is a form of scrying, which is gazing into a reflective medium, such as a crystal ball or mirror, to detect significant messages or visions. Fruitful crystallomancy might not be possible for all, but for those who want to try it, you will need a lot of patience and plenty of practice.

METHOD

Choosing a ball is the first step. For traditional crystal gazing, the larger the sphere the better—this allows you to better focus and fully see any images that might appear. Many out there are made from plain glass, but for divination purposes, look for a polished natural gemstone, such as quartz. In this, you need to go with

A quartz crystal ball set in a brass holder

your gut. If you are drawn to a particular one—even in an online photo—take that as a good sign. If you are familiar with gemstones, you might already have a feel for which stones resonate best with you. You can gaze holding it in your hands or use a holder to set it on a tabletop.

Once you have chosen your ball, forming a "rapport" with it can help you use it as a tool of divination. Before attempting a true gazing session, spend time just holding it, getting to know its intricacies. To clean your crystal ball, submerge it in water mixed with about a handful of sea salt. Let it soak for 24 hours, and then dry it with a lint-free cloth.

To try a reading, you need the ball, a journal, and a space to work undisturbed.

- First cleanse yourself, your ball, and your space, being sure to maintain an open and positive energy. It is best to do this under the light of the Moon at night if you are outdoors or in dim lighting, as from a small candle or a salt lamp, if you are indoors. Record the question you want to answer in your journal.
- Hold the ball in both hands or set the ball in its holder before you settle into your space, concentrating on your question. If you like, you can place your hands on the sides of the ball or hover them just over the surface.
- Turn your eyes to the ball, and allow your gaze to come in and out of focus.
- Without breaking your gaze, allow your mind to record any images or symbols that appear.
- When your session ends, jot down any images or impressions that you have received, and then again cleanse the ball.

INTERPRETING YOUR VISIONS

The next day, review what you have recorded in the journal, interpreting any meanings you can get from the images and symbols you saw. With practice, you will better able to divine hidden meanings and know whether to interpret your visions as literal representations or as symbolic ones.

Keep in mind that gazing into a crystal ball is not for everyone. Still, with dedication, you may find it a rewarding method of divination. Until you are comfortable and confident, limit practice sessions to once a week at most (but never ignore the ball for too long). If you find you have an affinity for the art, you can test your skills on others.

> **Insight** To cleanse your crystal ball before or after a reading, light incense, and wave it over your ball. Let the flames waft over it until you feel the smoke has freed it of any lingering energy. Extinguish the incense, and wipe the ball with a lint-free cloth.

As with any form of divination, interpreting what you see relies as much on intuition as it does on skill.

DIVINING with GEMSTONES

Using colored stones is a long-held practice for divining the future.

Lithomancy is an ancient form of divination that foretells the future using stones. The term is used to cover everything from simple two-stone and three-stone readings to far more complex readings involving many stones, including the 13-stone method that became popular in the British Isles.

METHOD

Gemstones are ideal for divination, with properties in each that can tell a reader much information. You can, however, use any kinds of stones, from beach pebbles to craft beads to precious gems. The key to many divination methods is to find ones of similar shape and size and that are as smooth as possible. You then cast the stones and read the patterns in which they fall. There are several methods of interpretation, depending on whether you cast them over a pre-drawn chart, such as one indicating the points of the compass or the signs of the zodiac or the planets, or just let them fall where they may.

The stones themselves represent various concepts, such as love or home life, and they align with the astrological planets of Mercury, Venus, Mars, Jupiter, Saturn, the Sun, and the Moon, as well as the seven chakras. When choosing stones to work with, keep these qualities in mind.

GEMSTONES and the ZODIAC

Many gemstones have affinities with the astrological signs. You can choose one to match your Sun sign or by the qualities possessed by that sign. Here is just a sampling of the many options available.

ARIES
- Aquamarine
- Bloodstone
- Carnelian
- Citrine
- Topaz

TAURUS
- Amber
- Aventurine
- Garnet
- Kunzite
- Rose Quartz

GEMINI
- Blue Lace Agate
- Citrine
- Honey Calcite
- Moonstone
- Tiger's Eye

CANCER
- Carnelian
- Chalcedony
- Moonstone
- Nephrite
- Rose Quartz

LEO
- Carnelian
- Citrine
- Peridot
- Sunstone
- Tiger's Eye

VIRGO
- Amazonite
- Amethyst
- Carnelian
- Chalcedony
- Peridot

LIBRA
- Aquamarine
- Blue Lace Agate
- Lapis Lazuli
- Peridot
- Pink Tourmaline

SCORPIO
- Amethyst
- Kunzite
- Labradorite
- Obsidian
- Unakite

SAGITTARIUS
- Citrine
- Lapis Lazuli
- Malachite
- Topaz
- Turquoise

CAPRICORN
- Chrysoprase
- Fluorite
- Garnet
- Jasper
- Lepidolite

AQUARIUS
- Amethyst
- Angelite
- Aquamarine
- Chrysoprase
- Lapis Lazuli

PISCES
- Amethyst
- Aquamarine
- Bloodstone
- Blue Lace Agate
- Fluorite

However you choose to use them, whether for divination or healing, gemstones are aesthetically pleasing to the eye.

Free Casting

In this method, you cast stones, each with a specific meaning, onto the ground or on a table and interpret them based on their relative positions to one another. You can choose an array of stones to correspond with the planets or the astrological signs or their meanings within lithomancy or randomly, basing the interpretation on the stone's intrinsic significance.

Casting with a Grid

Many practitioners prefer casting over a grid. There are many available, such as those based on the Bagua (the feng shui energy map), on the signs of the zodiac, or other patterns, such as simple grids, circles, or stars.

A Bagua map is used in feng shui and other disciplines to chart energy. Usually depicted as an octagon or square, you can use these grids to cast gemstones.

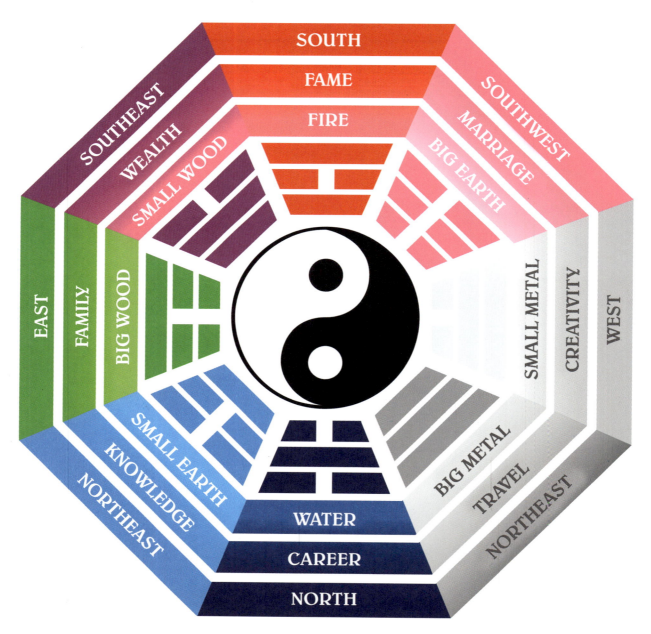

Quick Guide: READING with GEMSTONES

Insight There is no "right" or "wrong" way to read the stones. As you become familiar with your collection and understand both the stones' given meanings and what you absorb from them, it will become easier to forecast.

1 WEALTH ABUNDANCE	2 FAME	3 RELATIONSHIPS MARRIAGE MOTHER
4 FAMILY THE PAST	CENTER	5 CHILDREN CREATIVITY THE FUTURE
6 KNOWLEDGE SPIRITUALITY	7 CAREER	8 HELPFUL PEOPLE TRAVEL FATHER

BAGUA SQUARE READING

This method of gemstone divination uses a simplified Bagua square grid that you can easily draw out yourself. You can use it in many kinds of casting, but this one calls for you to just place stones on the grid. It works for a general life forecast.

1. Choose eight stones that have meaning to you, and place them in a pouch.
2. Without looking in the pouch, draw one out and place it in the top-left square. Continue placing stones, going from left to right and downward.
3. When all the stones are placed, read them according to both the meaning of the stone and its relationship to the theme of the square.

YES, NO, OR MAYBE READING

This is one of the simplest methods of casting, with one stone designated as "yes," one as "no," and one as "maybe." A fourth significator stone represents you.

1. Place the stone representing yourself on the ground or on a table before you.
2. Hold the other stones in one had, thinking of a question that can be easily answered (such as "Should I accept that job offer?).
3. Cast the stones in front of you.
4. The one that lands closest to your stone reveals the answer to your questions.

BEAD WISHING

This easy method of predicting if your wish will or will not come true in the near future doesn't require gemstones. Use simple craft beads or even pebbles. Just choose a few each of two colors, and decide beforehand which color represents which outcome. The sample below uses blue and white beads.

- Select several blue beads and several white.
- Hold them in your hands for a moment, concentrating on your wish as you do so.
- Place the beads in a deep bowl, and pour rice or semolina grains over the beads to completely cover them.
- Draw a triangle on the surface of the grains with your index finger.
- Close your eyes and fish out a single bead.

  - *Blue bead* Your wish will come true.
  - *White bead* Your wish won't come true.

CHOOSE YOUR LAYOUT

There are many options for casting over a grid or another pattern. Here is a sampling to help you find one that resonates with you.

ZODIAC GRID

Set up a grid that utilizes the signs of the zodiac and their associated meanings and significations.

2
TAURUS
HOUSE OF
POSSESSIONS

12
PISCES
HOUSE OF
THE UNCONSCIOUS

3
GEMINI
HOUSE OF
COMMUNICATION

1
ARIES
HOUSE
OF SELF

11
AQUARIUS
HOUSE OF
FRIENDSHIP

4
CANCER
HOUSE OF
HOME AND FAMILY

10
CAPRICORN
HOUSE OF
SOCIAL STATUS

5
LEO
HOUSE OF
PLEASURE

7
LIBRA
HOUSE OF
PARTNERSHIP

9
SAGITTARIUS
HOUSE OF
PHILOSOPHY

6
VIRGO
HOUSE OF
HEALTH

8
SCORPIO
HOUSE OF
TRANSFORMATION
AND SEX

THE PENTAGRAM

Associated with the occult and mysteries, this shape lends itself to gemstone casting. You can designate the areas to match your reason for casting, using such markers as compass points and their meanings, or even a "simple yes, no and maybe" arrangement.

COMPASS READING

In this method, you place various gemstones in a pouch, and then cast them over a chart marked with the compass points. Each compass point has a particular meaning, and the stone that falls near or on it will tell you what to expect.

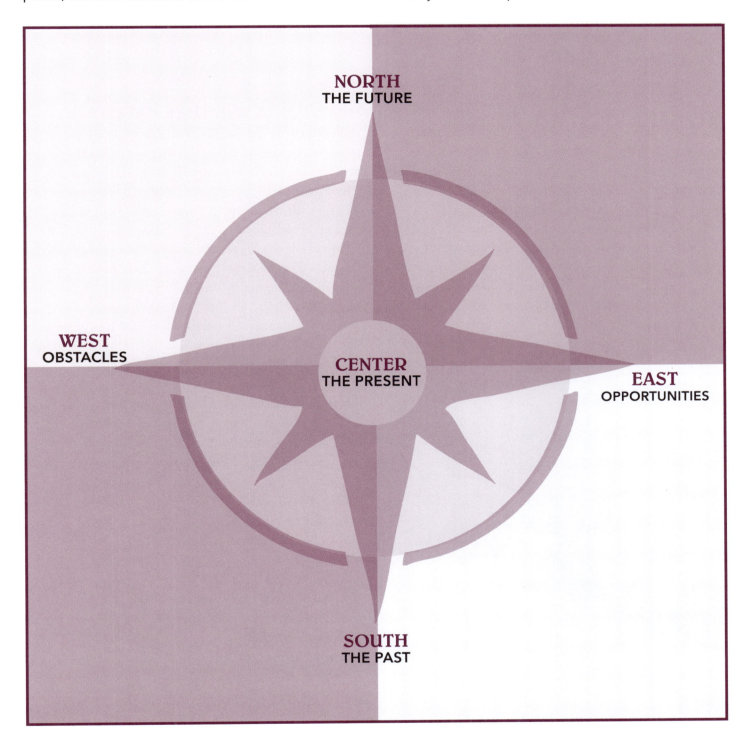

NORTH
THE FUTURE

WEST
OBSTACLES

CENTER
THE PRESENT

EAST
OPPORTUNITIES

SOUTH
THE PAST

CHOOSING GEMSTONES

With so many beautiful stones to pick from, finding the right ones for you can be difficult but a lot of fun.

When using gemstones for divination, the choices might seem overwhelming. There are simply so many captivating stones that finding the array that works for you can leave you a bit boggled. There are many ways to pick the ones you will use for divining the future. You might just choose simply by their looks—maybe blue is your favorite color and stones like lapis lazuli or blue lace agate catch your eye or green speaks to you, and you can't resist picking up that chunk of malachite. You may also just get a certain vibe when you hold a particular stone. It is never wrong to trust your intuition.

In certain casting methods, the color of a stone is all you need to know, other methods call for a deeper understanding of their meanings and associations.

GEMSTONES AND THE CHAKRAS

A chakra, from the Sanskrit for "wheel," is one of the focal points located along the spinal column that are used in a variety of ancient meditation practices. Chakras are said to rotate according to the force of energy within the breath. Breathing allows the body to absorb both positive and negative energy, with the right side of a body containing positive energy and the left taking in negative energy. Each chakra radiates light of a particular color, resulting in each of our bodies containing the full rainbow of colors.

Many gemstones are associated with one or more of the chakras. For divination, the chakras add another layer of meaning to the stones you choose.

TRADITIONAL BIRTHSTONES

It has long been a tradition to assign a gemstone to each month. These designations can help you chose your gemstones, whether you pick your own birthstone or those of your loved ones.

- *January* – Garnet
- *February* – Amethyst
- *March* – Bloodstone or Aquamarine
- *April* – Diamond
- *May* – Emerald
- *June* – Pearl or Moonstone
- *July* – Ruby or Carnelian
- *August* – Peridot
- *September* – Sapphire
- *October* – Opal or Tourmaline
- *November* – Topaz or Citrine
- *December* – Turquoise or Lapis Lazuli

The chakras align with all the colors of the rainbow, and there is a gem to fit each of them.

QUICK GUIDE: The CHAKRAS and a SAMPLING of THEIR GEMSTONES

Crown
"I UNDERSTAND."

Sahasrara
- **Knowledge**
- **Consciousness**
- **Fulfillment**
- **Spirituality**

- Alexandrite
- Amethyst
- Fluorite
- Rhodonite
- Rose Quartz
- Selenite

Third-Eye Chakra
"I SEE."

Ajna
- **Intuition**
- **Lucidity**
- **Meditation**
- **Trust**

- Angelite
- Azurite
- Clear Quartz
- Lepidolite
- Peacock Ore
- Sodalite

Throat Chakra
"I TALK."

Vishuddha
- **Communication**
- **Expression**
- **Creativity**
- **Inspiration**

- Amazonite
- Aquamarine
- Azurite
- Lapis Lazuli
- Rutilated Quartz
- Turquoise

Heart Chakra
"I LOVE."

Anahata
- **Acceptance**
- **Love**
- **Compassion**
- **Sincerity**

- Aventurine
- Chrysoprase
- Kunzite
- Malachite
- Peridot
- Unakite

Solar Plexus Chakra
"I DO."

Manipura
- **Strength**
- **Personality**
- **Power**
- **Determination**

- Amber
- Citrine
- Gold Topaz
- Labradorite
- Nephrite
- Tiger's Eye

Sacral Chakra
"I FEEL."

Svadhishthana
- **Sensuality**
- **Sexuality**
- **Pleasure**
- **Sociability**

- Carnelian
- Chrysoprase
- Gold Topaz
- Honey Calcite
- Red Coral
- Sunstone

Root Chakra
"I AM."

Muladhara
- **Energy**
- **Stability**
- **Safety**
- **Comfort**

- Bloodstone
- Garnet
- Jasper
- Obsidian
- Smoky Quartz
- Zoisite

QUICK GUIDE: GEMSTONES and THEIR ASSOCIATIONS

ALEXANDRITE
Green to brownish green or yellowish green; changes to red in certain light

ELEMENT Water

PLANET Mercury

SIGNIFICATION
- Hone your intuition and find your balance and creativity.

CHAKRA
- Sahasrara

AMAZONITE
Yellow-green to blue-green

ELEMENT Earth, Water

PLANET Uranus

SIGNIFICATION
- Let go of grief and dispel negative energy.

CHAKRA
- Vishuddha
- Anahata
- Manipura

AMBER
Deep golden, yellow-orange

ELEMENT Fire

PLANET Jupiter

SIGNIFICATION
- Stay optimistic and express yourself.

CHAKRA
- Sahasrara
- Vishuddha
- Manipura
- Muladhara

AMETHYST
Lilac pink to purple-red to deep violet, with white to gray striations

ELEMENT Water

PLANET Uranus

SIGNIFICATION
- Focus on goals and self-discipline

CHAKRA
- Sahasrara

ANGELITE
From colorless, white, bluish white, to violet or dark gray

ELEMENT Air

PLANET Uranus, Moon

SIGNIFICATION
- Maintain a calm and be clear and concise.

CHAKRA
- Sahasrara
- Ajna
- Vishuddha

AQUAMARINE
Bluish green

ELEMENT Water

PLANET Neptune

SIGNIFICATION
- Keep a cool head and ignore gossip.

CHAKRA
- Vishuddha
- Manipura

AVENTURINE
Jade green

ELEMENT Earth

PLANET Mercury

SIGNIFICATION
- Take a risk and start a new venture.

CHAKRA
- Vishuddha
- Anahata

AZURITE
Deep blue

ELEMENT Air

PLANET Saturn

SIGNIFICATION
- Find firm resolve and be ready for positive transformation.

CHAKRA
- Ajna
- Vishuddha

BLOODSTONE (Heliotrope)
Deep green with red inclusions

ELEMENT Fire

PLANET Mars

SIGNIFICATION
- Summon your courage and trust your heart.

CHAKRA
- Muladhara

BLUE LACE AGATE
Banded in layers of light blue, brighter blues, and whites

ELEMENT Water, Air

PLANET Neptune

SIGNIFICATION
- Expect news soon, so keep lines of communication open.

CHAKRA
- Vishuddha

CARNELIAN
Pale orange to deep red-orange

ELEMENT Fire

PLANET Mars

SIGNIFICATION
- Open yourself to joy, love, and creativity.

CHAKRA
- Manipura
- Svadhishthana
- Muladhara

CHALCEDONY
White to gray, grayish blue, yellow, or brown from pale to nearly black

ELEMENT Water

PLANET Moon

SIGNIFICATION
- Harmonize your mind, body and spirit.

CHAKRA
- Vishuddha

CHRYSOPRASE
Apple to pale green with gold intermixed

ELEMENT Water

PLANET Venus

SIGNIFICATION
- Heal and release your inner child.

CHAKRA
- Anahata
- Svadhishthana

CITRINE
Deep amber to pale yellow

ELEMENT Fire

PLANET Jupiter

SIGNIFICATION
- Expect you finances to improve.

CHAKRA
- Manipura

CLEAR QUARTZ
Colorless; transparent, translucent, or opaque

ELEMENT All elements

PLANET Sun

SIGNIFICATION
- Be honest and keep a focus on your goals.

CHAKRA
- All chakras

FLUORITE
All colors; can fluoresce blue, red, purple, yellow, green, or white under UV light

ELEMENT Air

PLANET Neptune

SIGNIFICATION
- Be clear in your decisions and seek mental clarity.

CHAKRA
- All chakras

GARNET (Almandine)
Dark red to orange, green to brown, pink and black

ELEMENT Fire

PLANET Mars

SIGNIFICATION
- Keep a balance between passion and serenity in your life.

CHAKRA
- Muladhara

GOLD TOPAZ
White to yellow, orange, red-brown

ELEMENT Fire

PLANET Jupiter

SIGNIFICATION
- Lead and inspire other in your life.

CHAKRA
- Manipura
- Svadhishthana

HONEY CALCITE

Warm yellow with white or creamy striations

ELEMENT Fire

PLANET Earth

SIGNIFICATION
- Regain your self-worth and overcome obstacles.

CHAKRA
- Svadhishthana

JASPER

Combinations of brown, red, orange, yellow, or green

ELEMENT Earth

PLANET Mars

SIGNIFICATION
- Stay grounded and keep things simple.

CHAKRA
- All chakras

KUNZITE

Translucent pink to violet

ELEMENT Water

PLANET Pluto, Venus

SIGNIFICATION
- Open your heart and release your joy.

CHAKRA
- Anahata

LABRADORITE

Pale tan that can show iridescent blue, green, yellow, copper, or gray

ELEMENT Air

PLANET Uranus

SIGNIFICATION
- Your wishes will come true, so be careful what you wish for.

CHAKRA
- All chakras

LAPIS LAZULI

Bright, rich blue that can be interspersed with white and tan

ELEMENT Air

PLANET Jupiter

SIGNIFICATION
- Think and research before you act.

CHAKRA
- Vishuddha

LEPIDOLITE

Mottled pinkish violet to brownish purple

ELEMENT Water

PLANET Sun

SIGNIFICATION
- Forgive yourself and learn from the past.

CHAKRA
- Ajna
- Anahata

MALACHITE

Swirls of light to dark green interspersed with black

ELEMENT Earth

PLANET Venus

SIGNIFICATION
- Give up grudges and let go of the past.

CHAKRA
- Anahata
- Manipura

MILKY QUARTZ

Cloudy white

ELEMENT Earth

PLANET Venus

SIGNIFICATION
- Let yourself relax, even if the issues are cloudy.

CHAKRA
- Sahasrara

MOONSTONE

Pearly shades of white, brown, peach, cream, and gray

ELEMENT Water

PLANET Moon

SIGNIFICATION
- Maintain balance and keep your emotions in check.

CHAKRA
- Sahasrara
- Anahata

NEPRITE (Jade)

White to dark green or black

ELEMENT Earth

PLANET Venus

SIGNIFICATION
- Dispel fear and enjoy an abundant, generous life.

CHAKRA
- Manipura
- Svadhishthana
- Muladhara

OBSIDIAN

Jet black, can be spotted or mottled with white and gray

ELEMENT Earth

PLANET Pluto

SIGNIFICATION
- Expect hidden feelings to rise to the surface in turbulent times.

CHAKRA
- Manipura
- Muladhara

PEACOCK ORE (Chalcopyrite)

Iridescent pink, blue, green-gold, and purple

ELEMENT Earth

PLANET Moon, Sun

SIGNIFICATION
- Show your confidence and be content.

CHAKRA
- All chakras

PERIDOT

Olive green, bottle green, or yellowish green

ELEMENT Fire

PLANET Mercury, Venus

SIGNIFICATION
- Let go of bitterness and open yourself to joy.

CHAKRA
- Anahata
- Manipura

PINK TOURMALINE

Various shades of pink

ELEMENT Water

PLANET Uranus

SIGNIFICATION
- Revel in feelings of joy, happiness and relaxation.

CHAKRA
- Anahata

RED CORAL

Deep red-orange

ELEMENT Air

PLANET Mars

SIGNIFICATION
- Feel at peace with yourself and unleash your imagination.

CHAKRA
- Svadhishthana
- Muladhara

RHODONITE

Various shades of pink to red, orange, and black

ELEMENT Air

PLANET Mars, Venus

SIGNIFICATION
- Develop your creativity and quick thinking.

CHAKRA
- Sahasrara
- Manipura

ROSE QUARTZ

Various shade of pink, from rose to salmon

ELEMENT Water

PLANET Venus

SIGNIFICATION
- Hone your intuition and find your balance and creativity.

CHAKRA
- Sahasrara

RUTILATED QUARTZ

Clear with brown to black strands within

ELEMENT Earth

PLANET Sun, Mars

SIGNIFICATION
- Seek harmony and support from loves ones.

CHAKRA
- All chakras

SELENITE
Most often transparent and colorless, but can be chalky and opaque

ELEMENT Air

PLANET Moon

SIGNIFICATION
- Be prepared in an unstable situation.

CHAKRA
- Sahasrara
- Ajna

SMOKY QUARTZ
Translucent brownish gray

ELEMENT Earth

PLANET Saturn

SIGNIFICATION
- Find you calm center and seek patience.

CHAKRA
- Muladhara

SODALITE
Blue with white to gray streaks blue with white

ELEMENT Air

PLANET Venus

SIGNIFICATION
- Connect with nature, allowing calm to help heal wounds of the past.

CHAKRA
- Ajna

SUNSTONE (Heliolite)
Mottled shade of bright orange

ELEMENT Fire

PLANET Sun

SIGNIFICATION
- Reflect on the qualities of light, openness, benevolence, and warmth.

CHAKRA
- Svadhishthana
- Muladhara

TIGER'S EYE
Bands of yellow to golden to brown

ELEMENT Earth

PLANET Saturn

SIGNIFICATION
- Allow your energy to burst forth and revel in your self-assurance.

CHAKRA
- Manipura

TURQUOISE
Blue to green with bands of copper to black

ELEMENT Earth

PLANET Jupiter

SIGNIFICATION
- Protect your physical and emotional health, as well as your personal safety

CHAKRA
- Vishuddha

UNAKITE

Mottled combination of various shades of pink and green

ELEMENT Earth

PLANET Jupiter

SIGNIFICATION
- Let go of negativity and seek emotional resilience and balance.

CHAKRA
- All chakras

ZOISITE

Green with ruby red and black swirls

ELEMENT Water

PLANET Venus

SIGNIFICATION
- Show your true self and joyfully engage with life.

CHAKRA
- Ajna
- Muladhara

PRECIOUS GEMS

Diamonds, rubies, emeralds, and sapphires are considered the "big four" of gemstones, placed in the precious gems category by jewelers. You can cast with these lovely stones if you have samples that are unset. As jewelry, they have a long history of use as amulets for protection and attraction.

- *Diamond* This famed precious gem is usually crystal clear and colorless, but there are varieties that exhibit subtle, pale hues of yellow, brown, blue, gray, pink, or green. Considered a highly powerful stone, it represents strength, clarity, and courage. It is a fire gem aligned with the Sahasrara chakra.

- *Ruby* Another fire gem, this brilliant red stone is said to promote fearlessness. Also associated with passion, it has been worn to attract love and admiration. It is aligned with the Muladhara chakra.

- *Emerald* The stone of hope and wisdom, this was once used in amulets to guard against unfaithfulness and to attract fidelity in love. This beautiful green water gem is aligned with the Manipura and Anahata chakras.

- *Sapphire* This air gem comes in an array of blue hues, from the palest sky blue to royal blue to blue-black. Often used as a protective amulet, it is aligned with the Ajna and Vishuddha chakras.

CASTING with RUNE STONES

Made from all kinds of materials, from polished marble and gemstones to many species of wood, rune stones offer a variety of casting methods.

Dating back as far as the first century CE, the tradition of rune stone divination rose in the proto-Germanic world and by the fifth century was adapted by the Vikings and Nordic tribes, spreading across Northern Europe. This method uses stones or wood carved with the 24 sigils of the Futhark runic writing system to seek guidance and foretell the future. Modern methods really date from only the 1980s.

METHOD

As with casting with gemstones or laying out tarot or playing cards, there is a wide array of possible layouts you can use to cast runes.

There is the simple yes-or-no option in which you pull a single stone from your pouch, having determined ahead of time which stones represent which answer to your question. Use this method

The choices for rune stone sets vary in materials and colors, from brilliant gemstones to utilitarian wooden or bone sets.

whenever you want to evaluate how your day is going or to get a quick answer to a specific question. In general, you will cast using an odd number of stones. Although there are five and seven-stone spreads, runes have been traditionally cast in multiples of three. As with other method of divination, there is also an option that you can use once a year to forecast what the coming 12 months holds using all 24 stones.

To cast the rune stones, you can either toss them onto a special piece of fabric, or, holding your rune pouch in your non-dominant hand, pull them out with your dominant hand and lay them out in the configuration you've chosen. The stones themselves represent various concepts, such as love, wisdom, family, or finances. As you read them, pay attention to their aspect in relationship to one another, whether they are reversed or in close proximity to runes with conflicting meanings. Keep in mind these concepts and weave them all into a coherent picture. With practice, as you get to know the meanings, it will become easier to divine the future and understand what advice the rune stones are offering.

Insight The word *rune* roughly translates as "secret" or "mystery." Although there are several runic writing systems, most rune sets available today are inscribed with Elder Futhark, which developed from an ancient form of the Germanic alphabet. This system consists of 24 runes, the first six of which spell out the word *futhark*.

QUICK GUIDE: LAYOUTS for RUNE STONE CASTING

THE THREE-RUNE LINE

This basic layout is versatile, offering an answer to a simple question or giving you insight into your feelings about an issue.

1. Hold the pouch in your non-dominant hand.
2. With your dominant hand, start at the center, and place a stone above and a stone below.
3. Read in order.

- Rune 1 – The question
- Rune 2 – Present influences
- Rune 3 – The answer

THE FIVE-RUNE CROSS

A five-rune spread is a good way to get a feel for rune casting. It is a versatile layout that can offer insight into a variety of questions, from those about relationships or work to just a general guide to the near future.

1. Hold the pouch in your non-dominant hand.
2. With your dominant hand, start at the center, and begin to lay the stones out in the shape of a small cross while concentrating on your question or the matter at hand.
3. Read in order.

- Rune 1 – Future influences
- Rune 2 – General influences
- Rune 3 – Problematic influences
- Rune 4 – Positive influences
- Rune 5 – The answer

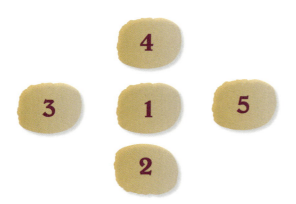

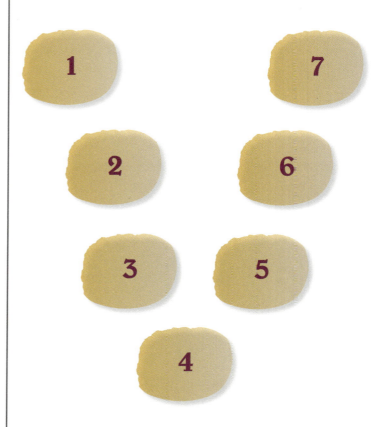

THE SEVEN-RUNE "V"

This spread takes the Five-Rune Cross a step further, adding a bit more depth to the answers and advice you are looking for.

1. Hold the pouch in your non-dominant hard.
2. With your dominant hand, begin to lay the stones out in the shape of a V while concentrating on your question or the matter at hand.
3. Read in order.

- Rune 1 - Past influences
- Rune 2 - Present situation
- Rune 3 - Future actions
- Rune 4 - Action for best outcome
- Rune 5 - Feelings and emotions
- Rune 6 - Problematic influences
- Rune 7 - The outcome

THE WORLD TREE

In Norse mythology, Yggdrasil is the world tree, an immense ash considered sacred. In this spread, you lay out 10 stones to give you insight into your general state, and it can also help chart a path to a particular goal.

1. Hold the pouch in your non-dominant hand.
2. With your dominant hand, start at the center top, and begin to lay the stones out in the shape of a tree while concentrating on your question or the matter at hand.
3. Read in order.

- Rune 1 – Positive influences and accomplishments
- Rune 2 – Present energy level
- Rune 3 – Emotions and physical feelings
- Rune 4 – Moral code
- Rune 5 – Recent achievements
- Rune 6 – Health and present concerns
- Rune 7 – Relationship and love influences
- Rune 8 – The mind and creative influences
- Rune 9 – Imagination and direction
- Rune 10 – Home influences

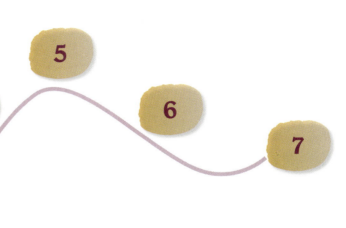

THE JÖRMUNGANDR

In Norse mythology, Jörmungandr, or the Midgard or World Serpent, is a huge monster that lives deep in the ocean. It grew so large it surrounded the Earth to grasp its own tail. It is said that when it releases its tail, Ragnarök, a series of disasters, will occur, after which the world will resurface anew. This layout is about learning to let go of things to renew ourselves.

1. Hold the pouch in your non-dominant hand.
2. With your dominant hand, start at the left, and work your way right.
3. Read in order.

- Rune 1 – Past emotions
- Rune 2 – Obstacles and struggles to overcome
- Rune 3 – Present emotions
- Rune 4 – Start of the journey
- Rune 5 – How to achieve your goal
- Rune 6 – Power and control
- Rune 7 – The outcome

THE RUNIC YEAR

Although most rune spreads are cast with an uneven number of stones, this one calls for you to take out your entire set of 24. This is a fun spread to cast on your birthday to prepare for the year ahead. This spread, which should be done only once a year, uses a 3-stone x 8-stone grid.

1. Hold the pouch in your non-dominant hand.
2. With your dominant hand, start from the top, and lay out the first row, working right to left.
3. Lay out the second row, working right to left.
4. Lay out the second row, working right to left.
5. Read in order.

ROW 1

- Rune 1 - How will I gain prosperity or secure financial security?
- Rune 2 - How will I achieve physical health and gain inner strength?
- Rune 3 - How will I construct defenses or tear down walls?
- Rune 4 - How will I gain wisdom?
- Rune 5 - What direction will my life path take?
- Rune 6 - How will I gain wisdom in the future?
- Rune 7 - What skills and gifts will I receive?
- Rune 8 - How will I find peace and happiness?

ROW 2

- Rune 9 - What changes are coming this year?
- Rune 10 - How can I achieve my goals?
- Rune 11 - What obstacles must I overcome?
- Rune 12 - Where will I succeed?
- Rune 13 - What will be my challenges and choices?
- Rune 14 - What inner skills will manifest?
- Rune 15 - Are this crises I must get through?
- Rune 16 - What energy will guide me?

ROW 3

- Rune 17 - Will I face legal challenges?
- Rune 18 - How can I grow and improve?
- Rune 19 - Will my relationships be rewarding?
- Rune 20 - How will my social status affect me?
- Rune 21 - How will my emotional status affect me?
- Rune 22 - What sexual influences will affect me?
- Rune 23 - How can I achieve balance?
- Rune 24 - What assets or wisdom will I gain in the coming year?

ROW 1

8	7	6	5	4	3	2	1
PEACE	SKILLS	FUTURE WISDOM	DIRECTION	WISDOM	DEFENSE	HEALTH & STRENGTH	MONEY

ROW 2

16	15	14	13	12	11	10	9
GUIDING ENERGY	CRISES	SKILLS	CHOICES & CHALLENGES	SUCCESSES	OBSTACLES	GOALS	FUTURE CHANGES

ROW 3

24	23	22	21	20	19	18	17
ASSETS & WISDOM	BALANCE	SEX	EMOTIONS	SOCIAL STATUS	FRIENDS	GROWTH	LEGAL

FOUR ELEMENTS CASTING

A great method to use outdoors, you can trace the four quadrants right into the earth. Each quadrant represents one of the elements—earth, water, air, and fire—with their corresponding meanings and associations. For this grid, you will cast with the entire set of 24 Futhark runes.

1. Concentrate on your question.
2. As you concentrate, draw out four squares in the ground or cast onto a pre-drawn grid.
3. Read all the stones that land face-up.

EARTH THE MATERIAL	AIR THE MIND
Finances Career Home Long-term events	Communication Wisdom Intellect Short-term events
WATER THE EMOTIONS	FIRE THE BODY
Relationships Intuition Spirituality Medium-term events	Energy Sexuality Health Unexpected events

Rose quartz rune set. Take your runes outdoors. There seems to be a natural connection between these symbols and the earth around us.

Quick Guide: FUTHARK RUNES and THEIR MEANINGS

FEHU
"CATTLE/WEALTH"

SIGNIFICATION
- Abundance
- Luck
- Hope
- Prosperity

REVERSED
- Financial loss

URUZ
"OX"

SIGNIFICATION
- Strength
- Endurance
- Health
- Courage

REVERSED
- Weakness

THURISAZ
"MALLET/GIANT"

SIGNIFICATION
- Defense
- Challenge
- Danger
- Crisis

REVERSED
- Protection

ANSUZ
"MESSAGE"

SIGNIFICATION
- Revelation
- Signs
- Visions
- Knowledge

REVERSED
- Miscommunication

RAIDHO
"JOURNEY"

SIGNIFICATION
- Progress
- Movement
- Evolution
- Perspective

REVERSED
- Standstill

KENAZ
"TORCH"

SIGNIFICATION
- Enlightenment
- Knowledge
- Passion
- Craftsmanship

REVERSED
- Blocked creativity

GEBO
"GIFT"

SIGNIFICATION
- Generosity
- Alliances
- Love affairs
- Agreements

REVERSED
- Extravagance

WUNJO
"JOY"

SIGNIFICATION
- Pleasure
- Celebration
- Comfort
- Bliss

REVERSED
- Stagnation

HAGALAZ
"HAIL"

SIGNIFICATION
- Destruction
- Uncontrolled forces
- Disaster

REVERSED
- No reversed meaning

NAUTHIZ
"NEEDS"

SIGNIFICATION
- Restriction
- Disagreements
- Delay
- Resistance

REVERSED
- Relaxed restrictions

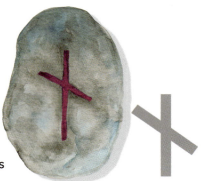

ISA
"ICE"

SIGNIFICATION
- Suspension
- Inertia
- Stillness
- Calmness

REVERSED
- No reversed meaning

JERA
"HARVEST"

SIGNIFICATION
- Conclusion
- Life cycle
- Good outcomes
- Perseverance

REVERSED
- No reversed meaning

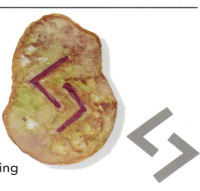

EIHWAZ
"YEW"

SIGNIFICATION
- Survival
- Inspiration
- Endurance
- Spiritual journeying

REVERSED
- No reversed meaning

PERTHRO
"DESTINY"

SIGNIFICATION
- Fate
- Mysteries
- Occult
- Chance

REVERSED
- Unluckiness

ALGIZ
"ELK"

SIGNIFICATION
- Protection
- Guardian
- Awakening
- Courage

REVERSED
- Vulnerability

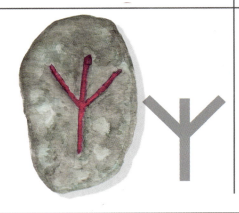

SOWILO
"SUN"

SIGNIFICATION
- Achievement
- Vitality
- Inspiration
- Justice

REVERSED
- No reversed meaning

TIWAZ
"VICTORY"

SIGNIFICATION
- Leadership
- Self-sacrifice
- Victory
- Honor

REVERSED
- Injustice

BERKANA
"BIRCH'"

SIGNIFICATION
- Fertility
- Growth
- Renewal
- Healing

REVERSED
- Barrenness

EHWAZ
"HORSE'"

SIGNIFICATION
- Progress
- Trust
- Movement
- Harmony

REVERSED
- Breakups

MANNAZ
"MAN"

SIGNIFICATION
- Humanity
- Social order
- Identity
- Community

REVERSED
- Poor adjustment

LAGUZ
"LAKE"

SIGNIFICATION
- Intuition
- Imagination
- Dreams
- New life

REVERSED
- Blocked help

INGWAZ
"FERTILITY"

SIGNIFICATION
- Pregnancy
- Sex
- Sensuality
- Inner growth

REVERSED
- No reversed meaning

OTHALA
"HERITAGE"

SIGNIFICATION
- Inheritance
- Spiritual growth
- Abundance
- Traditions

REVERSED
- Rejection

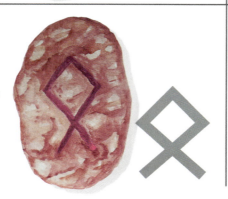

DAGAZ
"DAWN"

SIGNIFICATION
- Awakening
- Clarity
- Hope
- Balance

REVERSED
- No reversed meaning

Insight Many rune sets will come with a blank stone. Called the Odin's Stone or the Wyrd, this stone can represent the unknown in your readings.

Your rune set will likely come with a pouch, but you can also make your own. You should also keep a special piece of fabric or other material to cast on.

C·H·A·P·T·E·R 6

PENDULUM READING
and SPIRIT BOARDS

READING the PENDULUM

This simple form of dowsing allows you to seek answers and guidance through observing the movements of a pendulum.

Pendulums are objects suspended from a chain or string. Pendulum reading is a form of divination that focuses on their movements, which reveal answers posed to them. The answers are said to come from your intuition or "sixth sense." Pendulums can be made of a variety of materials, including gemstones, crystals, wood, glass, metals, and any found object.

A form of dowsing, pendulum divination allows you to reflect on questions and issues in your life. It may take a bit of practice to effectively use your tool, and you should try to hone the dowsing skills of concentration, intention, and grounding your energies.

METHOD

The simplest method of pendulum reading is asking clear yes-or-no questions. You can perform this kind of divination anywhere, indoors or out, but for some, setting a mood helps. Light a candle, put on some soothing instrumental music, burn a bit of incense—anything that helps you get into a calm, receptive mood for asking your question.

- Once you have cleared your mind, ready yourself for the reading by sitting up straight, with both feet planted on the floor or ground so that your body is as stable as possible.
- Determine your pendulum's responses. If you are asking a yes-or-no question, the following are common response signals.

  - *Yes* – Pendulum swings front to back.
  - *No* – Pendulum swings side to side.
  - *Maybe* – Pendulum swings in a circle.

- Once you have designated the signals, hold the pendulum in position, grasping it between your

Two gemstone pendulums. To protect yours, you can store it in a pouch or box when not in use. You can also wear it as necklace—this will allow it to absorb your energy.

Make Your Own Pendulum

There are so many lovely pendulums available, many made from crystals and gemstones. You can choose a stone with special meaning to you or you can make one yourself. All you need is a length of chain, string, cord, wire, or ribbon and a small object with enough weight to properly swing. The cord should be about a foot long and very thin. You can pick any object that appeals to you—a gemstone, of course, but also everyday objects like a bolt or key or even an heirloom ring. Once you've picked your object, just attach it to the cord, using jeweler's wire if necessary.

To get the most from your pendulum readings, practice establishing its motions, observing the pattern of it swings.

thumb and forefinger, and say, "If the answer is yes, move front to back" as you swing the pendulum in this pattern. Repeat the instructions for each signal. You can then ask unequivocal test questions, such as "Is it Thursday?" to verify the signal.

- Concentrate fully on your question for a moment, and then give a respectful statement of intent, such as "It is my intention to receive truthful answers." Then, ask your question. Try not to think about what you want the answer to be, but let the pendulum do its work of divination.

- Observe the pendulum's movement to determine the answer. Note, too, the force of its movement: decided swinging may point to a surer answer; small movements might be an answer a bit less certain.
- Touch the weight stone lightly to the palm of your free hand to clear the pendulum to move onto another question.

You can also use your pendulum to read for others. A common method is to hold the pendulum over the querent's hand as they ask their question.

A metal pendulum board inscribed with possible answers

QUICK GUIDE: MAKE YOUR OWN PENDULUM BOARD

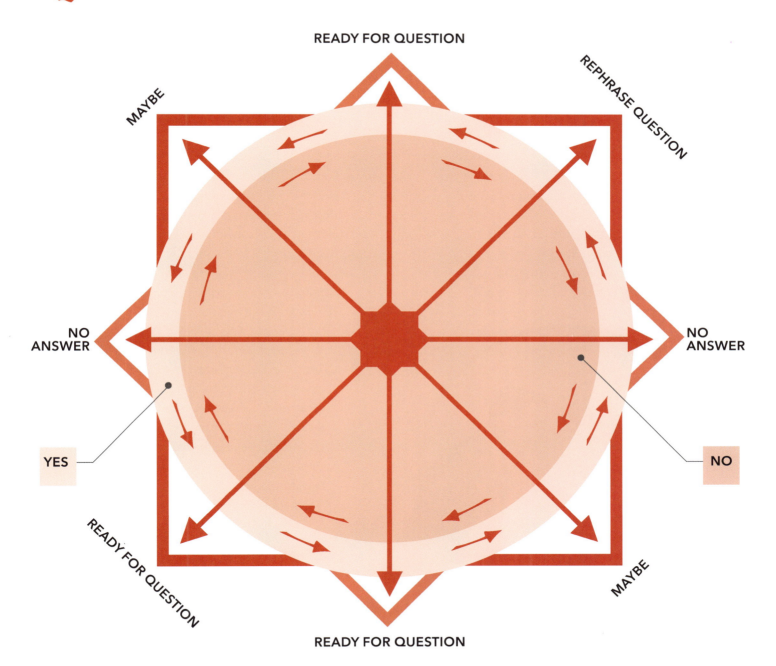

PENDULUM TAVOLA

To make your pendulum divination sessions more productive and the answers easier and clearer to read, you can use a special board marked with responses.

There are many available made from wood, metal, and other materials. It is also easy to make you own following the pattern above.

SPIRIT and TALKING BOARDS

Guided by our subconscious, spirit boards can help clarify questions of our future.

Many of us are most familiar with spirit boards in the form of the Ouija board that as children we played with as a parlor game. The game came into being in 1890 when businessman Elijah Bond decided to market a spirit board after taking note of the popularity of these kinds of boards among spiritualists in the United States. Toy company Hasbro later trademarked the name Ouija, but it is often used to refer to any talking board.

The spirit boards, also known as talking boards, that inspired Bond were used by spiritualists to facilitate faster communication with spirits during séances. In a time when so many people died early—women in childbirth, men in war, and children from an assortment of childhood diseases—these attempts to contact the spirits of lost loved ones was a comfort. The first marketed boards were intended as games, but by the 1920s, they were inextricably linked with the occult.

DO THEY WORK?

The claim that they could contact the dead drew much criticism, and numerous studies were conducted to verify these claims. The results concluded that there is no mystical reason for the movement of the planchette (a heart-shaped piece of wood or plastic) across the board, but instead the movement stems from the ideomotor responses of those using it. The "ideomotor response" refers to automatic muscular movements that take place without the conscious volition of an individual.

Does that mean spirit boards have no divinatory value? Not necessarily. As with any form of divination, we most often know

By the end of World War I and into the 1920s, Ouija boards were so commonplace that the Saturday Evening Post *featured a Norman Rockwell painting depicting a couple using one for the cover of the May 1, 1920 issue.*

A display of spirit boards at a Halloween fair in Rome, Italy, including a hand-made white skull decorated with Ouija symbols

Insight Given that we usually use the Ouija in a group, we are also getting the subconscious advice of our peers.

the answers to our questions before we ask them. Whether a reading of the tea leaves or tarot cards or a spirit board, the guidance we receive from many forms of fortune-telling helps us clarify how we really feel about an issue. It aids us in making decisions we don't always want to make and to face a situation as it really is and not how we want it to be.

Ouija boards come in many shapes, sizes, and patterns and can be made from a variety of materials, including laminated cardboard and wood. Top left: The original 1890 board; top right: a round, wooden board inscribed with both the Russian and English alphabets; bottom left: a free-form Halloween-themed board; bottom right: the "standard" Ouija board, or "Mystical Oracle," produced as a game.

METHOD

The Ouija is a flat board decorated with various mystical symbols and graphics and marked with the letters of the alphabet, the numbers 0 through 9, the words "yes," "no," and "good bye " and, occasionally, "hello," as well.

To use the board, participants place their fingertips on a planchette, and it is moved about the board to spell out words or point to "yes" or "no" in response to a question or series of questions.

C·H·A·P·T·E·R 7
The ART of DIVINATION THROUGH NUMBERS

MODERN NUMEROLOGY

Numerology is a method of analyzing the purposes and direction of an individual's life using the meanings of numbers.

Numerology is the study of the divine or mystical relationships between numbers and coinciding events. It uses the numerical values of the letters in words, names, and ideas to chart a person's personality and possible destiny. It has a long history, but William John Warner, better known as Cheiro, published *Cheiro's Book of Numbers* in 1926, helping to popularize the practice of numerology, as he did with palmistry.

METHOD

The practice relies on systems of assigning numbers to letters. Examples include the Arabic Abjad numerals, Hebrew numerals, Armenian numerals, and Greek numerals. The Jewish tradition of *gematria* assigns meaning to words based on their numerical values.

For the Latin alphabet, upon which Modern English and most European languages are based, there are various systems. The two most commonly used for modern numerology are the Chaldean and Pythagorean systems.

CHALDEAN SYSTEM

The Chaldeans were ancient people who ruled Babylonia from 625–539 BCE. Chaldean numerology is based on the energy of the numbers 1 through 8. The number 9, considered sacred, is not used for the alphabet's equivalent numerals, but it is used for divinatory and signification purposes. For students of the Chaldean system, there is also advanced studies of higher digits above 10.

Chaldean calculates your number using the name you currently go by, assuming that this name represents your energy at the time of the calculation. Three double-digit numbers do not get reduced in the Chaldean system: 11, 22, and 33. If your name number or birth number comes out to one of these master numbers, don't combine to form a single digit.

PYTHAGOREAN SYSTEM

Greek mathematician and philosopher Pythagoras (569–470 BC) may be the originator of Western numerology. His theory began with his discovery of numerical relationships between numbers and musical notes, or their "vibrations." The Pythagorean system is based on the numbers 1 through 9. Like the Chaldean system, it also recognizes the master numbers 11, 22, and 33, which you do not reduce to single digits.

With this method, you calculate your numbers using your full name as written on your birth certificate and your date of birth.

A bust of Pythagoras of Samos. Ancient Greek philosopher and mathematician Pythagoras posited that there is a divine relationship between numbers and events.

VALUES of the ENGLISH ALPHABET

1	2	3	4	5	6	7	8
A	B	C	D	E	U	O	F
I	K	G	M	H	V	Z	P
J	R	L	T	N	W		
Q		S		X			
Y							

1	2	3	4	5	6	7	8	9
A	B	C	D	E	F	G	H	I
J	K	L	M	N	O	P	Q	R
S	T	U	V	W	X	Y	Z	

In both the Chaldean and Pythagorean systems of numerology, three numbers—11, 22, and 33—are considered lucky master numbers, and they are not reduced to single digits.

UNDERSTANDING the NUMBERS

You only need basic mathematical skills or a calculator to determine some of the various personal options in numerology.

To best learn how to find your own numbers, follow the examples of just a few of the ways you can calculate them. Along with the foundational numbers of destiny or soul, which are based in your name, other aspects of your life can also be determined.

In the following examples, we use "Olivia Jane Jones," born on August 15, 1987. The numbers will vary, depending on the form of the name used and whether you calculate using the Chaldean system or the Pythagorean system (*see keys on page 209*).

SAMPLE CHALDEAN CALCULATIONS

DESTINY NUMBER

The destiny number shows you who you are and what you could become. To find this number, add together the values of the letters found in your name. Use whatever form of the name you most relate to. For Olivia Jane Jones, you would calculate the number as follows.

O	L	I	V	I	A	J	A	N	E	J	O	N	E	S
7	3	1	6	1	1	1	1	5	5	1	7	5	5	3

- First add the numbers of "Olivia."
  $7 + 3 + 1 + 6 + 1 + 1 = 19$, and then $1 + 9 = 10$; then $1 + 0 = 1$
- Then "Jane."
  $1 + 1 + 5 + 5 = 12$, and then $1 + 2 = 3$
- Then "Jones."
  $1 + 7 + 5 + 5 + 3 = 21$, and then $2 + 1 = 3$
- Add the three together.
  $1 + 3 + 3 = 7$
- The destiny number is 7.

You can break this down further:
- *First name number* Your personality; how you present yourself to the world; your interests and habits
- *Middle name number* Your hidden talents and desires
- *Last name number* The influence of your family

DREAM NUMBER

The dream number indicates your personality as other people perceive it; it's essentially the first impression you make upon the world and what you allow others to see. To calculate this number, you use the consonants of your name.

O	L	I	V	I	A	J	O	N	E	S
	3		6			1		5		1

$3 + 6 + 1 + 5 + 1 = 16$, and then $1 + 6 = 7$
- The dream number is 7.

HEART'S DESIRE NUMBER

Also know as the soul urge number, the heart's desire number indicates your hidden potential, inner resources, and unspoken desires—the things you may keep hidden from the world. To calculate this number, you use the vowels of your name.

O	L	I	V	I	A	J	O	N	E	S
7		1		1	1		7		5	

$7 + 1 + 1 + 1 + 7 + 5 = 22$
- The heart's desire number is the master number 22.

SAMPLE PYTHAGOREAN CALCULATIONS

SOUL PATH NUMBER

The soul path number tells you what your purpose in life is. To find it, add the figures found in your birth date. For the birth date of August 15, 1987, you would calculate the number as follows.

8 15 1987

- Add these figures together:

  8 + 1 + 5 + 1 + 9 + 8 + 7 = 39.
- Break that down to reach a single digit number:

  3 + 9 = 12, and the 1+ 2 = 3
- The soul path number is 3.

PERSONALITY NUMBER

The personality number shows you how you are best adapted to do what you came here to do. To find this number, you add the letters found in your legal name.

O L I V I A   J A N E   J O N E S
6 3 9 4 9 1   1 1 5 5   1 6 5 5 1

- First add the numbers of "Olivia."

  6 + 3 + 9 + 4 + 9 + 1 = 32, and then 3 + 2 = 5
- Then "Jane."

  1 + 1 + 5 + 5 = 12, and then 1 + 2 = 3
- Then "Jones."

  1 + 6 + 5 + 5 + 1 = 18, and then 1 + 8 = 9
- Add the three together.

  5 + 3 + 9 = 17, and 1 + 7 = 8
- The personality number is 8.

> **Insight** Your can't change your date of birth, but you can change your name, whether by marriage, for career, or simply because you prefer a different name. Any name change also changes your corresponding number—a new name can place you on a new path, partially charting a new course to your destiny.

THREE PREDOMINANT NAME NUMBERS

The three predominant name numbers show you what you will attract to yourself. You find the three predominant name numbers by selecting the three highest numbers repeated in a name.

O L I V I A J O N E S

- The highest number that is repeated is 9 (■).
- The second-highest repeated number is 6 (■)
- The third-highest number that is 5 ( )
- The three predominant name numbers are 9, 6, and 5.

If there are not three numbers repeated in a name, take the highest unrepeated numbers to finish out the full set. For example, taking the name John Fox:

J O H N F O X
1 6 8 5 6 6 6

- Taking the highest number repeated, you get 6.
- Because there are no other repeated numbers, you would use the other two highest. In this case the predominant name numbers would be 6, 8, and 5.

DESTINY NUMBER

The destiny number shows you your great objective in life, the thing you truly strive toward. To find the destiny number, add together the soul path, the personality, and the three predominant name numbers. Using the above example, Olivia Jones, born August 15, 1987, would have a destiny number of 1.

- Soul – 3
- Personality – 5
- Predominant name numbers 9, 6, and 5
- Destiny number – 3 + 5 + 9 + 6 + 5 = 28; then 2 + 8 = 10; and then 1 + 0 = Number 1

QUICK GUIDE: NUMBER SIGNIFICATIONS

NUMBER 1

PLANET	The Sun
GEMSTONE	Sunstone
COLOR	Red
TAROT CARD	The Magician

Life path / Soul path The Leader

Ones can be rather self-centered, but they make excellent leaders and are also musical and artistic. Ones are strong fighters, resent interference, and look out for number one, but are honest and frank, never hiding that fact. They like to delegate work, and make sure others perform to their own high standards. They most desire freedom and have a unique style. Ones do best in a career of original or creative effort of a public type or as managers and directors of firms.

STRENGTHS

- Motivated
- Revolutionary
- Creative
- Self-sufficient
- Driven
- Independent
- Responsible
- Determined
- Brave

POSSIBLE SHORTCOMINGS

- Aggressive
- Domineering
- Hasty
- Egocentric
- Exhibitionist
- Stubborn

NUMBER 2

PLANET	The Moon
GEMSTONE	Zoisite
COLOR	Orange
TAROT CARD	The High Priestess

Life path / Soul path The Peacemaker

Twos tend to choose a path where they can use the qualities of diplomacy, tactfulness, and arbitration. The affections and emotions and their effects in life are important to them. They naturally choose peaceful and quiet paths, and about the only time they would fight is in defense of a friend, a loved one, or a helpless person. They readily make friends and are good with people and so do best in jobs such as social worker, administrative assistant, accountant, or lawyer.

STRENGTHS

- Diplomatic
- Peace-loving
- Adaptable
- Creative
- Empathetic
- Sensitive
- Caring
- Modest
- Frank

POSSIBLE SHORTCOMINGS

- Melancholic
- Short-sighted
- Weak
- Shy
- Coy
- Nervous

NUMBER 3

PLANET	Jupiter
GEMSTONE	Amethyst
COLOR	Yellow
TAROT CARD	The Empress

Life path / Soul path The Creator

Threes tend to choose artistic ways to communicate. Theirs is the planning, the dreaming part of life, and if they can attach their dreams to a practical plan, things will work out. With their broad mental vision, they have great tolerance of other people's viewpoints and are attracted to other dreamers and planners. They are best suited to careers that allow them self-expression, such as painting, acting, music, sculpture, literature, designing, or journalism.

STRENGTHS

- Artistic
- Imaginative
- Intelligent
- Outgoing
- Hopeful
- Talkative
- Optimistic
- Tolerant
- Expressive

POSSIBLE SHORTCOMINGS

- Flighty
- Shallow
- Moody
- Hedonistic
- Unrealistic
- Scattered

NUMBER 4

PLANET	Uranus
GEMSTONE	Bloodstone
COLOR	Green
TAROT CARD	The Emperor

Life path / Soul path The Coordinator

The practical things of life appeal most to Fours. They are not afraid of some hardships and labor and can reap great rewards for their diligence. They are honest, reliable, and great organizers. Those around them often look to them for guidance or leadership. They do best in careers that allow them to show their meticulous skills, such as technical writer, engineer, chemist, electrician, cabinetmaker, builder, architect, manager, merchant, teacher, or businessperson.

STRENGTHS

- Fair-minded
- Hard-working
- Diligent
- Practical
- Pragmatic
- Disciplined
- Honest
- Ambitious
- Conscientious

POSSIBLE SHORTCOMINGS

- Acquisitive
- Moralistic
- Unimaginative
- Confrontational
- Self-important
- Harsh

NUMBER 5

PLANET	Mercury
GEMSTONE	Aquamarine
COLOR	Blue
TAROT CARD	The Hierophant

Life path / Soul path The Adventurer

Freedom-loving Fives love the journey and live to experience a variety of new things. With their bright minds, they are determined to try out all manner of temptations. Fives constantly seek out new adventures, following after every bright idea, to see if it is good or evil, high or low. They have splendid memories and do well in careers that take them off the beaten path, such as applied psychology, writer, teacher, archaeologist, entertainer, or linguist.

STRENGTHS

- Adventurous
- Unconventional
- Curious
- Freedom-loving
- Action-oriented
- Inquiring
- Resourceful
- Independent
- Versatile

POSSIBLE SHORTCOMINGS

- Impatient
- Discontent
- Anxious
- Hasty
- Impractical
- Restless

NUMBER 6

PLANET	Venus
GEMSTONE	Carnelian
COLOR	Dark Blue
TAROT CARD	The Lovers

Life path / Soul path The Humanist

With a knack of giving good advice, Sixes have a great desire is to be helpful, sympathetic, and sociable, which can result in others making demands on them. They are kind and always lend an ear to others' tales of woe. Music and some of the arts appeal to many Sixes. They do well in service, as heads of institutions or in healing and helping careers, such as social worker, insurance, undertaking, consultant, dressmaker, and hotel management.

STRENGTHS

- Warm-hearted
- Comforting
- Artistic
- Nurturing
- Sociable
- Empathetic
- Generous
- Compassionate
- Loving

POSSIBLE SHORTCOMINGS

- Vain
- Sanctimonious
- Mulish
- Domineering
- Opinionated
- Pushover

NUMBER 7

PLANET Neptune
GEMSTONE Fluorite
COLOR Purple
TAROT CARD The Chariot

Life path / Soul path The Seeker

Sevens are seekers of knowledge who want to absorb all they can. With their thirst for learning, they make excellent researchers, and crave a life of solitude and peace in which they can indulge their curious, bookish natures. Sevens possess a natural wisdom and do well as a counselors or the "power behind the throne." These perfectionists do well in careers that allow them autonomy, such as librarian, art shop manager, florist, horticulturist, clergyman, archivist, or writer.

STRENGTHS

- Inquisitive
- Philosophical
- Thoughtful
- Charismatic
- Analytical
- Inventive
- Thoughtful
- Refined
- Perceptive

POSSIBLE SHORTCOMINGS

- Secretive
- Suspicious
- Aloof
- Sarcastic
- Inflexible
- Oversensitive

NUMBER 8

PLANET Saturn
GEMSTONE Citrine
COLOR Pink
TAROT CARD Strength

Life path / Soul path The Analyst

Eights are analytical individuals and seekers of justice. Purposeful, they look for results and can be natural reformers, able to see a situation for what it is and how they can improve it. They possess mental fortitude, even to the point of being too headstrong or stubborn. Eights are eloquent public speakers and may find themselves in the front ranks of commerce or social movements and do well in careers, such as professor, attorney, judge, politician, or life coach.

STRENGTHS

- Authoritative
- Political
- Analytical
- Decisive
- Judicious
- Dignified
- Ambitious
- Driven
- Dominant

POSSIBLE SHORTCOMINGS

- Workaholic
- Dictatorial
- Impatient
- Materialistic
- Snobbish
- Callous

NUMBER 9

PLANET	Mars
GEMSTONE	Malachite
COLOR	Bronze
TAROT CARD	The Hermit

Life path / Soul path The Philanthropist

With their aspiring minds, Nines are keen thinkers with high ideals that can shade into zealotry. They value amity, and their generous spirits wish to change the world. Their sincere desire to make a difference can lead to a life of ups and downs, but they have the ability to weather the strife and continue to express generosity and artistry of all kinds, such as writing, teaching, and public speaking. They are suited to careers in the ministry or philanthropy, as well as creative efforts, such as sculpture and potter.

STRENGTHS

- Humanitarian
- Generous
- Helpful
- Giving
- Sincere
- Sympathetic
- Friendly
- Imaginative
- Artistic

POSSIBLE SHORTCOMINGS

- Scattered
- Conceited
- Irritable
- Spendthrift
- Attention-seeking
- Over-zealous

NUMBER 11

PLANET	Uranus
GEMSTONE	Garnet
COLOR	Silver
TAROT CARD	Justice

Life path / Soul path The Master Messenger

As one of the master numbers, Elevens tend to choose a path of deep idealism in the lines of religion and philosophy. They must take care to remain of this world, though, and not allow their desire to conquer the body and its passions to lead them to an overly ascetic existence. Elevens are likely to attract very spiritual people, and both sides will wish to share their message and wisdom with the other. Elevens to best in careers that allow them to communicate, such as lecturer, teacher, minister, and other spiritual leader.

STRENGTHS

- Charismatic
- Inspiring
- Perceptive
- Spiritual
- Observant
- Idealistic
- Mysterious
- Steadfast
- Original

POSSIBLE SHORTCOMINGS

- Moralistic
- Self-negating
- Mono-focused
- Pompous
- Obsessional
- Egotistical

NUMBER 22

PLANET Pluto
GEMSTONE Tourmaline
COLOR Gold
TAROT CARD The Fool

Life path / Soul path The Master Builder

The master Twenty-twos have a great desire for wealth and property and are willing to do the work to build those things in both large and small ways. They are doers and organizers, who enjoy the admiration and applause of the crowd—sometimes leading them to a mercenary type of mind. They do best in entrepreneurial careers and can excel as founders of companies and as architects, construction managers, high-tech workers, real estate investors, and small-business owners.

STRENGTHS

- Innovative
- Visionary
- Intuitive
- Hard-working
- Industrious
- Tireless
- Indefatigable
- Dynamic
- Energetic

POSSIBLE SHORTCOMINGS

- Unrealistic
- Greedy
- Mercenary
- Boastful
- Unscrupulous
- Overbearing

NUMBER 33

PLANET Neptune
GEMSTONE Diamond
COLOR Violet
TAROT CARD The Wheel of Fortune

Life path / Soul path The Master Teacher

As the sum of master numbers 11 and 22, kind-hearted Thirty-threes possess great power and an unlimited reservoir of spiritual energy. As teachers they seek to gain as well as share knowledge—their interests usually surpass their personal agendas. They like to push against boundaries and are highly sensitive to the needs of others. They should look for careers that call for nurturing and caring, such as the clergy, doctor, nurse, nun, salesperson, teacher, guidance counselor, wait staff, therapist, and psychologist.

STRENGTHS

- Unpretentious
- Gentle
- Understanding
- Conscientious
- Mystical
- Altruistic
- Selfless
- Peaceful
- Emotional

POSSIBLE SHORTCOMINGS

- Indulgent
- Careless
- Apathetic
- Chaotic
- Otherworldly
- Meek

C·H·A·P·T·E·R 8
INTERPRETING the FUTURE from DREAMS

The HIDDEN WORLDS of SLEEP

While we slumber our minds can take us to rich worlds that can bring us peace or also terrify us, but nearly every dream can also reveal important aspects of our lives.

Throughout history various cultures have placed more or less importance on dreams. For many, everything we see and everything that happens within them has important meanings. Ancient Babylonians and Egyptians believed dreams were supernaturally inspired, laden with signs, and could function as prophecy. As early as 325 BCE, Aristotle wrote about dreams, interpreting them as a window to one's soul. In medieval Islamic psychology, Muslim scholars also placed importance on dreams and sorted them into three categories: the false, the pathogenic (brought about by disease), and the true. The 16th-century Chinese book *Lofty Principles of Dream Interpretation*, among other things, raises the question of the relationship of reality to dream imagery.

It was Austrian neurologist Sigmund Freud, however, who undertook the first scientifically based research, publishing *The Interpretation of Dreams* in 1900, which posits that dreams are expressions of unfilled wishes. From there, others began in-depth dream analysis, with Carl Jung, the founder of analytical psychology, proposing that dreams mean even more, that they reflect the complexity of both an individual's unconscious and the collective unconscious. Since then, many areas of psychoanalysis have incorporated some form of dream analysis into their therapeutic protocol. Most dream analysts these days recognize a deeply personal aspect of dreaming, that they are based on an individual's particular life experiences, which can hold profound significance to them.

Not everyone remembers their dreams, but we all have them. Depending upon how long you sleep and how many REM (rapid-eye movement) cycles you go through, you can have as many as five or six a night, but only remember the most vivid ones. Most of us have, at some time or other, woken up to a feeling of calm, dread, joy, fear, or myriad other emotions brought on by our nocturnal adventures.

There is much scientists still don't know about the actual function of dreaming, but many could agree that they represent things relevant to the sleeper—people, places, ideas, emotions. They can also help us form memories and clarify our thoughts about the world and events concerning us.

THEMES OF DREAMS

Despite the deeply personal aspect of dreaming, many of us have similar imagery that regularly occurs. Who hasn't felt immensely relieved to wake up to find that, no, they are not naked in their old school's corridors desperately seeking the room in which a test they never prepared for is taking place? What about falling or flying? Losing our teeth or our hair? All these seem to happen in the dreams of so many of us. We have to wonder what these scenarios are revealing. There are many compilations of the symbols, images, and events that are common to many sleepers that attempt to ascribe specific signification to them.

Insight As with many forms of divination, dreams can reveal to us things we already know but have not yet consciously recognized in our waking lives.

The landscape of a dream can be weird, wonderful, and brilliantly colored, filled with bizarre imagery, but it can also be merely mundane and murky.

The MEANINGS of DREAMS

The meanings of dreams can vary according to source, but many agree on some common themes.

Interpreting the meanings of your dream might not tell you your future, but it can tell you what issues in your life need attention. The first step to interpretation is paying attention to the signs and symbols that occur. A dream journal or diary lets you record those so that you can begin to analyze them.

KEEPING A DREAM JOURNAL

How many of us try to relate a dream to someone else, only to find the details slip away even as we speak? Writing them down helps you to remember dreams, which can be so elusive the minute you open your eyes. A dream journal is simply a record of the imagery and events that fill your mind as you sleep. It lets you reflect on both the odd and the mundane aspects.

To capture the most detail, keep the journal by your bedside, and record everything you can recall as soon as you wake up (you can also use a phone app as your diary). As this practice becomes habit, you may find that you start to better remember your dreams. An added bonus will be an improvement in your memory skills in general. Keeping a dream journal has many benefits, including the following.

- It puts you in touch with your emotions. The tone of a dream can affect the following day. A pleasant dream can leave you feeling at peace, while a nightmare can mean an unsettled day ahead. Either can clue you into things that trigger your emotions.
- It can help you learn the practice of lucid dreaming. A lucid dream is one in which you become aware that you are dreaming. Lucid dreaming allows you to manipulate to some extent the events of the dream. This kind of control can extend into your waking life, so that you can better guide your feelings, freeing yourself to act in healthful ways.
- It can help you creatively solve problems. Dreams can inspire new kinds of solutions to the issues that otherwise might overwhelm you.

Once you are in the habit of consistently updating your journal you can review what you have recorded and look for elements that occur with some frequency. These patterns may be your subconscious trying to show you what you need to pay more attention to.

A dream journal decorated with an image of a dreamcatcher. Dreamcatchers were first used by First Nations cultures as protective charms to hang over a bed or cradle. They are still in use today, and they are believed to bestow good dreams.

Dreaming of falling from a great height is a quite common occurrence for many people.

Insight Use whatever method works for you to record your dreams, whether writing a narrative, making a bulleted list of symbols, or even sketching the images you can recall.

COMMON DREAMS and THEIR MEANINGS

There are several dreams that are common to many people. Here are 10 of them.

BEING CHASED
Often terrifying, these dreams may express a hidden desire to escape from your fears. They may also mean you are haunted by some aspect of your past.

DYING
A death of a loved one, or even yourself, can mean you fear the unknown, equating death with change.

FALLING
Dreams of falling are very common. This points to something wrong in your life—maybe you need to rethink a choice you've made, or you need to learn to let go of an issue.

FLYING
Often these dreams feel very liberating, although that might scare you, too. They may express a desire for independence or also a desire to escape a situation.

INFIDELITY
As distressing as these dreams might be, they shouldn't be taken literally. But they do point to the fact that your relationship might need some work.

LOSING TEETH
This might be as simple as exposing your worry that you are not attractive, but it can also point to a fear of a loss of power.

NAKED IN PUBLIC
These embarrassing dreams might signify that you are afraid to show your true self, wanting to hide your shortcomings from others.

PREGNANCY
This may be a positive signal that a period of creativity is about to begin, but it can also reveal worries about being a good mother or whether you should deepen a relationship.

TAKING A TEST
This common theme—whether you are late for a test or taking one you know nothing about or are otherwise unprepared for, means that you feel unprepared to face the challenges of your life.

UNABLE TO SPEAK
A dream in which you cannot speak points to a feeling of being ignored and the desire to learn how to communicate better or express yourself more fully.

QUICK GUIDE: DREAM SYMBOLS and SIGNIFICATIONS

Above Anything hanging above you, an improvement in your situation.

Absent person They will soon return.

Abuse A business dispute.

Abyss A warning; also accidents by traveling.

Accident Someone unexpected arrives.

Adultery Desire to escape or try something new.

Airplane A rapid change in your life; if missed, too many commitments.

Airport A period of transition is ahead.

Aliens An encounter with something unfamiliar or hostile.

Amputation Need for a more grounded life.

Angel Some are near you; also dream will come true.

Anger Powerful enemies; also good news.

Ants Bad luck.

Apes Malicious, though secret enemies.

Apparel Nice clothes, prosperity and happiness; if white, a sign of trouble; if black, business improves; if scarlet, honor.

Apples If sweet, joy; if sour, contention.

Arms If withered or lean, affliction, sickness, and poverty; if hairy, improved finances.

Attic Avoidance of fully using intellect.

Bacon Mischief from enemies; also a disappointment in love.

Baking Plans about to be enacted

Balding Fear of loss of vigor or a feeling of helplessness.

Ball Speedy receipt of money.

Balloon Business success.

Banana Wealth, love, and happiness.

Bank Financial woes.

Barefoot Issues about current life choices.

Barrels If full, wealth; if empty, poverty.

Bat A unsatisfactory journey.

Bathing Good luck in some undertaking; also change of residence.

Bear To see it, one or more enemies; if it attacks, you will overcome your enemy.

Beard A lawsuit; also if long and thick, success; if falling out, disgrace.

Beating A peaceful life.

Bed In bed, danger; a stranger in your bed, marital quarrels; if well-made, an established life.

Beer Domestic troubles.

Bees Success with lover.

Bells Ringing merrily, good news; tolling solemnly, bad news.

Belly If bigger and fuller than usual, family and money increase; if lean and shrunken, safety from a bad accident.

Betting Suffering from own imprudence.

Birds If chirping, good luck; if fighting, adversity; if flying overhead, prejudice by enemies.

Birds' nests If full, a good sign; if empty, great disappointment.

Blindness Overlooking an important issue.

Bloody nose Loss of goods; also loss of lover.

Board game Preference for a rule-bound life.

Boots If new, a new love; if old, separation; if dirty, sorrow.

Bottles Success in business; also speedy marriage; if broken, sorrow.

Bouquet To receive one, much pleasure; to give one, faithful lover.

Bread Good fortune, also a good match.

Breakfast An act you will be sorry for.

Breasts Great gain and profit.

Briars A dispute.

Bridge If crossing over, prosperity and success in love; if passing under, difficulties in both love and business.

Brothers A long life.

Building A new friend.

Bull Narrow escape from misfortune.

Buried alive Wealth and power.

Butter Good fortune mixed with sadness.

Butterflies Happiness and luxury.

Cakes A gift soon to come.

Can't find a bathroom Ignoring your own needs and wants.

Candle A creative spark or an innovative idea.

Candy A happy home.

Car If driving smoothly, consistent progress toward a specific objective; if out of control, a feeling of being trapped by a situation; if missing, loss of drive or ambition.

Cards Lucky in love.

Carrots Profit or inheritance.

Caterpillars Misfortune by secret enemies.

Cats Hidden enmity; if bitten or scratched, misfortune; if petting one, false friends.

Cave Reunion with a loved one.

Chair Sitting, an increase in your family; a rocking chair, better days ahead.

Cheese Profit and gain in business; in love, deceit.

Cherries Good news.

Chess Lying and deceit.

Chicken Business losses; deceit in love.

Child A rich legacy or other good fortune.

Chocolate Trouble by gossiping.

Church Joy and comfort.

Clams A happy relationship.

Climbing A rewarding but difficult challenge.

Clock Speedy marriage; if before noon, good luck; if after noon, bad luck.

Closet If exploring it, something hidden; if overstuffed, avoidance of critical issues.

Clouds Prosperity.

Coffee Loss of reputation

Concert Good health.

Corpse A long life.

Cow Great prosperity and unexpected success

Crabs Quarrel with a friend.

Cross Sadness.

Crow Misfortune.

Dancing Joyful news; also happiness in love.

Danger Success in life.

Darkness Loss.

Dawn Good fortune.

Deer Unexpected news.

Devil Dangers threaten you.

Diamonds Lover is unfaithful.

Digging Good luck.

Dinner A journey or change of location.

Dirt Someone will speak ill of you.

Divorce Need for balance.

Dogs If friendly, marriage and happiness; if barking, insults.

Doll A disappointment.

Door If you go through, success; if not, disappointment.

Dove Good fortune.

Drinking If cold water, good luck; if hot, sickness and hindrance; if wine, success in love.

Drowning Good fortune.

Drunkenness There will be loss in business ventures, but success in love affairs.

Duck A visitor.

Eagle Riches and honors: also love and marriage.

Ears Obedience; also good news ahead.

Earthquake Change of estate; injuries; also ambiguity, obscurity, and uncertainty.

Eating Successful business.

Eggs Many children.

Elephant Acquirement of riches and wealth; also speedy marriage.

Embracing Disappointments or treachery; also possible travel.

Empty room Untapped talents in reserve.

Explosion A sudden, drastic change.

Fairy A seduction.

Falling in love Lack of intimacy and passion

Fasting A quarrel; also success in love and business.

Fatigue Success in business.

Fear Courage.

Feasting A new acquaintance.

Feet Trouble of some kind.

Fever An inclination to strong drink; also, if your partner has a fever, affection and happiness.

Fighting A new enterprise; also increased pay.

Fingernails If longer than usual, profit; if shorter than usual, losses.

Fire If houses are burning, improved finances; if fire rages, losses and disappointments.

Fish Receipt of money.

Fishing Good fortune.

Flag Great danger from enemies; also or sickness.

Flies Insincere lover.

Flood Riches and plenty.

Flowers Successful in love.

Flute Trouble and contention with friends.

Fork A false friend.

Fountain Riches and honors; in love, happiness in marriage and romantic relationships.

Fox A cunning enemy; false friends.

Frog Good health.

Fruit Success in all worldly matters.

Funeral A wedding or lively party.

Gag A kiss is coming soon.

Gambling Poverty and disgrace.

Garden Good luck and abundance.

Geese Success and pleasure in your undertakings.

Gift Loss of something.

Globe A great traveler.

Goat Good luck.

Gold Increase of friends and business.

Goldfish A large sum of money coming soon.

Good-byes Painful news.

Grapes A good omen.

Grass If green, a long life; if cutting grass, great trouble and problems.

Grasshopper A long life.

Grief A jolly time.

Grinning Shame or embarrassment.

Groaning An entertaining outing.

Guitar Luck in love affairs.

Gun Strife and difficulty with a friend.

Hail A good bargain.

Hammer Good fortune.

Hand If beautiful hands, rapid career rise; if ugly, disappointments; if bloody, estrangement from family.

Hat Putting one on, be careful in love affairs; taking one off, secrets to be revealed.

Hatred The person hated has been talking bad about you.

Hawk A new enterprise.

Healing A romantic breakup or end of friendship.

Heat An attack or scold is coming.

Hiding A secret revealed.

Hill If going up, you will rise in the world; if going down, the reverse.

Hissing A sign of shame.

Honey A long and happy life.

Horse If riding, advancement in world; if thrown, disgrace.

House building A comfortable domestic life.

Hunger Successful new enterprise

Ice skating Difficulty that will soon be overcome.

Illness Someone will cheat you in some way.

Infant Joy and success generally.

Island A shameful act.

Itching Money comes soon.

Jealousy Your partner may betray you.

Joy Pain and trouble.

Kaleidoscope Travel in distant countries.

Key A secret told.

Kissing If just an acquaintance, a good omen; if a lover, they will soon insult you.

Kite You will contact a friend.

Kneeling Misfortune in business.

Knives Law suits and strife.

Ladder Going up, successful but not wealthy; going down, misfortune; falling, others envy you.

Lake Success, if smooth.

Lamp If dropping or breaking, disappointment; if lit in the distance; an invitation to visit.

Laughter Unfortunate business engagements; also domestic trouble.

Lawyer Misfortune; hindrance of business.

Laziness Sickness or loss.

Leaping Roadblocks to your present pursuits.

Leaves If green, a long and be happy; if fallen, sickness and death.

Legs If fat, sickness; if thin, good fortune.

Lemons Family problems and tension.

Leopard False friends.

Letter Praise.

Liar A benefit at the hands of a stranger.

Light Riches; also an amiable lover.

Lighthouse Seeking guidance in your life.

Lightning A pleasant trip.

Lion Upward mobility.

Lizard Secret enemies.

Log An upcoming move.

Love Ridiculous behavior.

Map Imminent arrival of a distant friend; also unexpected return of lover.

Marriage If to a stranger, anxiety over an upcoming commitment.

Mask Hypocrisy.

Milk Love on the horizon.

Mirror False friends.

Misfortune Luck and success: also a legacy.

Money If finding, you will soon get some; if receiving, good omen in love.

Monkey A silly new friend.

Moon If new, riches; if full Moon, happy marriage, if half Moon, loss of partner.

Moth New problems are cropping up.

Mother If quarreling, she will do something nice for you.

Mountain You will rise in the world, but face difficulties getting there.

Mouse Dishonesty and thievery.

Moving Financial loss.

Mud Gossip against you.

Mushroom If eating, a long life; if gathering, unstable finances from speculation.

Music Joy and happiness.

Necklace A seduction.

Needles Deceit of supposed friends.

New spaces Exciting opportunities.

Nose If big, a good omen; if small, a quarrel.

Numbers Good fortune.

Nurse Luck and plenty of cash.

Nuts Riches and happiness; luck in love.

Oak tree An inheritance.

Old people Good luck in business; also domestic happiness and a happy home.

Opera A journey.

Oranges Good health.

Owl A secret uncovered.

Oysters Money difficulties.

Painting Bad luck.

Pancakes Falling in love.

Panther Ungrateful friend.

Paper Success in love matters.

Parade Deceit or bad debts.

Parrot Flattery.

Party To give, losses and poverty; to attend, a plea to help a friend.

Paying rent Unexpected money.

Peaches Luck that will not amount to very much.

Peacock Empty-headed lover.

Peanuts Poor but contented.

Pearls Poverty and misery.

Pears Elevation in life or status.

Peas Health and thrift.

Pen A tattle-tale gossiper.

Peppers A match with an intelligent individual.

Pet A single, but ultimately fulfilling life.

Photographs Joy without profit.

Piano Domestic happiness.

Picnic Foolish crushes on unworthy targets.

Pie Pleasure and happiness.

Pig Increase in foreign business.

Pigeon Content and delight.

Pineapple Wealth; also hospitality.

Pitching Lies are being told about you.

Plants Success in life, also smart children.

Poet A foolish lover.

Poison Bad or unworthy company.

Police Disgrace.

Portrait or selfie Compliments on your attractive looks or appealing smile.

Praise A scandal.

Praying You will need a favor.

Prison Honor awaits you.

Procession A friend needs assistance.

Promise broken The person who broke the promise will benefit you somehow.

Puzzle Frivolity or silliness.

Quarrel With a stranger, a new friend arrives; with a friend, a good time with them; with a lover, more romance than ever.

Rabbits Many children.

Raccoon A legacy.

Racing If winning, success; if losing, disappointment.

Rage A pleasant event is coming.

Rain If gentle rain, a good omen; if stormy, trouble before success.

Rainbow Health and general prosperity; also happy marriage and riches.

Raspberries Health and riches.

Rats Loss from robbery.

Reading Successful in love and business.

Reptile Injured reputation; also false friends.

Rescuing Rising in the world by increased wealth or new honors.

Resigning Career advancement.

Resuscitation Public attention.

Revenge Disgrace.

Rhinoceros Great success in business matters, but many disappointment in love affairs.

Rich Bad luck.

Ring A wedding.

Rival Your lover prefers you.

River A splendid fortune.

Rocket A joyful event is coming soon.

Rooster A new lover; also great prosperity.

Rose Troubles ahead.

Rowing Good luck generally.

Running If swift, success in undertakings; if stumbling, accidents or misfortune.

Rust Destruction of property.

Sailing If sailing in pleasant weather, success in business; to lovers, happiness; if stormy, speedily settled quarrels.

Sawing An action soon regretted.

Scales A long, happy life.

School Advancement and good fortune.

Scissors Marriage.

Sea Fortunate in money matters.

Searching If for a person, desire to reconnect with true self; if a lost valuable, a loss of self-worth.

Secret A friend turns enemy.

Seduction A very sincere attachment.

Shark Escape from great danger.

Shaving Soon to be in debt.

Sheep Domestic happiness.

Shell If empty, losses in business; if full, success in all your undertakings.

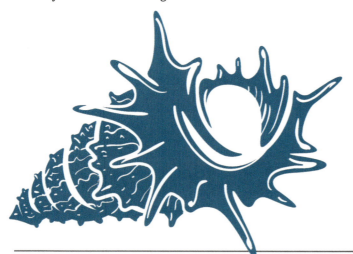

Shirt If new, a blow to your self-esteem.

Shoes If missing, indecision; if it has a hole in it, your partner prefers another; if untied, a kiss from a new acquaintance.

Shopping Expenses and great charges.

Shopping mall Need of money.

Skating Success and good luck.

Sky If clear, a happy marriage; if red, increase of wealth; if cloudy, misfortune.

Sleeping with coworker You feel admiration for that person.

Sliding An agreeable lover.

Smoke Angry controversy.

Snake A friend will injure you; also designing enemies or treacherous friends.

Sneezing A sign of long life.

Snow Joy and pleasure; also a pleasant journey or good health.

Soap Trouble in business.

Sores Great fortune.

Spider Someone will soon pay you money.

Sports A feeling of competition.

Squirrel Good fortune.

Stained clothing A scandal.

Stars Good friends; also many children or business customers.

Statue Advancement.

Stealing You will soon want what you steal.

Sting Injury from gossip.

Storm Losses and trouble.

Strawberries Success in love affairs; also a happy, loving marriage.

Sugar Purity.

Sun If bright, success in anything you may undertake; if dim, trouble and difficulties; if rising, good news and luck; if setting Sun, misfortune.

Swan Riches.

Swearing Downward mobility.

Swimming Success and good fortune generally.

Tea Happy home life.

Tears Someone is in love with you.

Telescope Upward mobility.

Theater A breakup.

Thirst A joyful life.

Thunder Successful speculation.

Tiger A treacherous friend.

Toad Smart children.

Tomatoes Prosperity.

Toothache Trouble ends by a piece of good luck.

Tower Inheritance or purchase of property.

Trap A dicey relationship.

Traveling Success in your business.

Trees Riches—the larger the trees, the better the fortune.

Triplets Good luck and success in love matters.

Tulips Abundance.

Turkey Considerable sum of money coming your way.

Turtle A long life.

Twins Good omen in love and romantic matters.

Umbrella A new lover.

Underground Riches and long life.

Vaccination Good health.

Vexation Soon to be pleased.

Vines Prosperity, journeys, or employment.

Vomiting Good health.

Wading A happy relationship.

Waking up Awaken yourself, an end to sorrow; to awaken another, love reciprocated.

Walking Bad temper and disappointment.

Walls If walking on or climbing over walls, a dangerous enterprise, trouble, and vexation await; if getting down is successful, success; if not, disappointment.

Walnuts Success and a good-tempered partner.

Warts Money coming.

Washing A change of location.

Wasp Thrift and abundance.

Watch Good luck and money-getting.

Well Finding a treasure.

Whale Great and abundant fortune.

Wig A new relationship is coming.

Wine An extravagant spouse.

Winning lottery A gain in wisdom.

Witch A sojourn among strangers.

Wolf Poor choice in relationship.

Wound Losses.

Writing a letter Visit from absent friends.

Wrong number Lack of connection; also communication with someone important to your life.

Yellow Wealth to come.

Zebra A quarrel.

GLOSSARY

Ascendant (AC) The zodiac sign that appears on the eastern horizon with reference to a specific place of birth at the exact time of a person's birth.

Astrological chart Diagram representing the positions of the Sun, Moon, planets, astrological aspects, and sensitive angles at the time of an event, such as the moment of a person's birth.

Astrology Divination by the movements of celestial bodies.

Bagua Eight symbols used in Taoist cosmology to represent the fundamental principles of reality; Bagua grids can be adapted for divination by gemstones or other methods.

Cartomancy Divination by cards, such as standard playing cards or tarot cards.

Chance line In palmistry, lines less commonly seen in an individual's hand.

Chirology Judgment formed from what appears in the palm of the hand

Chiromancy Divination by reading the lines and mounts of the palm as well as other qualities of the hand.

Cleromancy Divination by casting of lots, or casting bones or stones, such as runes.

Court card A card that depicts the king, queen, or jack of a suit; in tarot, the king, queen, knight, and page of a suit. See also face card.

Crystallomancy Divination by crystal ball; also called scrying.

Descendant (DC) The zodiac sign that descends on the western horizon with reference to a specific place of birth at the exact time of a person's birth.

Dowsing Divination conducted with the aid of a divining tool, such as a pendulum.

Earthly Branches Chinese ordering system used in various contexts, that divides the celestial circle into 12 sections to follow the orbit of Jupiter.

Face card A card that depicts a person, in traditional playing cards, the king, queen, or jack of a suit. *See also* court card

Feng shui Divination by earthen harmony.

Five Elements Theory In Chinese astrology, the belief that five elements play a crucial role in the balance of the universe and that all things that arise from and return to the universe are composed of them, forming a 60-year cycle of creation and destruction.

Futhark An alphabet originally of 24 and later of some 16 angular characters; probably derived from both Latin and Greek and used for inscriptions and magic signs by the Germanic peoples, from about the 3rd to the 13th centuries. The spelling futhark is from the first six symbols of the runic alphabet.

Glyph A mark used as a pictorial symbol, such as those used to represent the zodiac signs or the planets and other heavenly bodies.

Heavenly Stem Chinese system of ordinals that represent the names of the 10 days of the week.

Hierophant An interpreter of sacred mysteries and arcane principles; one of the cards of the Major Arcana of the tarot deck.

House Represents the path of the planets as they moved across in the sky at the time of a person's birth; usually listed as 12 in number,

Lithomancy Divination by stones or gems.

Major Arcana Also called the trump cards, this group consists of 22 cards numbered in Roman numerals from I to XXI from The Magician to The World; The Fool is sometimes placed at the beginning of the deck as 0, or at the end as XXII.

Minor Arcana Also known as the Lesser Arcana; the 56 suit cards in a tarot deck containing four court cards of each suit and pip, or numbered, cards from 1 (ace) to 10, along with court cards (or face cards) in each of four suits.

Moon sign Determined by the position of the moon at the time of a person's birth.

Mount In palmistry, the fleshy lumps of the palm evaluated to reveal characteristics of a querent.

Natal chart *See* astrological chart.

Numerology Divination by numbers.

Oneiromancy Divination by dreams.

Ouija board Trademarked name of spirit board marketed as a game. *See* spirit board.

Palmistry Divination by evaluating the lines and mounds on the hand.

Pendulum reading Divination by the reading the movements of a suspended object.

Piquet deck A French-style playing card deck containing 32 cards.

Planchette A small, heart-shaped device that, when moved across a surface by the light, unguided pressure of the fingertips, is supposed to trace meaningful patterns revealing subconscious thoughts, psychic phenomena, clairvoyant messages, and the like.

Querent The questioner; the one whose fortune is being told or whose question is being anwsered.

Rising sign *See* ascendant.

Rune casting or **runic divination** Divination by the casting of runes.

Scrying Divination by looking at or into reflective objects. *See also* crystal ball.

Significator An object that stands for the querent, such as a certain card in tarot reading or a certain gemstones in lithomancy.

Spirit board A board, usually marked with the letters of the alphabet, numbers 0 through 9, and the words *yes, no,* and *good bye;* answers to questions are spelt out by a planchette pointer or glass held by the fingertips of the participants and are supposedly formed by spiritual forces.

Spread Pattern in which you lay out a tool of divination, such as cards or stones, with each position representing a certain aspect or quality.

Suit One of the categories into which the cards of a deck are divided; each card bears one of several pips (symbols) showing to which suit it belongs. The suit may also be indicated by the color of the symbol. In playing cards, standard suits are Hearts (red), Clubs (black), Diamonds (red), and Spades (black); in tarot, they are Cups, Wands, Pentacles, and Swords.

Sun sign In Western astrology, the birth sign.

Talking board *See* spirit board.

Taromancy Divination by a form of cartomancy using tarot cards.

Tasseography or **tasseomancy** Divination by tea leaves or coffee grounds.

INDEX

IMAGE CREDITS

KEY

SS = Shutterstock.com   CC = Creative Commons*

PD = Public Domain**

t = top   m = middle   b = bottom   c = center

All illustrations by Lisa Purcell, unless otherwise noted

COVER

Front cover tl Fer Gregory/ss; tm Gluiki/SS; tr Dzhulbee/SS; ml Mercury Green/SS; mc Inked Pixels/SS, Dzhulbee/SS; mr Rumdecor/SS, immyIurii/SS; bl whiteMocca/SS; br baklykovadaria/SS

Back cover FotoHelin/SS

Front flap t Vera Petruk/SS; b New Africa/SS

Back flap Gluiki/SS

Contents 4–5 shutterstock_1902916732.jpg

Introduction 6–7 shutterstock_583428031.jpg

** Creative Commons Attribution-Share Alike 3.0 Unported
** These works are in the public domain in their country of origin and other countries and areas where the copyright term is the author's life plus 100 years or fewer.*

C·H·A·P·T·E·R 1
READING the FUTURE in the HEAVENLY BODIES

8–9 Vera Petruk/SS; 8 inset Bada1/SS; 10–11 Viacheslav Lopatin/SS; 13 l Fouad A. Saad/SS; 13 r My Portfolio/SS; 14 Vlada Young/SS; 15 Kaspars Grinvalds/SS; 16 Christos Georghiou/SS; 17 tl Taeya18/SS; 17 tr Vadim Sadovski/SS; 18 Christos Georghiou/SS; 19 tl Taeya18/SS; 19 tr J10/SS; 20 Christos Georghiou/SS; 21 tl Taeya18/SS; 21 tr J10/SS; 22 Christos Georghiou/SS; 23 tl Taeya18/SS; 23 tr J10/SS; 24 Christos Georghiou/SS; 25 tl Taeya18/SS; 25 tr robert_s/SS; 26 Christos Georghiou/SS; 27 tl Taeya18/SS; 27 tr J10/SS; 28 Christos Georghiou/SS; 29 tl Taeya18/SS; 29 tr J10/SS; 30 Christos Georghiou/SS; 31 tl Taeya18/SS; 31 tr 19 STUDIO/SS; 32 Christos Georghiou/SS; 33 tl Taeya18/SS; 33 tr J10/SS; 34 Christos Georghiou/SS; 35 tl Taeya18/SS; 35 tr J10/SS; 36 Christos

Georghiou/SS; 37 tl Taeya18/SS; 37 tr J10/SS; 38 Christos Georghiou/SS; 39 tl Taeya18/SS; 39 tr J10/SS; 40–41 Shokultd/SS; 44 Shokultd/SS; 45 tl Pand P Studio/SS; tr J10/SS; 46 Shokultd/SS; 47 tl Pagina/SS; 47 tr J10/SS; 48 Shokultd/SS; 49 tl Pand P Studio; 49 tr J10/SS; 50 Shokultd/SS; 51 tl Pagina/SS; 51 tr J10/SS; 52 Shokultd/SS; 53 tl Pagina/SS; 53 tr Vadim Sadovski/SS; 54 Shokultd/SS; 55 tl Pagina/SS; 55 tr J10/SS; 56 Shokultd/SS; 57 tl Pagina/SS; 57 tr J10/SS; 58 Shokultd/SS; 59 tl Pagina/SS; 59 tr J10/SS; 60 Shokultd/SS; 61 tl Pagina/SS; 61 tr robert_s/SS; 62 Shokultd/SS; 63 tl Pand P Studio/SS; 63 tr J10/SS; 64 Shokultd/SS; 65 tl Pagina/SS; 65 tr J10/SS; 66 Shokultd/SS; 67 tl Pagina/SS; 67 tr 19 STUDIO/SS

C·H·A·P·T·E·R 2
CARTOMANCY and the ART of the TAROT

68–69 HikaruD88/SS; 68 inset Oksistyle/SS; 70 Maisei Raman/SS; 70 Maisei Raman/SS; 71 Maisei Raman/SS; 74 l gakhuashvili/SS; 74 m IANINAS/SS; 74 r KUCO/SS; 75 l Pushkin/SS; 75 r LanaN/SS; 76 PD; 81 all boxed images PD except Kilom691/ CC_SA_3.0 [Shields], Kilom691/ CC_SA_3.0 [Roses]; 81 b Radowitz/SS; 82 PD; 83 t bigjom jom/SS; 83 b Alina Vaska/SS; 84–85 n_defender/SS; 86 Vera Petruk/SS; 87 anakondasp/SS; 88–93 LaInspiratriz/SS; 94 t duddili/SS; 94 bl Astrologer/SS; 94 bm duddili/SS; 94 br Astrologer/SS; 95 t, m, b PD; 96–101 delcarmat/SS; 101 b wavebreakmedia/SS; 102 La-Catalina/SS; 103 bigjom jom/SS; 104 bigjom jom/SS; 105 Mindful Photography/SS; 106 t bigjom jom/SS;106 b Pavel_

Kostenko/SS; 107 bigjom jom/SS; 108 bigjom jom/SS; 109 bigjom jom/SS; 110 bigjom jom/SS; 111 bigjom jom/SS; 112 bigjom jom/SS; 113 bigjom jom/SS

C·H·A·P·T·E·R 3
PALMISTRY, CHIROLOGY, and the ART of CHIROMANCY

Basic hand image throughout chapter Krakenimages.com/SS; 14–115 Rumdecor/SS; 114 inset d_odin/SS; 117 vectortatu/SS; 120–121 photka/SS; 122 Ann Baldwin/SS; 124 reddees/SS; 125 Julian Bohorquez/SS; 126 tl J10/SS; 126 ml J10/SS; 126 bl robert_s/SS; 126 tr J10/SS; 126 mr J10/SS; 126 mr J10/SS; 127 t Vadim Sadovski/SS; On Page 127 b J10/SS; 128–129 n_defender/SS; 131 Mariya Volochek/SS; 132 Dado Photos/SS; 137 PD; 145 DedMityay/SS

C·H·A·P·T·E·R 4
READING the TEA LEAVES and COFFEE GROUNDS

146–147 pixeldreams.eu/SS; 146 inset Maya Kruchankova/SS; 149 Africa Studio/SS; 150 justyle/SS; 151 Helen Adamova/SS; 152 tl Helen Adamova/SS; 152 bl Helen Adamova/SS; 152 tr Tatiana Akhmetgalieva/SS; 153 tl DGIM studio/SS; 153 bl Mario Pantelic/SS; 153 tr DGIM studio/SS; 153 br Aliaksei Design/SS; 154 tl Alexkava/SS; 154 iana kauri/SS; 154 tr Arcady/SS; 154 br Naddya/SS; 155 tl Gluiki/SS; 155 bl archivector/SS; 155 bl SS; 155 tr brullikk/SS; 156 tl TRONIN ANDREI/SS; 156 bl DGIM studio/SS;156 tr buchandbee/SS; 156 mr iana kauri/SS; 156 br OLYVIA/SS; 157 tl Les Perysty/SS; 157 bl Neda/SS; 157 br Kastoluza/SS; 157

tr Artfury/SS; 158–159 justyle/SS; 160 Bermek/SS; 161 Rugged Studio/SS; 162 kattytekin/SS; 163 t Jr images, Evgeny Karandaev/SS; 163 b Levent Konuk/SS; 164 tl Masterlevsha/SS; 164 mr Helen Adamova/SS; 164 tr TRONIN ANDREI/SS; 164 mr DGIM studio/SS; 164 br shuttersport/SS; 165 tl Airin.dizain/SS; 165 bl Mallinka1/SS; 165 tr Sabelskaya/SS; 165 br Svetlana Ivanova/SS

C·H·A·P·T·E·R 5
CRYSTAL GAZING and the ART of READING STONES

166–167 Bruce Rolff/SS; 166 inset FotoHelin/SS; 168 Danny Smythe/SS; 169 Inked Pixels/SS; 170–171 vetre/SS; 172 Pushnova/SS; 176 FotoHelin/SS; 177 Jerome-Cronenberger/SS; 178 tl David Weinberg/CC_SA_3.0; 178 ml vvoe/SS; 178 bl New Africa/SS; 178 vvoe/SS; 178 mr New Africa/SS; 178 bl vvoe/SS; 179 tl vvoe/SS; 179 ml vvoe/SS; 179 bl vvoe/SS; 179 tl vvoe/SS; 179 mr vvoe/SS; 179 br vvoe/SS; 180 tl New Africa/SS; 180 ml vvoe/SS; 180 bl vvoe/SS; 180 tr vvoe/SS; 180 mr La corneja artesana/SS; 180 br vvoe/SS; 181 tl Miriam Doerr Martin Frommherz/SS; 181 ml vvoe/SS; 181 bl vvoe/SS; 181 tr vvoe/SS; 181 br vvoe/SS; 181 mr vvoe/SS; 182 tl Elena Noeva/SS; 182 ml vvoe/SS; 182 bl vvoe/SS; 182 tr vvoe/SS; 182 mr vvoe/SS; 182 br galka3250/SS; 183 tl vvoe/SS; 183 ml vvoe/SS; 183 bl vvoe/SS; 183 tr Martina Osmy/SS; 183 mr vvoe/SS; 183 br vvoe/SS; 184 tl vvoe/SS; 184 ml vvoe/SS; 184 bl vvoe/SS; 184 tr vvoe/SS; 184 mr vvoe/SS; 184 br vvoe/SS; 185 tr vvoe/SS; 185 tl vvoe/SS; 185 b Africa Studio/SS; 186–187 andregric/SS; 191 Nakaya/SS; 192–194 Rata Blanca/SS [stones], vonzur/SS [glyphs]; 195 Borys Vasylenko

C·H·A·P·T·E·R 6
PENDULUM READING and SPIRIT BOARDS

196–197 Vera Petruk/SS; 196 inset Monika Wisniewska/SS; 198 Mercury Green/SS; 199 Happy_Nati/SS; 200 Couperfield/SS; 201 Patrizia magni/SS; 202 PD; 203 Edward R/SS; 204 snow toy/SS; 205 tl PD; 205 bl EVGENII LEONTEV/SS; 205 tr EVGENII LEONTEV/SS; 205 br overjupiter/pixabay

C·H·A·P·T·E·R 7
The ART of DIVINATION THROUGH NUMBERS

206–207 Dzhulbee/SS; 206 inset HALINA GOLD/SS; 208 blackboard1965/SS; 209 FotoHelin/SS; 212–217 Tomash Sugint/SS

C·H·A·P·T·E·R 8
INTERPRETING the FUTURE from DREAMS

218–219 Gorbash Varvara/SS; 218 inset marina shin/SS; 221 Bruce Rolff/SS; 222 Ice lemon/SS; 223 MP2021/SS; 224 l DGIM studio/SS; 224 b Alexander_P/SS; 225 l Olga Olmix/SS; 225 r CloudyStock/SS; 226 l Anabela88/SS; 226 r mahmuttibet/SS; 227 l SS; 227 r insima/SS; 228 l A-spring/SS; 228 r Shtefan Yelizaveta/SS; 229 l benntennsann/SS; 229 r varoken/SS; 230 l vectortatu/SS; 230 r Rakhimov Edgar/SS; 231 l Naddya/SS; 231 r Apostrophe

Acknowlegments Tanya Antusenok

ACKNOWLEDGMENTS

The author would like to thank Nancy Hajeski for both her contributions to this book and her encouragement thoughout the writing process. Thank you to Deborah McHugh for Sunday walks. And thanks to Susen Saullo, whose enthusiam for all things divination has never waned since she first read my tarot cards so many years ago. You all provided motivation and much-needed insight.

And to baby Joe, may your future always be bright.